The Dictionary of
AMERICAN BIRD NAMES

THE DICTIONARY OF
AMERICAN
BIRD NAMES

REVISED EDITION

ERNEST A. CHOATE

REVISED BY
RAYMOND A. PAYNTER, JR.

THE HARVARD COMMON PRESS
A Gambit Book
HARVARD AND BOSTON, MASSACHUSETTS

To Elaine and Shirley

The Harvard Common Press
535 Albany Street
Boston, Massachusetts 02118

Printed in the United States of America.

Library of Congress Cataloging in Publication Data
Choate, Ernest A. (Ernest Alfred)
   The dictionary of American bird names.

   "A Gambit book."
   1. Birds—Nomenclature—Dictionaries.   2. Birds—
Nomenclature (Popular)—Dictionaries.   3. Birds—
United States—Nomenclature—Dictionaries.   4. Birds—
United States—Nomenclature (Popular)—Dictionaries.
I. Paynter, Raymond A.   II. Title.
QL677.C5   1985   598′.014   84-28975
ISBN 0-87645-065-6
ISBN 0-87645-117-2 (pbk.)
10   9   8   7   6   5   4   3   2

Contents

Preface to the Revised Edition

Ten years after the publication of the first edition of this book, the sixth edition of the American Ornithologists' Union's *Check-list of North American Birds* made its long-awaited appearance. It had been twenty-five years since the fifth edition of this authoritative reference, a quarter of a century during which there were many changes in how ornithologists classified birds. Moreover, the committee in charge of the new *Check-list* made a vigorous attempt to standardize vernacular names and to provide each species with a name not duplicated elsewhere in the world. This all resulted in a plethora of changes and even the coinage of new common names.

Because Ernest Choate had used the fifth edition of the A. O. U. *Check-list* as the authority for modern common and scientific names, when the sixth edition of the *Check-list* appeared, his book suddenly became badly outmoded.

My task has been to bring the book into conformity with the current A. O. U. *Check-list,* and to correct those errors in the derivations and origins of names that have come to light. Although this has resulted in many changes, I have taken special care to preserve the wry humor, subtle *double-entendres,* and classical scholarship of Ernest Choate, characteristics that have made this delightful book so popular and useful.

Raymond A. Paynter, Jr.
August, 1984

Preface to the First Edition

And smale foweles maken melodye,
          Chaucer, The Canterbury Tales, *Prologue*

This is to seyn, the foules of ravyne
Were hyest set, and then the foules smale,
That eten as hem nature wolde enclyne,
As worm or thyng, of which I telle no tale;
And water-fowl sat lowest in the dale,
But foul that lyveth by seed sat on the grene
And that so fele that wonder was to sene.
          Chaucer, The Parlement of Foules, *The Proem*

The writings of Chaucer are preeminent not only for their literary worth and their portrayal of the social life of the time, but also as a philological "monument." This is the term that language specialists attach to a noted body of writing in a given language from a specific period in the past, in this case the period of Middle English. At that time, quite evidently, a prominent member of the court of Edward III could use such spelling variations as *foweles* or *foul* and *yeer* or *yere* with no social penalty. The "monument" also shows that while the ways of letters in some words were already set, the spelling of others might vary until the custom of "correct" spelling became a matter of concern to school teachers and dictionary makers, as in our present period of Modern English. We can also note that *foul* (*foule, fowel, foghel*) in Chaucer's time meant all clothed in feathers, as *bird* does today. Chaucer's *briddes* was shifting away from its contemporary meaning of "young birds"and was gradually beginning to replace the then more inclusive *fowl*, which is now more commonly applied to the larger edible game birds and poultry, and likely to be found in combination with other words, as in waterfowl, wildfowl or wild fowl, or barnyard fowl.

The suggestion of a shift of meaning for *brid, briddes* in Chaucer's time is found in his "Parlement of Foules":

> On every bough the *briddes* herde I synge,
> With voys (voice) of aungel (angel) in her armonye (harmony);
> Som besyede (beside) hem (them) hir (their) *briddes* forth to brynge.

The first *briddes* means adults in the present sense of the term, while the second evidently means the young, an older connotation. A few lines later, Chaucer with his inconsistent spelling has "every bryd cometh ther to chese (chase) his make (mate)," and "the goshawk that doth pyne (pain) to bryddes." The spelling *brid* and *byrd* both came into Middle English from Anglo-Saxon where the word was derived from *bredan*, "to breed." The transposition of the *r* changing *brid* to *bird* occurred first in the Northumbrian dialect, which gradually supplanted the older spelling. Although the new spelling prevailed in Shakespeare's time, the old meaning of young had not been dropped, as evidenced by:

> And, being fed by us, you us'd us so
> As that ungentle gull, the cuckoo's bird (young),
> Useth the sparrow;

which we find in *Henry IV*.

The gradual three-century-long change in the meaning of *bird* has at long last ended. Both spelling and meaning have attained a modicum of solitary distinctness when applied to a feathered animal. Its former meaning is archaic, and it is, from the linguist's historical viewpoint of language, quite a new word. What does the future hold? Doting grandmothers while supervising the photographing of their wriggling charges have been heard to say, "Look at the birdie" (spelling and meaning). Youth in our institutions of higher learning have been recorded as exclaiming, "College isn't what those old birds (meaning) say it is."

Ernest A. Choate
August, 1973

Introduction

The purpose of this book is to promote an appreciation of the common and scientific names of North American birds. It aims to do this through an exploration of their origins and their meanings in the past, with the hope that this will give an understanding and in turn an added pleasurable dimension not only to the words themselves, but also to the recognition of the birds of which they are the voiced and written symbols. Thus we may become involved both in linguistics, the science of language, and in ornithology, the science of birds.

Modern linguistics looks upon a spoken language as a continually changing group of dialects which have enough in common for those using them to be able to understand one another. Attempts have been made to standardize a language by giving official sanction to a preeminent dialect, as Parisian for the French language, Castillian for Spanish, and Tuscan for Italian. No such thing has been attempted for the English language, although schools and mass media have had a strong unifying influence. We are here chiefly concerned with American English, a major dialect of the mother tongue. It contains words from many languages, ancient and modern. It is constantly adding new ones and dropping old ones. It carries not only an enormously rich cultural heritage, but also a tremendous body of scientific knowledge. This sumptuous and varied load is stored in and communicated through language.

In English the written word is not necessarily an exact reflection of the spoken one so far as the spelling is concerned. There is sometimes quite a gap between the two. More technically, the written language instead of being phonetically functional may use a spelled word as a recognized and conventional symbol of the spoken word, carrying a meaning rather than just a series of letters representing the exact sound of the spoken word. For example, *c* in English may be used for the sound of either *s* or *k*, as in *circus* or *concern*, or combined with *h* for still another sound, *ch*, as in *church*. *Ghoti* could spell *fish* if we use the *gh* sound in *enou(gh)*, the *o* sound in *w(o)men* and the *ti* sound in *mo(ti)on*. The point is that the phonetic inexactness of written English in recording words makes the task of working with their origins and meanings complicated and at times futile.

When dealing with the problem of transliteration, words passing through more than one language compound the difficulty. Greek has no *c*, but Latin does. Greek has *k* (kappa), but the Latin *k* was introduced only in later days when authors began using Greek words with Greek spellings. A hard-sounding Greek *k* generally became a hard *c* in Latin and passed into English as a sound which might or might not be the same as the original. Thus Greek *kuklos* becomes Latin *cyclus* and then English *cycle*. As our aim is to enrich the background of meaning in American bird names rather than to trace the vagaries of philological transliteration, we have chosen the spellings which we hope make it easiest to see word relations. We thus avoid a pedantic overload of explanations of differences in words due to cases of nouns, irregularities and tenses of verbs, varied transliterations of letters from one language to another, and the occasional spelling errors in words from dead languages. Although this arbitrary and somewhat inexact way of handling things may result in such spelling variations as

Progne, Prokne, and Procne, we hope that the young lady in question can be recognized although she at times appears in a different dress.

A work of this type is made possible only through the activities of a vast number of writers through a succession of milleniums, from the Egyptians, who first made paper from papyrus, to the authors of the latest field guides for birds. Wilson found and named new birds, Linnaeus invented a system of nomenclature that made possible a scientific organization in naming living organisms, and Darwin explained how life changes and evolves. A word of appreciation is also in order for the philologist, the linguist, and the lexicographer, whom Samuel Johnson defined as "a harmless drudge."

The black and white illustrations are from Thomas Bewick's *A History of British Birds*. The woodcuts illustrating his book for both their accuracy and artistry made the work an outstanding contribution to ornithological literature.

Among those who have given more immediate help and encouragement are the late J. d'Arcy Northwood, Floyd Oliver, Charles H. Rogers, James Reid, Lester S. Thomas, and C. Brooke Worth.

Eugene Eisenmann, Curator of Ornithology at The American Museum of Natural History and Chairman of the Committee on Classification and Nomenclature of the American Ornithologists' Union, and Raymond A. Paynter of the Museum of Comparative Zoology at Harvard deserve special commendation for their help on the section on scientific names.

The editor, Lovell Thompson, has been most helpful. His many pertinent suggestions broadened the dimensions of the book. His patience and understanding made working with him most enjoyable.

Language
Abbreviations

The scheme used below follows in the main that used by Jaeger.

Ar.   Arabic
AS.   Anglo-Saxon, c.450–c.1200
D.   Danish
Du.   Dutch
E.   English
F.   French
G.   German
Gr.   Classical Greek
H.   Hebrew
HG.   High German, the language spoken in southern Germany before it evolved into modern German.
I.   Italian
Ic.   Icelandic
IE.   Indo-European, the ancestral language of most classical and modern European languages as well as classical Sanskrit.
L.   Latin, Classical Latin, the language of the Romans until about 200 A.D.

LG.   Low German, the dialect of the low countries of north-
       ern Germany, particularly along the coast. It was basi-
       cally Saxon, but gradually gave way to High German.
LL.   Low Latin, the Latin of the early church fathers and
       the Middle Ages, c.200–c.1500.
ME.   Middle English, c.1200–c.1500
ML.   Modern Latin, c.1500, includes a host of scientific
       names, especially in biology. Words from many lan-
       guages are latinized by the addition of Latin endings.
Nor.   Norwegian
OF.   Old French, c.800–c.1500
ON.   Old Norse
Per.   Persian
Por.   Portuguese
Prov. Provençal, an old southern French dialect which was
       the first French to contain a considerable amount of
       written material of literary worth. It was the language
       of the troubadors.
S.   Swedish
Sa.   Sanskrit
Sp.   Spanish

Common Names

Background

Just to contemplate the sheer number of common names for all birds is overwhelming. Kalmbach, in "An Ornithological Treasure Awaits Resurrection" (*The Auk,* vol. 85, no. 4, October 1968), tells of Waldo Lee McAtee's work, *American Bird Names and Their Histories and Meanings.* The unpublished data consist of 1,697 manuscript pages for volume one. The material for volume two is "recorded on about 153,000 slips and 4,100 bibliography cards in 90 file drawers." The grand total of names is estimated to be about half a million, and McAtee admitted it was by no means complete. It would seem possible for a reader to become completely befuddled by an article in which only the rarer bird names were used. In actual practice there was some confusion in understanding, as different common names for the same bird were widely used in different parts of the country. The problem was particularly vexing as local and state bird organizations were prone to use only the common names.

As the interest in birds developed beyond the local level, the need for a widely acceptable list of common names of North American birds became apparent. The American Ornithologists' Union went a long way toward filling this need by including in the fifth edition of its *Check-list of North American Birds* (1957) one common name for each species and by eliminating common names for subspecies, as had been the custom earlier. In the sixth edition of the *Check-list* (1983) a concerted effort was made to be certain that each common name was unique and not duplicated by another species elsewhere in the world. This led to the demise of such familiar vernaculars as White-necked Raven, now the Chihuahuan Raven, Common Gallinule, now Moorhen, and the various tree ducks, now called whistling ducks. Stability in vernacular names has never been achieved, in spite of vigorous proselytizing, and whether this latest attempt will be successful remains to be seen.

The task of selecting one common name for each bird was a formidable one. From the sidelines it would seem less difficult to choose a name for a rare bird than for one that was widespread and abundant. There would be on the surface fewer names to choose from. A very rare species might be more familiar to professional ornithologists than to bird watchers. In such cases the scientific name would be better known and its reflection in the common name justified. This process is by no means limited to rarer species, and may come about independent of scientific influence. For example, vireo, which might be considered a scientific name, has crowded out greenlet, which was in vogue to some extent in the last century. Pyrrhuloxia seems to have come from the genus end of *Pyrrhuloxia sinuata* while Merganser may likely have arisen from the specific portion of *Mergus merganser*. So even the common names with a scientific name in their ancestry, like Topsy, just grew up.

At the other end of the philological spectrum are the names of the familiar, abundant, and widely distributed species. Many, local in origin, have either remained so or have fallen into disuse. The use of some names has spread and become widely accepted. Other names have changed both in their degree of usage as well as in their form. Some appellations, reflecting a fond intimacy, originated as pet names. We have quite a few: Jackdaw, Jay, Jenny Wren, Magpie, Martin, Parakeet (little Peter), Philip Sparrow, Robin, and Tom Tit. Several of these still remain in the realm of the nickname while others have attained the status of preferred acceptance. Jay came into English from French, beyond which the derivation is obscure. It is remotely possible that the word in French is derived from the Latin, *gaius,* which carries the implication that it was a "joy" about the Roman home. Magpie was Shakespeare's Magot-pie. Magot along with Maggot, Margot, Mag, Maggie, and Peg were all nicknames for Margaret. Robin, a common pet name, first preceded Redbreast as a mark of endearing familiarity and gradually took over; Redbreast, then Robin Redbreast, and finally Robin. The more literate the speakers of a language and the more general and widespread their education, the slower are the changes in their language. Thus whatever tendency there might be for Jenny to gradually supplant wren, the present state of our culture suggests that it will take a long, long time.

Aside from their use as names for species, vernacular terms and words have other important functions in ornithology. They are useful in describing variations and aberrations which do not warrant categorical scientific attention. We use the terms red-brown phase or gray phase for the plumages of the Screech-Owl. We use light and dark phase for the different plumages of the Rough-legged Hawk. Common terms may well be used for variations in a species whose particular segments of population do not warrant scientific subspecific status. Vernacular words used correctly are just as accurate in conveying meaning as scientific terms and are, of course, indispensible. Without common names familiar to most people, communication about birds would be nonexistent, unless, of course, birders became as at ease using scientific names as are the gardeners (e.g., forsythia, chrysanthemum, poinsettia, rhododendron, etc.).

Common names are used not only to identify individual species, but also to show relationships in a kind of vernacular binomial nomenclature. Although until recently placed in different genera, all three members of the scientifically termed family Phalaropodidae have the same common name, phalarope. Our three American jaegars, which belong to the same genus, have the same second common name. Showing the relationships in such common names as duck, gull, swallow, hawk, or sparrow is not so much or at all the expression of a need for terms of this type, but rather a reflection of the degree of most people's interest in birds. Only bird watchers, who are rather a unique minority, require a more specific vocabulary for their esoteric communication.

List of Common Names

Accentor. A local name for the Ovenbird. For the penetrating song in which the first note of each two-syllable phrase is accented as it calls, "TEACHer, TEACHer, TEACHer."

Albatross. In its present form since the seventeenth century. Obsolete E. *alcatras* (Hawkin's voyage, 1564), *alca* changing to *alba* possibly by the influence of L. *alba*. Por. *alcatraz*, "sea fowl, cormorant, albatross, but most frequently a pelican"; Por. *alcatrus*, "bucket, bucket or trough on a waterwheel," with a second meaning, "pelican," for the shape of the bill in which it was believed to carry water for its young. Ar. *alquadus*, also primarily a "bucket on a waterwheel" and secondarily a "pelican"; *al* is the Ar. definite article and *quadus*, "bucket." Gr. *kados*, "jar," possibly of Semitic origin, cf. H. *kad*, "bucket." Newton says that the name was spelled *albitross* in *Shelvache's Voyage* (London: 1726), wherein (pp. 72, 73) is recorded the incident that, on Wordsworth's suggestion, Coleridge immortalized in the "Rhyme of the Ancient Mariner." **Black-browed A.** for the dark line over its eye. **Black-footed A.** for the black color of its feet. **Laysan A.** for the island where the first specimen was obtained. **Short-tailed A.** for its short tail. **Shy** or **White-capped A.** for its presumed nature and white crown. **Yellow-nosed A.** for its yellow beak.

Anhinga. Same as the scientific name. A South American (Tupi) native name for the Water Turkey.

Ani. Brazilian name for the bird. **Smooth-billed A.** for its smooth-surfaced bill in contrast with the **Groove-billed A.**

Auk. Occurs also as alk, ON. *alka*. A name given to several northern sea birds. **Great A.** extinct. The largest of the auks, not a name of great antiquity in English, is referred to by Willughby (1678) as, "the bird called penguin by our seamen." **Little A.** British and occasional American name for the Dovekie, one of the smallest sea birds.

Auklet. For auk (see above) plus *-let,* diminutive suffix, hence "little auk." **Cassin's A.** for John Cassin (see Appendix). **Crested A.** OF. *creste,* L. *crista,* "crest on a rooster or plume on a helmet." E. *crestfallen* is a cockfighting term. When applied to horses the word slips from the top of the head to the ridge of the neck. **Least A.** for its small size. **Parakeet A.** for the almost circular bright red bill of its breeding period which suggests the bill of a Parakeet (see Parakeet). **Rhinoceros A.** for the pointed growth on its bill during summer. **Whiskered A.** for the facial plumes. Whisker from the likeness to a small brush, a whisk.

Avocet. F. *avocette,* I. *avosetta,* "avocet." Quite possibly from L. *avis,* the suffix suggesting small and graceful. American, a different species from the European.

Baldpate. A popular name for the American Wigeon. (For bald, see Eagle, Bald E.) Pate, origin unknown. The white feathers on the crown suggest a bald head or pate. The name is also used, according to Newton, by the English in the West Indies for a dove with a white head.

Bananaquit. Another name for the Honeycreeper. Banana, possibly a Carib name; no connection with the banana tree or fruit. *Quit,* possibly for the note of the bird, but more likely it is a West Indian name for small birds in general, as there are grassquits, a Long-mouthed Quit, etc.

Basketbird. The Orchard or Northern Oriole. From the resemblance of the woven nest to a basket.

Becard. F. *bec,* "beak"; *-ard,* HG. *hart,* "bold, hardy," an intensifying suffix, hence "big beak." **Rose-throated B.** for the rosy throat of the male.

Bee-bird. The Kingbird. For taking bees near their hive.

Bee-martin. Another name for the Kingbird.

Bellbird. The Wood Thrush. For its clear and ringing song.

Big Cranky. The Great Blue Heron. Possibly for its rather aloof habit of fishing, suggesting by its pose a dour disposition.

Bill-willie. The Willet. For its call.

Bird. The earliest ancestor of our word "bird" is unknown. We first meet it in Old English as *brid*, meaning generally the young of animals. Newton gives as early illustrations Wycliff's *Translation of Matthew XXIII*, "eddris and eddris briddis," which in the King James version is rendered, "ye serpents, and generation of vipers." We find in other quotes from Newton: "In temperat yeres ben fewe byrdes of been (bees)," "All fysshe (fish) fede and keep theyr byrdes," and "The Woolfe and Woolfe-birdes (cubs) suld (should) be slaine." Thus it seems that *brid*, in one form or another, could mean the young of reptiles, insects, fish, or animals. For a fuller understanding of the word's evolution we are fortunate to have a comparative wealth of material in the writings of Chaucer (see Preface).

Bittern. A variety of OE. forms: *bitoyre, bittour, bytoure, botor, buttour;* became crystallized into *bittern* soon after the English translation of Willughby's *Ornithology* appeared in 1678. He says, "It is called by later writers Butorius or Botaurus because it seems to imitate *boatum tauri*, the bellowing of a bull. The common people are of the opinion that it thrusts its bill into a reed, by the help whereof it makes that lowing and drumming noise." **American B.**, smaller and slightly different in appearance from the European B., a different species. **Least B.** for its small size.

Blackbird. For the predominant color. **Brewer's B.** for Thomas M. Brewer (see Appendix). Retained as the common name although dropped from the scientific one originally given by Audubon. **Red-winged B.** for the red and yellow epaulets of the male. **Rusty B.** for the rusty tinge of the fall plumage. **Tricolored B.** as the red and white epaulets of the male add two colors to the bird. **Yellow-headed B.** for the bright yellow head of the male.

Bluebill. A secondary name for the Ring-necked Duck, the Ruddy Duck, and both Scaups, their blue and whitish bills.

Bluebird. For the predominant color. **Eastern B.** for its range. **Mountain B.** for its habitat at high elevations. **Western B.** for its range.

Blue Crane. A colloquial name for the Great Blue Heron.

Blue Darter. Either the Sharp-shinned or Cooper's Hawk. For the slate-blue color of the male.

Blue Peter. Either Coot or Purple Gallinule, for the dark gray-blue color.

Bobolink. Bent suggests that the name is an abbreviation of "Robert O'Lincoln" from the poem by William Cullen Bryant. This is hardly creditable. It likely originated in imitation of the bird's unpatterned bubbling song, and is certainly preferable to Skunk Blackbird suggested by the color pattern of its back.

Bobwhite. In imitation of its call.

Bogbumper. American Bittern. Probably for its call (see Stake Driver).

Bonxie. A Shetland name for the Great Skua.

Booby. Sp. *bobo*, "stupid"; L. *balbus*, "stammering," hence by Roman logic "stupid." Being unfamiliar with men on its isolated nesting sites, it was unaware that the intrusion was a threat to its safety and therefore acted indifferently. This was considered stupid by the seamen, who quite correctly deemed any living thing that trusted them foolish, and so named the birds boobies or fools. **Blue-faced B.** for the slate-blue color of the exposed skin near its bill. **Blue-footed B.** for its bright blue feet. **Brown B.** for the dark brown upper parts and head. **Masked B.** another name for the Blue-faced B. **Red-footed B.** for the color of its feet. **White-bellied B.** another name for the Brown B.

Bottle-head. Local name for the Black-bellied Plover. For its comparatively large round head.

Brant. Other species in England were called *brent goose* or *brand goose;* cf. G. *brand gans,* literally *"burnt goose."* Possibly from AS. *bernan, brennan,* "burned," referring to the dark brown color of the plumage. **Black B.** for the western subspecies which has a dark belly and sometimes is treated as a distinct species.

Bristle Tail. A hunter's name for the Ruddy Duck. For its stiff upright tail.

Broad-bill. A hunter's name used indiscriminantly for the Shoveler, Redhead, both Scaups, and the Ruddy Duck.

Buffalo-bird. A name, alas, no longer appropriate for the cowbird. Por. *bufalo*, L. and Gr. *boubalos*, "a kind of antelope," incorrectly given to the American bison.

Bufflehead. For the shape of the duck's head suggesting that of a buffalo (see Buffalo-bird).

Bulbul. Per. *bulbul*. In imitation of its note. The name was applied to various species by the English in India, one of which has been introduced into the continental United States. **Red-whiskered B.** for the red mark below the eye.

Bullbat. Nighthawk. For its crepuscular habit which it shares with bats. Bull, for its comparatively large size and noisy habit.

Bunting. An early name for the British Corn Bunting and now given to several sparrow-like birds in Britain and in America. The origin is obscure. MacLeod suggests it may be cognate with G. *bunt*, "mottled," and may apply to the Corn Bunting. Weekley thinks it is possibly derived from a double diminutive of F. *bon-et-on*, and a pet name, as for a child in the old nursery rhyme, "Bye, Baby Bunting." **Indigo B.** L. *indicum*, Gr. *indicon*, "Indian," for the country of origin of indigo dye, a bluish powder obtained from plants. For the color of the male's plumage. **Lark B.** as it sings on the wing like a lark. **Lazuli B.** ML. *azulus*, "azure," a term generally used in connection with the semiprecious stone, lapis lazuli. For the blue color of the male's plumage. **McKay's B.** for Charles McKay (see Appendix). **Painted B.** as it appears to be painted in a variety of colors. **Snow B.** for the color of the plumage with wintry associations. **Varied B.** for the different shades of the male's plumage.

Burgomaster. A name for both the Glaucous and Great Black-backed Gull. Du. *burge-moester*, "town master," possibly suggested by the manner in which these large gulls dominate their lesser associates.

Bushtit. ME. *bush*, "a thicket," for the bird's habitat; *tit* (see

Titmouse). Both **Black-eared B.** and **Common B.** have been dropped as both are considered belonging to one species with the name **Bushtit.**

Butcher-bird. A name for the shrike. For its habit of impaling its food.

Buzzard. L. *buteo* through F. *busard*. In Britain a common name for the larger soaring hawks. The early colonists coming from a country devoid of vultures bestowed the name on the large soaring American vultures, giving us Turkey Buzzard, Black Buzzard and even Mexican Buzzard for the Caracara.

Calico-back. Hunter's name for the Ruddy Turnstone. This name still persists along the sandy coasts where there are no stones to turn, although hunting of the shore birds is now a thing of the past. For the striking and colorful pattern of the back, especially in flight. E. *calico* formerly *calicut* from the dappled pattern of the cloth imported from Calicut (now Kozhikode), a port of the southwestern coast of India. Cf. calico cat.

Camp Robber. One of a variety of common names used by the hunter, trapper and backwoodsman of the north for the Gray Jay, the term most familiar to the ornithologist. According to Bent, "the 'camp robber' will eat anything from soap to plug tobacco, for it will, at least, steal and carry off such unsavory morsels; some Indians have said, 'Him eat moccasins, fur cap, matches, anytink.'" He goes on to quote William Brewster's journal (1937): ". . . they spend the greater part of each day carrying food back into the woods. They seemed to prefer baked beans to any other kind of food . . . and next to beans, oatmeal. . . . Of baked beans they regularly took four at one load, three in the throat and one held in the bill." Bent goes on to quote a letter from Manly Hardy: "I know of nothing that can be eaten that they will not take, and I had one steal all my candles, pulling them out endwise one by one from a piece of birch bark they were rolled in, and another pecked a large hole in a cake of castile soap. A duck which I had picked and laid down for a few minutes had the entire breast eaten out by one of these birds.

I have seen one alight in the middle of my canoe and peck away at the carcass of a beaver I had skinned. They often spoil deer saddles by pecking into them near the kidneys. They do great damage to the trappers by stealing the bait from traps set for martins and minks and by eating the trapped game; they will spoil a martin in a short time. They will sit quietly and see you build a trap and bait it, and then, almost before your back is turned, you hear their hateful 'ca-ca-ca' as they glide down and peer into it."

Canary. Our wild birds get the name from their resemblance to the caged birds first introduced into Italy from the Canary Islands in the sixteenth century. F. *Canarie,* Sp. *Canaria,* L. *insula Canaria;* L. *canis,* "dog," the islands being so named, according to Pliny, for the dogs found there. **Blue C.** for the Indigo Bunting. **Wild C.** for either the American Goldfinch or the Yellow Warbler.

Canvasback. For its whitish back.

Caracara. Probably a South American native name in imitation of its call, a low rattle.

Cardinal. L. *cardinalis,* "important," from L. *cardo, cardin-,* "hinge," which came to mean "important" as it was something on which an object or idea depended or hinged. Cf. Gr. *cardan,* "to swing." LL. *episcopus cardinalis,* originally the designation of one in charge of an important (cardinal) church in Rome and member of the council electing the Pope. Now a name for high church officials whose robes and hats are red. Hence a name for the bird whose plumage is that color.

Catbird. For one of its notes which resembles the mewing of a cat.

Cedar Bird. The Cedar Waxwing. For one of its favorite habitats.

Chachalaca. In imitation of the bird's call.

Chaparral Cock. A name in general use for the Roadrunner over most of its range. Sp. *chaparra,* "evergreen oak," which has evolved in southwestern United States into a name for dense scrub made up of a variety of plants. The "chaps" of a cowboy, the tough overtrousers worn to protect his legs from thorny undergrowth, are a shortening of chaparral. This name for the bird comes from its habitat. A modern dictionary states that the female is called the chaparral hen; not so, as the sexes are alike in plumage. Cock, AS. *cocc,* "adult male chicken, rooster," probably imitative of its cry, a shortening of cock-a-doodle-do. The name became associated with other birds with or without reference to the sex and for no apparent reason, as in Cock Robin. The aggressive and jaunty character of the cock has given us "cocky," and the jauntiness implied in cocked hat for the tilt, which, if happening to the eye, is rendered "cockeyed."

Chat. In England used with a prefix for bird names, as in *Stonechat, Whinchat.* The Stonechat gets its name from its persistent call of harsh notes resembling, according to Newton, the clicking of stones together. Although the American chat resembles the European bird in size only, some of its notes may have suggested to the colonists the bird of the Old World. On the other hand, the American name may have come about independently, as chat for chatterer, which the bird surely is, with its unique and amazing conglomerations of whistles, squeaks, squeals, musical single notes and phrases, and harsh chattering in varied sequence and timing, poured out in unpremeditated artlessness. Stone claims he identified in the song, "the rasped call of the kingfisher, . . . trill of the tree toad, call of the yellowlegs, and a distant auto horn." **Yellow-breasted C.** for its bright yellow breast. **Long-tailed C.** another name for the Yellow-breasted, for its long tail.

Chebec. For its call, which is one of the surest means of identifying the Least Flycatcher.

Cherry Bird. The Cedar Waxwing. For one of its favorite foods, the wild cherry. It has been observed squeezing the juice into the open mouths of its nestlings for their first feedings.

Chewink. An alternative name for the Rufous-sided Towhee, also imitative of its call.

Chickadee. Onomatopoeic. **Black-capped C.** for the black crown. **Boreal C.** L. *borealis, Boreas;* Gr. *Boreas,* "god of the north wind." Boreas fell in love with the nymph Crithyia, but his breathing was so harsh that it repelled her, not being in concordance with her maidenly ideas of a lover's sighs. True to his rough-and-ready character, Boreas soon lost his patience and carried her off. This name for the chickadee does not imply a virile harshness but a northern range. **Carolina C.** a place name first used for the colonies when Charles II was king of England. L. *Carolus,* "Charles." Also a loose term of the naturalists meaning "southern," for the range of the bird. **Chestnut-backed C.** for the rich brown color of the back. **Gray-headed C.,** which was also known as **Siberian C.** and is now called **Siberian Tit**, for its gray cap. **Mexican C.** for its southern range. **Mountain C.** for its range in the Rocky Mountains.

Chicken. ME. *chiken,* AS. *cicen,* "chicken," related to the word cock. **Greater Prairie-C.** F. *prairie,* "meadow," a name given by the early French explorers to the great central plains; L. *pratum,* "meadow"; Greater as it is slightly larger than the **Lesser Prairie-C.** Prairie is a habitat name for both birds.

Chippy. A familiar name for the Chipping Sparrow (see Sparrow, Chipping S.).

Chuck-will's-widow. In imitation of the bird's call.

Chukar. Hindu *chakar,* "the Indian Hill Partridge," a range name for one of the twenty geographic races of the species whose total range extends from the Alps to the Himalayas. It is used in America for the racially mixed introduced species.

Clam Bird. For the food preference of the American Oystercatcher. It could easily be called Mussel Bird as it also feeds on mussels.

Cock of the Woods. The Pileated Woodpecker. For its red crest resembling a comb, and its habitat.

Coffin-bearer. For the Great Black-backed Gull or Burgomaster who, indeed, seems to walk at a deliberate and mournful pace.

Collective names.

Bevy: In late ME. *bevy,* "a company of roes (deer), larks, quails or ladies"; as in a bevy of beauties.

Brace: As in a brace of partridges. L. *brachio* (pl.), "two arms," came to mean that which held things together as by a string, hence two birds tied together. We find another use of the term in embrace.

Brood: AS. *brod,* "the hatching and the care of the young," hence a number of birds from one nest.

Clutch: Used for the young hatched from one set of eggs or for the number of eggs in one nest; formerly also a number of chickens. From Scottish and Provincial E. *cleck,* "to hatch," allied to "cluck" of a hen.

Colony: For birds breeding together. It may be refined to denote the breeding sites for some species, as in heronry or rookery. L. *colonia,* "a farm or settlement."

Congregation: L. pp. of *congregare,* "to collect in a flock," more commonly used in Britain for an assemblage of Rooks.

Covey: F. *couvée,* "brood"; pp. of F. *couver,* "to brood, to hatch." Now a sport term for a foraging flock of partridges, bobwhites or pheasants.

Creche: F. *crêche,* "A hospital for foundlings, or public nursery where working mothers can leave their children." The term has been adopted by ornithologists for aggregations of young birds such as the Flamingo and the Emperor Penguin of the Antarctic.

Flock: AS. *flocc,* "a company of sheep, and other animals as in a flock of geese or teal." AS. also used the word for a gathering of men, but not as in E. where usage is generally limited to members of a church. The most usual term for a number of birds of the same kind.

Murmuration: A falconry term for a flock of Starlings, an echoic word. F. *murmurer,* L. *murmurare,* "to murmur."

Raft: A large and rather closely packed number of ducks on water.

Skein: For the resemblance of a line of geese in flight to a length of thread.

Spring: For a number of teal, possibly from the impression given by their quick takeoff as they spring into flight.

Wisp: For the resemblance of a wavering line of shorebirds in flight to a thin column of smoke.

Condor. Sp. *cóndor,* from Peruvian *cuntur,* "condor." **California C.** for the state where the bird is found. It is not the same species as the Andean Condor.

Coot. Of uncertain origin and perhaps cognate with scout and scoter. Used in ME. for various waterfowl and still in general use for all three scoters. **American C.** as it is a different species from the European.

Cormorant. F. *cormoran,* "cormorant," (in some patois, *cor marin*); L. *corvus,* "crow." L. *marinus,* "pertaining to the sea." As the final *t* is not found in any source of the word, it is labeled spurious by etymologists. **Brandt's C.** for J. F. Brandt (see Appendix). **Double-crested C.** for the almost invisible crests. **Great C.** is the cormorant common in Europe. Americans add the adjective to differentiate it from the Double-crested C. **Olivaceous C.** alludes to the dull green color which is not distinctive. **Pelagic C.** Gr. *pelagos,* "the sea," but not more so than other cormorants. **Red-faced C.** has more and brighter red in the face than the Pelagic C.

Corn Crake. Corn is the British word for grain. AS. *corn,* "corn," a habitat word for the grain fields frequented by the birds. Crake imitates the bird's call, probably from AS. *cracian,* "to make a noise"; cf. crack, creak.

Cowbird. In England, the Yellow Wagtail. In America, the bird which associates with cattle. Catesby says it is an abbreviation of Cowpen-bird. "They delight much to feed in the pens of cattle, which has given them their name." The plumage of both sexes has a light bronze sheen. **Bronzed C.** for the metallic sheen of its plumage. **Brown-headed C.** for the male's brownish head. **Common C.** another name for the Brown-headed C. **Red-eyed C.** alternative name for the Bronzed C.

Cowcow. Onomatopoeic name for the cuckoos.

Crane. AS. *cran,* "crane," ultimately from an ancestral Indo-European root, *gar, ker,* "to cry out." That such a word once existed is inferred from the number of words similar in form and meaning in the same language family. Thus, besides the parental relation in AS. *cran,* we find its first cousins in other Teutonic languages: Du. *krean,* G. *kranich,* "crane," and among second cousins in the Romance languages, the descendents of Latin, F. *grue,* I. *gru,* from L. *grus,* all meaning "crane." Another second cousin, Greek, has *geranos,* "crane." We call these cousin words cognates to denote common ancestry. E. *geranium,* so-called because its seed pod resembles a crane's bill, comes directly from Greek with only the last syllable undergoing a Latin change. E. *pedigree* comes from L. *ped,* "foot," and L. *grus,* "crane," with maybe a brief stop in France where we find it in old Anglo-French as *pe de gru* and in French, *pied de grue.* The meaning comes from the sign, the foot of the crane, used to indicate relationships in the family tree. The number of the bird's toes depended on the number of children in the family. Words develop figurative meanings which are paralleled, as Gr. *geranos* means a lifting machine, which *crane* does in English. L. *grus* also means battering ram, as its long pole suggests a crane's neck. We crane our necks, have a crane-fly for its birdlike silhouette, and a crane-fly orchid for its crane-fly–like appearance. **Sandhill C.** probably from its congregating on a low hill for its courtship dance. **Whooping C.** from the bird's note. F. *houper* from the cry *houp* used to command dogs and horses as *hup* was used to get horses moving. The original form was *hoop.* And a child with the whooping cough does sound like the Whooping Crane and vice versa.

Creeper. From its habit of moving up tree trunks. **Brown C.** for the predominating color of the back. **Tree C.** the British name for a similar species, possibly to differentiate the bird from a nuthatch, which is also called creeper.

Crossbill. OE. *cros,* L. *crucem,* "cross." After the Roman gallows became a religious symbol, the Latin word for it spread in various forms over Europe, making it difficult to trace the direct route from one language to another. Preoccupation with the word as a religious symbol accounts for the legend that the bird acquired the shape of its bill while attempting to withdraw the nails that held Christ to the cross; and in so doing the bird became so splattered with blood that its plumage became ever after generously hued with red. The name for the bird comes from the overlapping ends of the beak, which make it appear crossed. This shape makes it a specialized tool for extracting seeds from cones. AS. *bile,* "a bird's beak"; allied to AS. *bill,* "sword, axe." **Crossbill** British name for the American **Red Crossbill,** which is red with the exception of the dark brown wings and tail. **Two-barred C.** British name for the American **White-winged C.** whose wings are dark brown with two white wing bars.

Crow. AS. *crawe,* "crow," in imitation of the call, although we find it comfortable to say "a crow caws" and "a rooster crows." An individual "crows" when unduly bragging and "eats crow" when he finds it necessary to retract an ill-considered assumption. Age puts "crow's feet" beside the eyes. We have "crow berry" for the evergreen plant with black fruit and the "crow-foot violet" from the shape of its leaves. "Jim Crowism" is a term for the doctrine and practice of discrimination against blacks. The crow's habit of flying rather directly to its roosts seems to account for the expression "straight as the crow flies." **American C.** a good name for this widely distributed bird. **Carrion C.** a local name in America for the Black Vulture but a species of crow in Britain. **Fish C.** generally found near the seashore where it scavenges for many kinds of food. **Northwestern C.** for its range in northwestern United States.

Cuckoo. An imitative name so appropriate that there are practically no others in English or foreign languages which have kindred words: F. *coucou,* G. *kuckuck,* Gr. *kokkus,* Sa. *kokila;* in OE. and ME. we find *coccou, cuccu, cukkow, cocow.* The European Cuckoo of parasitic fame is a different species from the American birds. **Black-billed C.** for the color of its bill. **Black-eared C.** another name for the Mangrove Cuckoo, for the black feathers behind the eye, an excellent field mark. **Ground C.** the Greater Roadrunner which is closely related to the cuckoo. **Mangrove C.** for one of its favorite habitats, the mangrove thickets. **Yellow-billed C.** for the bill's color.

Curlew. F. *corlieu,* "curlew," in imitation of the call. **Bristle-thighed C.** for the barbless feather shafts projecting from its flanks. **Eskimo C.** from the name of its human cohabitants. **Hudsonian C.** once in general use for the Whimbrel. **Long-billed C.** for the bill which is about a third of the bird's length. **Spanish C.** for the White Ibis, as the bill is shaped somewhat like a curlew's.

Cutwater. A local name for the Black Skimmer. For its manner of flying with its bill in the water. Also used for the shearwaters.

Cygnet. L. *cygnus,* "swan," plus the diminutive *-et,* hence "little swan." For the young of the swan, generally the Mute Swan.

Dabchick. Formerly dap or dopchick. AS. *dop-snid,* "dipping duck," a name in Britain for the Moorhen as well as the sanctioned name for the Little Grebe. In America it is a local name for the Pied-billed Grebe.

Daddy-long-legs. The Black-necked Stilt whose legs, excepting the flamingo's, are the longest in proportion to the size of its body than those of any other bird.

Darter. Local name for the Anhinga. **Blue D.** Cooper's Hawk. **Little Blue D.** Sharp-Shinned Hawk.

Devil Downhead. Local name for the nuthatches. For its going head-first down tree trunks, in the sense of a daredevil.

Dickcissel. In imitation of its song.

Dipper. Quite possibly not from its dipping into the water to feed, but from its dipping motion when perched on a stone in a stream. Suffix *-er,* "one who," hence, "one who teeters." **American D.** as it is a different species from the Eurasian. See, also, Ouzel.

Dotterel. The diminutive of "dolt," ME. *dote,* "to be foolish," especially in old age as in dotage. Swann quotes Ray as saying, "It is a very foolish bird, and is taken in the night time, by the light of a candle, by imitating the gestures of the fowler, for if he stretches out an arm the bird stretches out a wing, if a foot, the bird likewise a foot; in brief, whatever the fowler does, the bird does the same, and so being intent upon the man's gestures it is deceived, and covered with the net spread for it." This is, of course, nonsense to anyone who has observed the birds. Newton points out that it is the fowlers imitating the birds and not vice versa. "We call a foolish, dull person a Dotterel, and on this account our people also call it Dotterel, as if they were to say doting with folly." **Eurasian D.** in spite of its name also breeds in Alaska.

Dove. Probably from AS. *dufan,* "to dive." From the bird's swift and irregular flight. In the past in England a general term for "wild pigeon." **Ground-D.** where it is generally seen. **Inca D.** found from southwestern United States to northwestern Costa Rica. In Mexico it is called *coquito common,* which suggests that it is fairly abundant in the land of the ancient Aztecs. The common name of the bird reflects the scientific name given it by Larson. It appears that he confused the land of the Aztecs with the land of the Incas in Peru. **Mourning D.** for its forlorn call. **Ringed Turtle-D.** for the dark line of feathers on the back of the neck; turtle from AS. *turtla,* "turtle dove," imitating the cooing of the bird. Chaucer tells us of "the wedded turtil with her hearte trewe." To the confusion of the nonliterary, the bible reminds us that "the voice of the turtle was heard in the land." Beginning in the sixteenth century and increasingly in the seventeenth, we find the name of the bird appearing as turtle dove. Although this marriage of words enlarged the meaning to show the relationship with the larger doves, the more potent reason was that another meaning for turtle came into the language. English sailors of the period became acquainted with the large sea tortoises of the Caribbean. This animal became known to them as turtle, possibly from their corruption of F. *tortue* or from their idea that the neck of the turtle resembled that of the turkey. Gradually the word turtle by itself came to be used for the creatures having shells and the name for the small dove became the two-word turtle dove. **Rock D.** is the progenitor of the domestic pigeon, which got its name from nesting in rocky cliffs.

Spotted D. most likely for the lacy pattern of the neck.
White-fronted D. F. and L. *frons, front,* "forehead" which
was its original sense in English, here retained for the white
forehead of the bird, but, alas, there are other doves with
this characteristic and the name has been changed to **White-
tipped D.** in reference to its tail. **White-winged D.** for the
large white wing patches on the secondaries. **Zenaida D.**
Charles L. J. L. Bonaparte (see Appendix), the nephew of
Napoleon, came to America with his wife, Zenaide, a niece
of Napoleon, and her father, Joseph Napoleon, following
the decline of the family fortunes after Waterloo. Charles,
an eminent ornithologist, was employed by the Academy of
Natural Sciences in Philadelphia, Pennsylvania. In reorgan-
izing the classification of American birds, he gave his wife's
name, Zenaide, to the genus of doves in which he placed
this one. Latinized to Zenaida, it has become, in addition to
the genus name, the common name for this species (see
Appendix under Zenaide).

Dovekie. As in "dove" plus *-kie,* a diminutive suffix giving us
"little diver."

Dowitcher. Before crystallized into its present spelling, it was
dowitchee, doewitch, and dowitch from Deutsher (German)
or Duitsch (Dutch) snipe to distinguish it from the English
(common) snipe. Coues says the name was associated with
Dutch traditions in New York. In Stroud we find "its odd
name 'Deutacher snipe' may derive from its popularity as a
food in Revolutionary times with the Hessians." While this
is possible, it seems unlikely that the Hessians stayed long
enough in one place to establish a lasting impression on the
language from an item on their menu. The Dutch, on the
other hand, played an important role for a considerable period of time in colonial New York and may have contributed
to the name. Maybe both played a part or neither, as the
name may be of Indian origin. The British name, Red-
breasted Snipe, is much simpler. **Long-billed D.** its bill is
on the average longer than that of the Short-billed D. with
considerable overlapping in size. Competent bird watchers
(and listeners) find that the weak crisp notes of the Long-

billed D. distinguish it from the two- or three-syllabled liquid call of the **Short-billed D.**.

Duck. AS. *duce,* "diver." Also a female duck with drake as the male. With *-ling,* the diminutive suffix, *duckling,* "a young duck." **American Black D.** for the very dark brown plumage. **Black-bellied Whistling-D.** for the black underparts. Formerly **Black-bellied Tree-D.** Often perches in trees and sometimes nests in them. **Dusky D.** another name for the Mottled D. **Fulvous Whistling-D.** L. *fulvus,* "reddish-yellow," for the color of its plumage. Until recently was **Fulvous Tree-D. Gray D.** a name for the Gadwall. **Harlequin D.** for the variegated plumage which recalls the pantomime costume of the Italian stage. **Labrador D.** for the breeding area of this extinct bird. **Masked D.** for the pattern of the male's face. **Mexican D.** for the main area of its range, although currently merged with the Mallard. **Mottled D.** for its streaked and speckled plumage. **Ring-necked D.** for the faint line of lighter color at the base of the neck. **Rock D.** another name for the Harlequin Duck for its frequenting of rocky shores. **Ruddy D.** for the striking color of the male's breeding plumage. **Whistling D.,** or Whistler, a popular name for the Goldeneyes and both wigeons, but now used for what were Tree-ducks. **Wood D.** for its nesting in hollows of trees.

Dunlin. AS. *dunn,* "dark"; *-lin* (having dropped a terminal *g*) the diminutive suffix, giving us "the little dark one" for the bird in the breeding plumage. Formerly Red-backed Sandpiper.

Eagle. F. *aigle,* L. *aguila,* "eagle," originally black eagle from L. *aguilus,* "dark"; also L. *aquilo,* "the north wind," which darkened the sky; used by imperial Rome as a military standard. Aquiline describes a rather large and somewhat hooked nose which suggests the beak of the bird. **Bald E.** although *bald* now means bare and hairless, in ME. *balled* meant "shining white." The present meaning is the one used for this bird in describing its head, although the bald appearance is due to the white feathers rather than to a lack of them. This bird is the official symbol of the United States, appearing on its seal. The choice of this bird was deplored by Benjamin Franklin who was familiar with its robbing the Osprey and termed it a bird of "bad moral character." His choice of bird was the Turkey. **Golden E.** from the color of the feathers of the neck and head.

Egret. F. *aigrette,* "egret"; Old High German *heigir,* "heron," the *-ir* was replaced by the suffix *-ette,* a diminutive which suggests that the name originally meant the Little Egret of the eastern hemisphere. **Cattle E.** for its associating with cattle. **Common E.** the former American name for the bird; called in Britain the Large Egret. The British Ornithologists' Union says this more appropriate name, used in India and elsewhere in the Old World normal range for this species, is preferred to the Great White Heron of British bird books. The choice for the former American name may have been because it is widespread. The American Ornithologists' Union now prefers **Great Egret**. **Reddish E.** for the color of the neck plumage. **Snowy E.** for the white plumage.

Eider. Ic. and ON. *aedr,* "eider." The "down" in eiderdown is also from Old Norse *dunn.* **Common E.** the British call this bird the Eider Duck. The American Ornithologists' Union dropped "Duck" from the name, which was established in English, and added the innocuous adjective "Common," apparently for its presence locally in large numbers off the New England coast in winter. It is rare elsewhere. **King E.** as it has raiment fit for a king. **Spectacled E.** for the white patch bordered by a black rim, around the eye of the male. **Steller's E.** for George W. Steller (see Appendix).

Eyas. A falconer's term for a young hawk obtained from the nest, generally the female. F. *niais,* "nestling"; L. *nidus,* "nest." The *n* was lost and the ME. *ey,* "egg," mistakenly added. The spelling may also have been influenced by a mistaken association with *eyry.* The name for the male bird taken from the nest was eyas tiercel. Some say it was so-called because it was a third smaller than the female, while others maintain the reason was that every third bird in the nest was a male. OF. *tierce,* L.*tertius,* "a third." The superstition that the third egg laid in a clutch produced a male is also found as a justification for the name.

Eyrie, Eyry, Aerie. Nest of an eagle or other large bird in a high place. No one derivation seems certain. Several words may have been contributed as sources: L. *ager,* "field," with the connotation of birthplace; L. *aer,* "air," and ME. *ei,* "eggs."

Falcon. L. *falx, falcis,* "sickle," for the curved beak and talons. The name is now used for the swift flying hawks with long and pointed wings, in the genus *Falco.* In falconry the female peregrine was called the "falcon gentle" while the male was the "tiercel gentle." **Aplomado F.** Sp. *aplomar, plomado,* "to plumb"; L. *plumbum,* "lead." As a lead weight on a string was used to obtain an accurate perpendicular line, the term "plumb" came to mean this method of obtaining such a line. The stoop of this falcon after prey in almost straight vertical descent suggests the derivation of its name. Sp. *plomo,* "lead"; L. *plumbum,* "lead," for its lead-colored plumage or its vertical stoop, the bird plummeting on its prey. **Peregrine F.** L. *per-,* "through"; L. *ager, agri,* "field"; L. *-inus,* "having to do with." The word peregrine, which to the Romans meant "foreign, wandering," evolved into E. *pilgrim.* Ray, writing in 1713, is quoted by Swann: "It took its name either from passing out of one country into another, or because it is not known where it builds." **Prairie F.** for its habitat.

Finch. AS. *finc,* "finch" which it has been called since the ME. period. It has a Teutonic ancestor as evidence in Du. *vink,* G. *fink,* S. *fink* and D. *finke.* Its most likely origin is onomatopoeic. **Black Rosy F.** for its two predominant colors. **Brown-capped Rosy F.** for the male's plumage. **Gray-crowned Rosy F.** for the male's plumage. These three now considered to be subspecies of **Rosy F. Cassin's F.** for John Cassin (See Appendix). **House F.** as it is commonly found around dwellings. **McGregor's House F.** for R. C. McGregor (see Appendix). It is now considered a subspecies and is extinct. **Purple F.** L. *purpureus,* "crimson" or other reddish color; Gr. *porphura,* "a shellfish," from which the

Tyrean purple dye was obtained. This was the imperial purple of the Romans, and to them it meant either the color or the cloth so colored. The togas of their senators were bordered with it. In ancient times wearing crimson signified royal rank. So in the classical sense of the word, the name of the color is correct for the bird's plumage. Now E. *purple* means a color obtained by mixing red and blue and indicates a color less reddish.

Flamecrest. Local name for the Golden-crowned Kinglet.

Flamingo. Sp. *flamenco,* Por. *flamingo,* "flamingo"; L. *flamma,* "flame," for the bright red plumage.

Flicker. AS. *flicerian,* "fluttering of birds." This seems to have been the original meaning of the word, which persisted at least until the time of Chaucer, who observed, "Above hir heed hir dowves flikernge." Cf. AS. *flacor,* "a flight of arrows," in some semblance of its original form. Later the meaning applied to a wavering light such as that of a candle in a draft and then to a passing feeling as in a "flicker of fear." The name Flicker for a bird seems to have been preempted solely by this bird. While the bird, being common, noisy, and conspicuous, has local names numbering in the hundreds, none rival Flicker in popularity. **Gilded F.** for the yellow in its wings and tail. **Northern F.,** formerly **Common F.** is now the specific name which includes the two following that are now classified as subspecies. **Red-shafted F.** for the color of the shafts of feathers which show in flight and which distinguish it from the **Yellow-shafted F.**

Flinthead. For the dark, featherless scaly head and neck of the Wood Ibis, which is not an ibis but a stork. (See Ibis, Wood I.)

Flycatcher. A name for a number of birds that prey on insects in the air. **Acadian F.** the name suggests a northern breeding range, Acadia being the old French name for Nova Scotia, the scene of the beginning of Longfellow's "Evangeline." This is singularly inappropriate for a range name as the bird's range is the most southern of the three empidonax flycatchers, the Mason-Dixon line being a rough northern boundary. The name is also inappropriate if it is meant to suggest a habitat of "murmuring pines and hemlock." The bird prefers thickets along streams in swampy hardwood areas. Its name may be accounted for by the confusion of early ornithologists in identifying the three small similar flycatchers. **Alder F.** for its habitat. Formerly another name for Traill's F., it is now considered a full species. Its members sing, "fee-bee-o." **Ash-throated F.** for its whitish-gray throat. **Beardless F.** for the absence of bristles about the base of the bill common to flycatchers, but now changed to **Northern Beardless-Tyrannulet** which is about as long as the bird. **Brown-Crested F.** a new, more descriptive name for Wied's Crested F. **Buff-breasted F.** just a shade more so than others of the group. **Coues' F.** for Elliott Coues (see Appendix). **Dusky F.** not particularly so when compared with the other empidonax. **Dusky-capped F.** a replacement name for the less specific Olivaceous F. **Fork-tailed F.** for the tail. **Gray F.** about as helpful as the name for the Dusky F. **Great Crested F.** one of the larger flycatchers with a crest. **Hammond's F.** for William A. Hammond (see Appendix). **Kiskadee F.** for its call. Now known as **Great Kiskadee. Least F.** as it is the smallest flycatcher in the eastern U.S. **Olivaceous F.** as most flycatchers are dark olive-gray, the name is no more distinctive than the plumage and has been replaced by more meaningful Dusky-capped F. **Olive-sided F.** for the dark streaks on the side of the belly. **Scissor-tailed F.** for the long outer tail feathers which suggest scissor blades. **Sulphur-bellied F.** for the rather dull yellow, heavily streaked underparts. **Traill's F.** for Thomas S. Traill (see Appendix). This name may still be used for this bird and the Alder F. where circumstances do not permit specific identification. This practically means all the time when either one is not singing. **Vermilion F.** for the brilliant plumage of the male. **Western F.** for its breeding range in North America. **Wied's Crested F.** for Prince Maximilian zu Wied (see Appendix), now replaced by Brown-crested F. **Willow F.** this is a new common name for "fitz-bew" singing members of the former Traill's F. **Yellow-bellied F.** for its dull yellow underparts.

Fly-up-the-creek. For the Green-backed Heron's habit of flying along a water course with a squawk when startled.

Forest Chippy. For the habitat of the Worm-eating Warbler and the resemblance of its song to that of the Chipping Sparrow, which is not a bird of the woods.

Frigatebird. A shortened version of the official name, **Magnificent F.**. Magnificent, through F. *magnifique*, from L. *magnus*, "great"; L. *facio*, "make"; Frigate, through F. *fregate*, from I. *fregata*, "a frigate." The name was originally given to the bird by seamen for its habit of pursuing and robbing other birds.

Fulmar. Swann says, "The name is said to be derived from the Gaelic, *fulmair*, but Mr. Harvie-Brown decides that the Gaelic is derived from the English and not the English from the Gaelic." The English name is of uncertain derivation; Swainson thought it akin to *foumart*, a polecat, meaning a foul martin, from the peculiar and disagreeable odor of the bird, owing to the oil which it emits and the rankness of its food. The oil vomited by this bird when caught is highly valued by the natives of St. Kilda as a cure for all diseases (Gray). Most authorities agree on ON. *ful*, "foul"; ON. *mar*, "maw," "gull." Noteworthy is the medicinal fortitude of the natives of the Outer Hebrides. Because there are two species, ours is now **Northern F.**

Gadwall. Coues says: "The name Gadwall was formerly Gaddel, Gadwall, Gadwale, Gadwell; origin obscure and etymology unknown." MacLeod agrees and then ventures, "Perhaps it is connected with AS. *gad*, a point, with reference to the fine tooth-like projections on the edges of the bird's mandible."

Gallinule. L. *gallinula*, "little hen." **Common G.** more numerous in the United States than the brighter colored **Purple G.** The British name for the Common G. is **Moorhen.** The American Ornithologists' Union has recently adopted **Common Moorhen.**

Gannet. AS. *ganot,* "little goose," which it was thought to be not only popularly but scientifically, being classed with the geese. An old name for the bird was solan goose, probably from ON. *sula,* "gannet"; ON. *ond, and,* "duck"; and E. *goose.* This gives us three bird names for one bird (see Goose).

Gnatcatcher. AS. *gnatt,* "a small insect," in imitation of the buzzing of the wings of the insect. OF. *chasier,* "hunt"; L. *capio, captum,* "take," for the birds habit of catching insects. **Black-tailed G.** for the color of its tail. **Blue-gray G.** for the color of its plumage.

Goatsucker. A name for the Whip-poor-will and its relatives from a superstition going back at least to Aristotle, who said: "Flying to the udders of she-goats, it sucks them, and thus gets its name. They say that the udder withers when it has sucked at it, and that the goat goes blind." Pliny gives us his version: "Caprimulgi, as they are called, look bigger than a Merula (thrush), and act as thieves by night; by day they even lack the power of sight. When I was in Switzerland I saw an aged man, who fed his goats upon the mountain, which I had gone up in search for plants. I asked him whether he knew of a bird the size of a Merula, blind in the day-time, keen of sight at night, which in the dark is wont to suck goats' udders, so that afterwards the animals go blind. Now he replied . . . that he had suffered many losses from those very birds; so that he had once had six she-goats blinded . . . but they now had flown away . . . to Lower Germany. . . . But possibly that aged man was jesting with me." Swann in 1912 felt called upon to tell us, "The story has long been refuted."

Gobbler. The male Turkey, in imitation of its call.

Godwit. Origin uncertain. It may be from AS. *god,* "good"; AS. *whita,* "animal," "bird," and more literally "good eating," although Coues says this is too easy to be true. **Bartailed G.** for the black and white bars on the tail. **Hudsonian G.** because the original specimen came from the Hudson Bay region. **Marbled G.** for the mottled back.

Goldcrest. A popular name for the Golden-crowned Kinglet.

A British bird of the same name in the same genus is not the same species.

Goldeneye. For the bright yellow iris. **Barrow's G.** for Sir John Barrow (see Appendix). **Common G.** as it is more widely distributed than Barrow's G.

Goldfinch. For the bright yellow plumage. The British have the same name for a yellowish finch of a different species. **American G.** to distinguish it in name from the European G., and put on the American Ornithologists' Union *Checklist* for a colony on Long Island which was once thought to be permanently established but has since disappeared. **Lawrence's G.** for George N. Lawrence (see Appendix). **Lesser G.** for the smallest goldfinch.

Goosander. The British name for the Common Merganser, rarely used in the United States.

Goose, Geese. AS. *gos, ges,* "goose." Cf. Du. *gans,* G. *gans,* ON. *gas,* Sp. *ganso,* cognate with L. *anser,* Gr. *ken,* E. *gander* (the male goose) and *gannet* are all derived from the same root, one of the few such for bird names. The Aryan root has been given as *gha,* "to gape or yawn," and may be the remote ancestor of such words as chasm, chaos. The vigorous old root is still producing a variety of descendants, albeit with a taint of slang: goose flesh or bumps, take a gander, cook one's goose, a goose egg (a zero score). **Barnacle G.** the name for the bird seems to have come from an old superstition that it hatched from the shellfish, called barnacles, *Lepas anatifera,* the scientific name also originating in the tale. Turner (1544) says: "When after a certain time the firwood masts or planks or yard-arms of a ship have rotted on the sea, then fungi, as it were, break out upon them first, in which in course of time one may discern evident forms of birds, which afterwards are clothed with feathers, and at last become alive and fly." He cites Gyraldus (1175) as bearing witness to the phenomenon and goes on to say, "by reason of the rarity of the thing I did not quite credit Gyraldus. . . . I took counsel of a certain man, whose upright conduct, often proved by me, had justified my trust, a theologian by profession and an Irishman by birth, Octavian by name, whether he thought Gyraldus worthy of belief in this affair. Who, taking oath on the very gospel which he taught, answered that what Gyraldus had reported of the generation of this bird was absolutely true, and that with his own eyes he had beholden the young." This seemed to satisfy Turner, who goes on to say that "the generation of the Bernicle will not appear so very marvellous to those who may have read what Aristotle wrote about the flying creature called Ephemerus." It seems it did not enter Turner's head to ask his Irish friend about the validity of Aristotle. Gerard in his *Herball,* or *Generall Historie of Plantes* (1597), not only goes into detail but also gives an illustration entitled, "The Barnacle Goose Tree." An excellent account of the fable may be found in Harting's *The Birds of Shakespeare* (1871). **Blue G.** for the dark-bluish hue of the back. Considered a morph (color phase) of the Snow Goose. **Cackling G.** a name for the smallest race of the Canadian G., for its distinctive call. **Canada G.** for the breeding range. **Emperor G.** although considered our "handsomest" goose, the reason for the name is obscure. **Ross' G.** for Bernard R. Ross (see Appendix). **Snow G.** as it is white. **Tule G.** a common name for the Greater White-fronted G., from its habitat. **Greater White-fronted G.** for the white forehead, distinguished from Old World Lesser White-fronted G.

Goshawk. AS. *gos,* "goose"; AS. *havoc,* "hawk," for one of the birds on which the bird might prey. Cf. ON. *gas-haukr.* **Mexican G.** also called Gray Hawk.

Gosling. AS. *gos,* "goose"; plus the diminutive suffix *-ling,* "little." For the young goose.

Grackle. ML. *gracula,* L. *graculus,* "jackdaw," "chough," also "cormorant." Adapted from a former scientific name for the genus in America but now for a genus, in another family, found in southern Asia of which the best-known member is the Hill Myna. Fairly common, it is popular as a pet, being an exceptional mimic. **Boat-tailed G.** in flight the middle of the large tail is depressed, giving it a resemblance to the keel of a boat. **Bronzed G.** formerly a separate species but now classified as a race of the **Common G.**

which includes the **Purple G.** formerly also classified as a distinct species. **Great-tailed G.** a new name for a former subspecies of the Boat-tailed G.

Grebe. F. *grebe*, which MacLeod suggests may come from Breton *krib*, "crest," which some grebes have. **Eared G.** for the light-colored tufts on the side of the head in its breeding plumage. **Holboell's G.** another name for the Red-necked G.; for Carl Peter Holboell (see Appendix). **Horned G.** for the buffy tufts on the side of its head. **Least G.** for its small size. **Mexican G.** for the Least Grebe's range. **Pied-billed G.** for the parti-colored bill. **Red-necked G.** for the color of the neck in its breeding plumage. **Western G.** for its range in western North America.

Greenlet. An old name which has lost ground to the more popular Vireo.

Grosbeak. F. *grosbec*, "grosbeak"; F. *gros*, "large"; F. *bec*, "beak." We might eliminate the French from the word and call the bird Grossbeak. **Black-headed G.** for the head coloring of the male. **Blue G.** for the male's bluish plumage. **Evening G.** a reflection of the scientific name, *vespertina*, which may mean either "western," the bird's range, or "evening" or "evening song" for its song in the evening. **Pine G.** for its habitat. **Rose-breasted G.** for the male's plumage.

Ground Chat. As it favors low vegetation and resembles the Yellow-breasted Chat in color.

Grouse. The ancestry of the word is vague, complicated by the confusion as to what bird was meant: bustard, godwit, crane, or grouse. Newton says: "The most likely derivation seems to be from the old French word *griershe, greoche* or *griais* (meaning speckled, and cognate with *grisius*, "grey") which was applied to some kind of partridge." **Blue G.** as it has a hint of blue on its underparts. **Ruffed G.** for the tufts on its neck resembling the neckware in vogue in the sixteenth century, which began as a ruffle on the wrist and gradually worked its way up. From *ruffle*, "to wrinkle," as the wind ruffles the water. It also seems to be related to the last syllable in dandruff, from ON. *hrufle*, "to scratch," an activity which ruffled (wrinkled) the skin. **Sage G.** for its habitat, the sage brush. **Sharp-tailed G.** for its pointed tail. **Spruce G.** for its habitat in spruce woods.

Guillemot. F. *Guillaume,* "William." A nickname with the transformed last syllable acquiring a *t,* suggesting a rendering of "little William" for the whole word. **Black G.** for the breeding plumage. **Pigeon G.** for its resemblance in size and shape to the domestic pigeon.

Gull. OF. Celtic origin: Cornish, *gullan;* Welsh, *gwylan;* Breton, *gwelan;* "a gull." Breton, one of the Celtic dialects, had the word, *goelaff,* "weep," which suggested to one etymologist that the word might originally have been imitative. Welsh *gwylan* also means "throat" as does L. *gula.* From the latter via OF. *goule,* "throat," we have gotten such words as gulp, gullet, and gullible. This suggests that "gull" might be related to the bird's indiscriminate scavenging; it appears willing to swallow almost anything. **Bonaparte's G.** for C. L. J. L. Bonaparte (see Appendix). **California G.** for the locality of the type specimen which came from around Stockton, California. **Common Black-headed G.** Chocolate-brown would be closer to the color of the head. **Franklin's G.** for Sir John Franklin (see Appendix). **Glaucous G.** for its silvery-blue plumage. **Glaucous-winged G.** for the color of its plumage. **Great Black-backed G.** from its size and plumage. **Heermann's G.** for A. L. Heermann (see Appendix). **Herring G.** this scavenger might occasionally eat a herring. **Iceland G.** breeds in Iceland whence came the original specimen in 1822. **Ivory G.** for its all-white plumage. **Laughing G.** for the resemblance of its cry to derisive human laughter. **Little G.** for its small size. **Mew G.** OE. *mew,* "a gull"; the bird the British call the Common Gull. **Ring-billed G.** for the dark ring on the bill of the mature bird. **Ross' G.** for Sir James C. Ross (see Appendix). **Sabine's G.** for Sir Edward Sabine (see Appendix). **Thayer's G.** for John E. Thayer (see Appendix). Formerly classified as a subspecies of the Herring G.; it is now a valid species. **Western G.** for its range on the west coast of the United States.

Gyrfalcon. The first syllable, the root *gyr,* seems to have caused a great diversity of opinions among etymologists. Here are some: (1) *Webster's New World Dictionary,* Germanic, *ger,* "spear"; (2) Albertus Magnus, L. *gyro,* "to circle," from the bird's habit of circling; (3) *Funk and Wagnalls New Standard Dictionary,* Gr. *hieros,* "sacred," as only royalty might hunt with them; (4) Skeat traces the word after several steps back to HG. *gir-* for *giri,* "greedy" (whence also G. *geier,* "a vulture"); (5) Coues quotes the *Century Dictionary,* "not connected with L. *gyrus,* 'a circle' but with G. *geier,* 'greedy'"; (6) The *Oxford Dictionary of English Etymology* says, "The first element (of gyrfalcon) is obscure." Various forms "have led to unjustifiable attempts to relate the first syllable to L. *gyrare,* 'gyrate,' and Gr. *hieros,* 'sacred.'" In spite of the fact that the term *Hierofalco* Cuvier, an early generic name, seems to lend some sanction to the Greek origin, it is most likely that the first element in the word is related to the G. *geier,* "greedy"; (7) Weekley suggests ON. *verthr,* "worthy," and that *gyr* is due to wrong etymology, confused with gyrate. Various spellings of the word have not contributed to its etymological clarity, as Coues notes that we have in English, "gerfaulcon, gerfaucon, gerfawcon, jerfaucon, gierfalcon, girefaucon, gyrfacoun, and gerfauk among others with many identical or similar forms in other European languages." He remarks on the spelling as follows: "*Gyrfalcon* is the worst, *gerfalcon,* the better, *jerfalcon* the best spelling of the name, if we regard the etymology of the word." It is quite possible Coues was not overfamiliar with the terms used in falconry which differentiated between the male and the female. Despite the welter of words, *gyrfalcon* was commonly the proper name for the female, as Swann states: "The male being formerly called the Jerkin (either diminutive of Jer or else from Jerkin, a short coat, hence indicating inferior size)." With Dr. Coues thus disregarded we can appreciate the contribution of the American Ornithologists' Union *Check-list* for standardizing the common bird names.

Hag, Hagdon, Hagdown, Haglet. Local names for the bird

called Greater Shearwater by Americans and Great Shear-water by the British.

Haggard. A falconer's term for a hawk caught wild in adult plumage.

Handsaw. See Heron.

Hangnest. The orioles, as several species have distinctive hanging nests.

Harrier. A British name for the hawks which usually hunt by flying low over the ground. The English names of *harnier* or *hen-harnier* came from the bird's harrying of poultry. The name appears first used for birds, in the sixteenth century. While there are four European species, there is only one American, the **Northern Harrier**, a newer name for the Marsh Hawk.

Hawk. AS. *hafoc,* "a hawk," cognate with *have* in the sense of grasp or seize. **Black H.** for its color. Has been renamed **Common Black-hawk**. **Broad-winged H.** for its wide wings. **Cooper's H.** for William Cooper (see Appendix). **Duck H.** for the bird on which it is supposed to prey. A name in general use for the Peregrine Falcon. **Ferruginous H.** for its reddish color. **Fish H.** a very popular name for the Osprey. **Gray H.** for its color. **Harlan's H.** for Richard Harlan (see Appendix). This is now a subspecies of the Red-tailed H. **Harris' H.** for Edward Harris (see Appendix). **Marsh H.** for its habitat. Now called **Northern Harrier. Pigeon H.** primarily a bird eater, it is named after one of the many species on which it preys. This is the same species called the Merlin in Britain and now the approved American name. **Red-shouldered H.** for the coloring on the bend of the wing. **Red-tailed H.** for the adult's red tail. **Rough-legged H.** for the feathered tarsi. **Sharp-shinned H.** the long, thin front of the lower leg of a man is a shin. The long, thin part of the lower leg of this bird suggests a shin, although it is below rather than above the ankle. The raised ridge on the front of the bird's tarsus (shin) is rather unique as the cross-section of the tarsus of most land birds is rounded. It is the reason for calling the shin sharp. **Short-tailed H.** for its short tail. **Sparrow H.** for its occasional prey. It is in the same subgenus as the Kestrel of Europe. The European Sparrow H. is an accipiter and not a falcon as the American. Although changes come slowly, American Kestrel has been substituted for Sparrow H. Nevertheless, it would be a comfort to those with orderly minds if the English and Americans could have more uniformity with ornithological nomenclature. A beginning could be made by calling all eagles, eagles; falcons, falcons; buteos, buzzards; accipiters, hawks; and harriers, harriers. **Swainson's H.** for William Swainson (see Appendix). **White-tailed H.** for the white tail. **Zone-tailed H.** for the wide tail band.

Heath Hen. A name for the eastern race, now extinct, of the Greater Prairie-Chicken.

Hell-diver. A name for grebes, particularly the Pied-billed Grebe.

Heron. ME. *heroun, heiron, harn,* OF. *hairon,* HG. *heiger,* "heron." I. *aghirone,* "heron," is credited with contributing to the final syllable. *Hern* is found in place names, surnames, crossword puzzles, and in poetry. *Heronshaw* or *hernshaw* according to Skeat should mean a young heron and by confusion a heronry. This is due to a false popular etymology: E. *heron,* "a heron" and *shaw,* "a wood." We are now able to understand the old taunt, "not able to tell a hawk from a handsaw" (*Hamlet,* Act II, Scene 2). A handsaw was not a tool for cutting wood but an end product of linguistic mutilation from OF. *herounceau* from older *herouncel,* the *-ceau* and *-cel* being diminutive, "a young heron." So it seems reasonable in the days when falconry was a popular sport to consider anyone who confused a hawk with a heron to be rather dimwitted. **Black-crowned Night-H.** for the feature which differentiates it from the Yellow-crowned, and Night for its nocturnal habits, especially its loud cries which advertise its presence while flying in the darkness. **Great Blue H.** for its size and color. **Great White H.** once treated as a separate species, but now as a color morph of the Great Blue H. This is the largest North American heron. **Green H.** some have remarked that it is also called the Little Green Heron because it has so little green in its plumage, but it does have some. It is now known as the **Green-backed H**. **Little Blue H**. for its size and color. **Louisiana H**. so-called by Wilson who had a penchant for naming birds after the place where they were first collected. In describing the birds collected on the Lewis and Clark expedition, of which this was one, Wilson named the bird for the vast area of the Louisiana Purchase and not for the state of Louisiana. **Tri-colored H**. frequently used nowadays for the Louisiana Heron. **Yellow-crowned Night-H**. for its distinctive yellow crown.

High-hole. Another of the many common names for the Common Flicker.

Honeycreeper. AS. *hunig,* "honey," for the bird's fondness for sweets; AS. *creepen,* "to crawl," for its ability to move along tree trunks as though it were creeping. Now officially the Bananaquit.

Hummingbird. For the sound of the buzzing wings. **Allen's H**. for C. A. Allen (see Appendix). **Anna's H**. for Anna, Duchess of Rivoli (see Appendix under Anna). **Black-chinned H**. for the dark chin. **Blue-throated H**. for the male's blue throat. **Broad-billed H**. maybe in comparison with another three-inch hummingbird. **Broad-tailed H**. as Coues says, the tail is "ample." **Buff-bellied H**. for the tawny color of the male's underparts. **Calliope H**. for Calliope, one of the nine muses, each of whom was head of some particular department in literature, science or the arts. Calliope was the muse of epic poetry. Any way you look at it, epic means big. But the Calliope is the smallest of the hummingbirds. From tip of bill to end of tail, it averages about two and three quarters of an inch. If Gould, who named the bird, admired the muses, why did he not choose Euterpe, the muse of lyric poetry? Lyrics are short and sweet. But maybe I am doing the namer of the bird an injustice. He could have had in mind the musical instrument, the calliope, which works by forcing steam through pipes. This interpretation is still more difficult to justify. **Costa's H**. for the Marquis de Costa (see Appendix). **Lucifer H**. meaning the torchbearer. **Rivoli's H**. for the Duc di Rivoli (see Appendix), unfortunately, now replaced by **Magnificent H**. **Ruby-throated H**. for its red gorget. **Rufous H**. for its rufous back. **Violet-crowned H**. for its distinctive violet crown. **White-eared H**. for the white patch behind its eye.

Ibis. L. *ibis*, Gr. *ibis*, "ibis," probably of Egyptian origin. It was mummified and also used in hieroglyphics. Thoth, the god of learning, had the head of an ibis. **Glossy I**. for the glimmering sheen on the dark plumage. **Scarlet I**. for the brilliant red color. **White I**. as only the wing tips are black. **White-faced I**. for the white lines on the face in breeding plumage. **Wood I**. for its nesting in woods. The bird is not an ibis but a stork. The name is sanctioned by usage as we call our red-breasted thrush a Robin. As **Wood Stork** avoids misleading taxonomic implications, the American Ornithologists' Union now prefers it to Wood I.

Jacana. A native South American name.

Jaeger. G. *jager*, "hunter." E. *yacht* has the same origin, coming into the language from Holland. **Long-tailed J**. as it has the longest tail of these birds. The British name is Long-tailed Skua. **Parasitic J**. no more a robber than the others. British name, Arctic Skua. **Pomarine J**. Gr. *poma*, "a lid"; Gr. *rhynchos*, "beak"; for the growth at the base of the bill in the breeding season. British name, Pomatorhine Skua.

Jay. F. *geai*, "jay." Although the origin is unknown, two possibilities are suggested. The first is that it was a Roman pet name from the name *Gaius*. The bird has such names as F. *Jacques*, "James," and G. *Wouter*, "Walter." The second is that the name is for the gay (bright) plumage. **Arizona J**. an obsolete name for the Gray-breasted J. **Blue J**. for its color. **California J**. formerly thought to be a separate species but now considered the Scrub J. **Canada J**. a name in general use for the Gray J. **Florida J**. like the California J., now a race of the Scrub J. **Gray J**. for the color of its plumage. **Gray-breasted J**. for its underparts. **Green J**. for its color. **Mexican J**. for its main range, although now called Gray-breasted J. **Pinyon J**. a Spanish name for the pine which the bird frequents. **Santa Cruz J**. for its locale; now considered a race of the Scrub J. **Scrub J.** for its habitat, scrubby growth. **Steller's J.** for George Steller (see Appendix).

Junco. L. *juncus,* "a rush." Derived from the scientific name for the genus, which is certainly not partial to reeds. **Dark-eyed J.** this is the enlarged species name. **Gray-headed J.** for the color of its head. **Oregon J.** for its range. Both are now subspecies of the Dark-eyed J. **Mexican J.** for its range, now a race of Yellow-eyed J. **Slate-colored J.** for its dull color. ME. *slat, sclat,* from OF. *esclat,* "a splinter, a slice of wood," hence a slice or flake of stone, from the most common color of the stone. This is now a subspecies of Dark-eyed J. **Pink-sided J.** another name for the Oregon J. **Red-backed J.** a local name for the Yellow-eyed J. **White-winged J.** for the two white wing bars, a race of Dark-eyed J. **Yellow-eyed J.** for its distinctive eyes. The second American junco species.

Kestrel. Since there are single records from Massachusetts and New Jersey, the **Eurasian K.**, this cousin of our American K., is in the American Ornithologists' Union *Check-list.* Weekley says, "F. *crecerelle,* dim. of *crecelle,* both used for kestrel. Originally a noisy bell or leper's clicket." He goes on to quote T. Cooper who in 1573 said, "Tinnunculus: a kinde of haukes; a kistrell or kastrell; a steyngall. They use to set them in pigeon houses, to make doves to love the place, because they fear away other haukes with their ringing voice." Thus it seems that the bird's name may come from its call. **American K.** quite a few Americans prefer this name to Sparrow Hawk. The American Ornithologists' Union now sanctions this preference.

Killdeer. In imitation of the call.

Kingbird. AS. *cyning,* "king." Possibly for the little crown, usually invisible like that of the Ruby-crowned Kinglet, of reddish gold feathers on the top of the head, or more probably because of the aggressive, dominating nature of the bird. **Arkansas K.** a once-popular name for the Western K. **Cassin's K.** for John Cassin (see Appendix). **Couch's K.** for Darius N. Couch (see Appendix). **Eastern K.** for its range in the eastern United States. **Gray K.** for its predominant color. **Thick-billed K.** an apt description. **Tropical K.** for its southern range. **Western K.** for its range in western United States.

Kingfisher. Literally chief of the fishers. AS. *cyning*, "king"; AS. *fisc*, "fish"; *-er*, suffix denoting "one who." **Belted K.** for the belt of colored feathers across the breast. **Green K.** for the greenish back. **Texas K.** an obsolete name for the **Ringed K.** for its white necklace.

Kinglet. AS. *cyning*, "king"; *-let*, diminutive suffix referring to the bright feathers of the bird's head and to its small size. **Golden-crowned K.** AS. *gold*, "gold"; ME. *corona* from OF. *corone*, from L. *corona*, "a wreath," from Gr. *coronis*, "a wreath," as the Greeks crowned their heroes with a garland of leaves. **Ruby-crowned K.** OF. *rubi*, from L. *rubinus*, "a ruby," from L. *rubeus*, "red," the color of the stone which is the color of the feathers on the bird's crown.

Kiskadee. Name descriptive of its call. The **Greater K.,** one of the two species in the genus (the other, obviously, the **Lesser K.**), once known as Kiskadee Flycatcher.

Kite. AS. *cyta*, "a kite." MacLeod suggests, "probably from the Aryan root *skut*, to shoot, go swiftly, with reference to the way in which the bird swoops on its prey." The *Oxford Dictionary* points out that the name corresponds to the G. *kauz*, "screech owl," and suggests the name may come from an imitation of the bird's plaintive voice. **American Swallow-tailed K.** for the shape of its tail. **Black-shouldered K.** for its distinctive epaulets. **Everglade K.,** a race of Snail K., for its range in Florida although it is also found in Cuba and the species south to Argentina. **Mississippi K.** for the state where Alexander Wilson found it. **Snail K.** preferred name for Everglade K. **White-tailed K.** for the color of its tail, a race of Black-shouldered K.

Kittiwake. Imitates the call. **Black-legged K.** for the leg color. **Red-legged K.** for the leg color distinguishing it from the above.

Knot. See scientific name *Calidris canutus*. Drayton's *Poly-Olbion* (1622) says: "The knot was called Canutus bird of old, of that great king of Danes, his name that still doth hold, his appetite to please, that farre and neare was sought, for him (as some have said), from Denmark hither brought." Weekley says the naming of the bird for Canute is baseless.

Lanner. F. *lanier*, L. *laniare*, "to dissever." A falconer's term for the immature female peregrine. The male was called the Lanneret.

Lapwing. AS. *hleapewince*, "one who turns about in running or flight," from AS. *hleapan*, "run," and *wincian*, "wink"; for the bird's twisting flight. **Northern L.,** a Eurasian species casual in North America and distinguished from **Southern L.,** its South American counterpart.

Lark. AS. *lawerce*, "lark," ME. *laverock*, "a lark." **Horned L.** for the tufts of head feathers. **Shore L.** an Old World name for the Horned Lark.

Limpkin. Probably from *limp*, for the bird's odd gait, and *-kin*, a diminutive suffix.

Log-cock. Local name for the Pileated Woodpecker.

Longspur. For the elongated rear claw. **Chestnut-collared L.** for the color of the back of the male's neck. **Lapland L.** whence came the first specimen. **McCown's L.** for J. P. McCown (see Appendix). **Smith's L.** for G. Smith (see Appendix).

Loon. As the call of the bird suggests the wild laughter of a demented person, many are inclined to associate its name with lunatic, as in the phrase "crazy as a loon." Loon is a corruption of Shetland, *loom*, from Ic. *lomr* and D. or S. *lom*, "lame," for the awkward walk of the bird on land. **Arctic L.** OF. *artique*, from L. *ar(c)ticus*, from Gr. *arktikes*, "the bear, the pole star," for the bird's range. **Common L.** ME. *commun*, OF. *comun*, L. *communis*, from L. *com*, "with," and L. *munus*, "bound," meaning obligatory services, a widespread obligation. Hence "usual" when applied to this loon. **Pacific L.** another name for the Arctic Loon. **Red-throated L.** for the dark red throat patch in the breeding season. **Yellow-billed L.** for the yellow color of the bill.

Magpie. Also called Magpye, Magotpie, Maggotypie, and

Maguerite. All dictionaries agree that *mag* is a pet form of E. *Margaret*, F. *marguerite*, L. *margarita* and Gr. *margarites*, "a pearl." The etymologists do not speak as one concerning *pie*. Skeat says, "ME. *pie*, F. *pie*, L. *pica*, "a magpie." MacLeod goes one step further in stating that the name may have been first imitative of the bird's call. Weekley says, "It has been suggested that it (the bird's name) may have to do with the magpie's habit of making miscellaneous collections." We are warned that the name seems to have no connection with the bird's habit of picking maggots from the backs of sheep. The British, having only one member of this genus, call their bird simply "Magpie." **Black-billed M.** although this bird is the same species as the one found in Britain, it is so called because the color of the bill is the main difference between it and the one other American magpie, the **Yellow-billed M.** The Black-billed M. is sometimes called the **American M.** The L. *picus*, "woodpecker," possibly comes from the same source. This supposition is reinforced by Sa., *pikas*, "Indian Cuckoo." L. *pipio*, "chirp," is also most likely related, indicating that the ancestral word was imitative of the bird's voice. At any rate, the magpie has long been known for its fairly continuous chattering. It gave rise no doubt to the old legend that it was the only bird that refused to enter the ark, preferring a perch on its roof from which it could jabber about the discomfiture of those caught in the rising flood. Leviner records that Aristotle was impressed by the bird's loquacity, stating that "the pica often times changes its notes, for almost every day it utters different cries." We are certain Pliny was referring to the magpie when he made the following improbable contribution to ornithological lore: Turner translates Pliny, "Not only do they learn, but they delight to talk, and meditating carefully and thoughtfully within themselves hide not their earnestness. They are known to have died when overcome by difficulty in a word, and, should they not hear the same things constantly, to have failed in their memory, and while recalling them to be cheered up in wondrous wise, if meanwhile they have heard the word." One modern philologist has the ornithological effrontery to suggest that our word "pie" for the pastry, a collection of edibles in one dish, is derived from observing the magpie's habit of collecting miscellaneous objects. He is in error as the bird does not, but to balance this he informs us that the "pie" in "piebald" when applied to the pattern of a horse's coat comes from the contrasting light and dark of the bird's plumage.

Mallard. ME. *malard* from OF. *malard,* "the mallard." From OF. *male,* "male," which derives from L. *masculinus,* extended from L. *masculus,* "male," and L. *mas,* "a male," plus the intensifying suffix *-ard* from HG. *hart,* an adjective meaning "bold, hardy," akin to the E. *hard.* It generally has a pejorative sense as in drunkard, dullard, and sluggard. The suffix seems to fit well the mallard male who exemplifies in his relations with the female a singular concentration on the physical union alone. The female, after she is snatched bald-headed, gets the eggs to hatch, the ducklings to raise, and her drake's name. The Mexican Duck is now considered a subspecies of Mallard.

Man-o'-war Bird. A name in general use for the Magnificent Frigatebird.

Marsh Hen. Used for both the Clapper Rail and the American Coot.

Martin. F. *Martin,* "Martin," a proper name in French as in English. It originated as a pet name derived from L. *Mars,* the stem of which is *mart.* Add to this the diminutive suffix *-in* and we have Martin or little Mars. Robin is derived in the same manner from Robert. The pet name is found not only in F. *Martin* but also in F. *martinpecheur,* "the king fisher." It appears also in F. *martinet,* "swift." We can conjecture that the nickname Martin had become established as a proper name and in making it into a pet name the second time, another diminutive suffix *-et* was added, giving us the F. *Martinet* "little little Mars." Making its way into English as a bird name, the word seems to have dropped its connotation of swift in favor of the swallows, as we have in the British dialect of English House Martin and Sand Martin. That this was a gradual evolution is suggested by an old term for the House Martin which appears in Shakespeare's *Merchant of Venice*: "like the martlet builds in the weather on the outside walls." Although the Americans superseded Sand Martin with Bank Swallow, they found a use for the word martin by naming their largest swallow the Purple Martin. The French not only call their swifts martinets to this day, but have commemorated their patron saint, St. Martin of Tours, in their name for the Hen Harrier, Busard Saint Martin. Did the Romans call the swallows and swifts "little Mars" because they appeared at the time of the first month on their calendar, when the dancing priests of Mars, the Salii, took out their sacred shields and spears to initiate the warring season? If no war was contemplated for the winter the weapons were stored away at a time commemorated by another festival. This festival was a very popular one and metamorphosed into Martinmas, November 11th, which is the feast day of Saint Martin. Not only is he the patron saint of France, but of innkeepers, drinking companions and reformed drunkards. Could it be possible that the erratic flight of swifts and swallows, bringing to mind the wavering walk of the dedicated celebrants of Saint Martin, was the inspiration for the nickname of the bird, "little Martin"? **Purple M.** for the male's dark plumage.

Meadowlark. AS. *mead,* "a place where grass was cut"; the longer form, meadow, is due to the addition of a case inflection and refers to the bird's habitat. AS. *lawerce* through ME. *laverock,* to E. *lark,* "a lark." The English colonists probably called our eastern bird a lark because its fine song reminded them of the song of the Old World Skylark. Our American birds, however, are in the blackbird and oriole family and are not true larks. **Eastern M.** for the species whose range is in eastern North America. **Western M.** for the species with the more western range.

Merganser. L. *mergus,* "a diver"; L. *anser,* "a goose"; hence "diving goose." **Common M.** Common is meaningless. **Hooded M.** AS. *hod,* "a hat," allied to E. *hat,* for the bird's crest. **Red-breasted M.** referring to the breast of the male.

Merlin. OE. *marlin, marlion,* "merlin"; in the days of falconry the term for the female bird. OF. *esmerillon*. Merlin is the name approved by the British Ornithologists' Union for the same species of bird for which the American Ornithologists' Union till 1973 approved the name Pigeon Hawk. Both organizations approve the same scientific name. As the American Ornithologists' Union nomenclature committee has made some effort to erase dialect differences between the common names of some species, as in giving its stamp of approval to Whimbrel and Dunlin, it is now gratifying that the name Pigeon Hawk has given way to Merlin, which is already in general use.

Mockingbird. One of the meanings of mock is to imitate in fun, although the connotation of derision still lingers in the meaning. ME. *mokken* from OF. *mocquer,* where it had both the meanings "to wipe the nose" and "to deride"; from LL. *muccere,* "to wipe the nose." I. *moccare* means both "to wipe the nose" and "to mock." The word is likely onomatopoeic for the sound of a nose being blown like a trumpet. The name is appropriate as the bird imitates the songs of many species.

Moorhen. A British name recently adopted by the American Ornithologists' Union, but modified as **Common M.**, for the Common Gallinule.

Mother Carey's Chicken. A sailor's name for petrel. Yarrell, who wrote *A History of British Birds* in 1843, stated, "The name was given by Capt. Carteret's sailors, from some unknown hag of that name." It has also been suggested that she is a witch of the sea accompanied by imps in the form of the little black birds. According to others she is the aunt of Davy Jones. Weekley conjectures that the term is English sailor's corruption of I. *madre cara,* "dear mother," to whom the sailors of southern Europe were wont to breathe a prayer when the gales began to blow.

Mud-hen. Local name for the coot. For its habitat, the muddy marsh.

Murre. Probably of Celtic dialect for a guillemot or auk. **Common M.** about as equally common as the Thick-billed M. **Thick-billed M.** for its heavy bill.

Murrelet. Diminutive of murre, a little murre. **Ancient M.** for its gray coloring. **Craveri's M.** for F. Craveri (see Appendix). **Kittlitz's M.** for F. H. Kittlitz (see Appendix). **Marbled M.** for the black and white winter plumage, reflecting the scientific name. **Xantus' M.** for John Xantus (see Appendix).

Nighthawk. ME. *night,* "night," for the bird's hunting insects in the dusk. For hawk, see Hawk. **Common N.** as its range is over most of North America. **Lesser N.** for its smaller size.

Night-heron. See Heron.

Nightjar. A provincial name in America for the Whip-poor-will but the common name in Britain for the European member of the same genus. The song of the European Nightjar is, according to Peterson, "a loud rapid churring, rising and falling and sustained for as long as five minutes." Its effect is jarring and E. *jar* is likely derived from imitation of the song. **Buff-collared N.** another name for Ridgway's Whip-poor-will.

Noddy. See Tern, Black Noddy and Tern, Brown Noddy.

Nonpareil. F. *non pareil,* "not equal." For the Painted Bunting whose plumage is unequaled in splendor.

Nutcracker. Another poor name as one of its favorite foods is the nut of the piñon pine, which it swallows whole as it does other seeds. **Clark's N.** for Captain William Clark who discovered the bird near Kamiah, Idaho, on August 22, 1805 (see Appendix).

Nuthatch. AS. *hnutu,* "a nut"; *hatch* is from *hack* for the bird's occasional technique of wedging a nut too large for it to swallow whole into a crevice and hacking it into small pieces. **Brown-headed N.** for the brown crown of the male. **Pygmy N.** for its small size. **Red-breasted N.** for its plumage. **White-breasted N.** for its plumage.

Oldsquaw. AS. *eald,* OE. *ald,* "old"; Massachusetts Indian, *Squa,* "woman." Bent states, "If there is any one thing for which the old squaw is justly notorious it is for its voice. It is certainly a noisy and garrulous species at all seasons, for which it has received various appropriate names, such as old

squaw, old injun, old wife, noisy duck, hound, etc. . . .
The names south-southerly, cockawee, quandy, coal and
candle light" as well as many others suggest its notes. With
all this Bent says he would prefer the name Long-tailed
Duck. We might as well add more names for this bird which
few can equal in evoking such a lengthy, humorous and
poetic list: long-tailed hareld, swallow-tailed duck, south-
southerland, old granny, old molly, old Billy, John Con-
nally, Uncle Huldy, my Aunt Huldy, cowhen, calaw, calloo,
scoldenore, scolder, and quandy. And finally, the Crees
called the bird Hah-ha-way, which we prefer to Mr. Bent's
prosaic Long-tailed Duck, which is also the British name.

Oriole. The American orioles got their name because of their
similarity in appearance to the European Golden Oriole.
ML. *oriolus,* "golden," from L. *aureolus,* "golden"; L. *aurum,* "gold." The Old World orioles belong to the family
Oriolidae, while ours belong to the family Icteridae, which
includes the blackbirds and meadowlarks. **Altamira O.** formerly Lichtenstein's O. Sp. *alta,* "high"; Sp. *mira,* "look-
out." Called Altamira by Ridgway because his subspecies,
tamaulipensis, has its type locality in Altamira, Tamaulipas,
Mexico. **Audubon's O.** for the famous bird artist. **Baltimore O.** Mark Catesby, in his *The Natural History of Carolina, Florida and the Bahama Islands* published in 1731,
made a plate of the bird which he called the Baltimore-Bird.
He so named the bird because its colors were the same as
those of the Baltimores, the colonial proprietors of Mary-
land. It is interesting that Catesby did not call the bird an
oriole in either the common or scientific name he gave it.
Linnaeus used Catesby's plate as the basis of his description. It is now a subspecies of the Northern O. **Black-
headed O.** a helpful name for the bird watcher as it is the
only northern oriole with a black head whose black does not
extend down the back below the neck. Unfortunately, the
American Ornithologists' Union has substituted nondescrip-
tive Audubon's O. for this. **Bullock's O.** for William Bullock (see Appendix). This is now a subspecies of the
Northern O. **Hooded O.** for the yellow plumage at the top

of the head. **Lichtenstein's O.** for M. H. Lichtenstein (see Appendix), now an outmoded name for the Altamira O. **Northern O.** a new species name including both the Baltimore and Bullock's Oriole. **Orchard O.** for its preference for orchards. AS. *wort, "plant"*; AS. *geard*, "yard." OE. *oregeard*, "orchard." **Scott's O.** for Winfield Scott (see Appendix). **Spot-breasted O.** for its plumage.

Osprey. L. *ossifragus, ossifraga*, "an osprey," from L. *os*, "bone," and L. *frangere*, "to break." The bird the old Romans called ossifragus is not the fish hawk. The ossifragus mentioned by Pliny was the Lammergeier, a German name, which means literally "lamb vulture." It received its Latin name from its habit of dropping bones and even tortoises from a height in order to fragment their ossified body parts. It is difficult to tell when the word came into English, when it obtained its present form, and when it came to mean the particular bird it now does. Latin and French (a modified Latin) words came into English in immense numbers from 1300 on. As most literary Englishmen of the fourteenth and fifteenth centuries were adept in both tongues, they may have borrowed from either for any word. Turner in 1544 and Aldrovandus in 1599 use osprey or an approximation of it for the Osprey. Things then become puzzling. The writers of the King James version of the bible in 1610 have: "And these are they which you shall have in abomination among the fowls; they shall not be eaten, they are an abomination: the eagle, and the ossifrage, and the ospray" (Leviticus, 11, 13) ends the list of proscribed fowls. It is explained in the foreword of most current editions of the bible that the center column running down each page contains references, "an aid in clearing up for the reader obscure passages." Here one finds that the ossifrage is "a species of eagle" and the osprey is "the black eagle." The introduction also contains suggestions on where to find "a cure for ignorance," "aid when discontented," and "sustaining faith when facing difficulty." The commentators responsible for the column were no better ornithologists than the writers of the King James version. This seems a bit odd as Shakespeare had not long before written in *Coriolanus,* "As is the osprey to the fish, who takes it by sovereignty of nature." Willughby and others of his time (1676) still confuse it with the Sea Eagle. His name for the osprey was Baldbusardus anglorum. Tristram is quoted by Driver: "The eagle is really the griffonvulture; the ossifrage, the bearded vulture, the largest and most powerful of the vulture tribe." This latter is the Lammergeier. Driver goes on to say that the Osprey is the Shorttoed Eagle. One is inclined to think that this great Hebrew scholar of the turn of the century did a bit of bird watching. Aeschylus, the Greek tragic dramatist, is said to have been killed by a Lammergeier (ossifrage) dropping a turtle on his bald head which it mistook for a stone. This cannot be verified as the Athenian mortuary records along with most of the plays of Aeschylus have been lost.

Ouzel, Ousel. AS. *osle,* "blackbird." Another name for the American Dipper. A name used in the past in Britain for their blackbird but now used only for the Ring Ouzel, a thrush which is a close relative of the European blackbird. The European Ring Ousel, which resembles the blackbird in coloration and size in Europe, was also called the Water Ouzel. This name was also used for the Dipper found in America.

Ovenbird. For the resemblance of the bird's nest on the forest floor to a miniature dome-shaped oven. AS. *ofn,* "oven." Our ovenbird is a warbler, whereas in Latin America the name is applied to the family Furnariidae, members of which build large clay nests more nearly resembling primitive ovens.

Owl. The statement that *owl* is simply a Cockney shortening of *howl* suggests what happened in the development of the original root of the word and what has occurred repeatedly in several languages. The word is onomatopoeic and derived from the bird's call. Our word is from AS. *ule,* "an owl." This is cognate with L. *ulula,* "a screech owl," found in Pliny. From L. *ululo,* "to cry out in pain." Related also to Gr. *alale,* "an outcry," and Gr. *ololuge,* "an outcry" although this is tied up with *ololugon,* "the croaking of frogs."

Sa. *uluka,* "an owl," suggests the antiquity of the word's origin. Cf. E. *owlet, howl, halloo, hallabaloo,* and *hallelujah* which we have borrowed from Hebrew. **Common Barn-O.** for one of its favorite nesting sites, "common" to distinguish it from species elsewhere in the world. **Barred O.** for its striped throat. **Bog O.** the Short-eared O. **Boreal O.** from its range in the north. **Burrowing O.** for its nesting in burrows. **Elf O.** as it is small and elusive. **Ferruginous Pygmy-O.** for its reddish color and small size. **Flammulated O.** from the scientific name "reddish." **Great Gray O.** for its large size and gray plumage. **Great Horned O.** from the resemblance of the feather tufts to horns. **Hoot O.** another name for the Barred and Great Horned Owls for their calls. **Long-eared O.** for the feather tufts on its head. **Monkey O., Monkey-faced O.** local names for the Barn O. **Northern Hawk-O.** the bird appears to be half hawk and half owl. **Pygmy-O.** for its smallness. **Saw-whet O.,** currently divided into **Northern Saw-whet O.** and the Central American Unspotted Saw-whet O. Their notes resemble the sharpening of a saw. **Screech-O.** now split between **Eastern Screech-O.** and **Western Screech-O.** The name is rather a libel on this bird which has a liquid, wavering whistle for its call. **Short-eared O.** as the ears or feather tufts are almost invisible. **Snowy O.** for its white plumage. **Spotted O.** for the whitish dots on its back. **Whiskered O.,** or more correctly the **Whiskered Screech-O.,** from the thin, hairlike feathers of its "moustache."

Oystercatcher. Coues says, "Oyster opener would be a better name, as oysters do not run fast." Other ornithologists also belittled the sprinting ability of the oyster. The word has been traced back to Mark Catesby, 1731, and it is interesting to note the opposite of the usual practice in this case of naming the European bird after its American counterpart, not only in English but also in French, *huitrier,* and German, *austermann.* Although it is too late to edify Dr. Coues, the verb "catch" need not imply that the victim is on the run. Someone may be caught unawares or in an indefensible position. Mark Catesby had probably observed the Oystercatcher feeding upon bivalves at low tide when the shell is partially open, allowing the bird to insert its beak and then cut the adductor muscles. To do this it had to catch the bivalve at the right time. **American O.** a location word given before it was realized there was another species on the west coast of America. **Black O.** from its plumage.

Parakeet, Paroquet. E. *parakeet* or *paroquet* is most likely from F. *parroquet* or OF. *paraquet,* which may have come from Sp. *periquito* or I. *parocchetto.* Although the relationship is uncertain the meaning in all was "little Peter," a pet name for a little parrot. **Carolina P.** for the range of this now extinct bird. **Monk P.** a reflection of the scientific name meaning "monk or solitary," probably referring to the hood on the head rather than to the nature of the bird, as it nests in colonies and flies about in small flocks. It was first recorded in 1967 or 1968 in the vicinity of the New York transoceanic airports. This has led to the conjecture that some birds escaped from a South American shipment. It has spread to New Jersey and Connecticut, and has been recorded as far west as Ohio. As its normal range is partially in temperate South America, it may be able to survive over winter in its incipient new range. It is a serious agricultural pest in its homeland; attempts to eliminate the bird from the United States are underway.

Parrot. F. *Perrot,* "little parrot," a nickname, diminutive of F. *Pierre,* "Peter." L. *petrus,* Gr. *petros,* "a rock." **Sea P.** the Common Puffin. **Thick-billed P.** for the heavy bill.

Partridge. Partridge upset Ingersoll who says, "Partridge is the most abused word in American Bird-talk; abused in form, spelling, pronunciation and significance; it is a distorted descendant of *perdix.*" First of all, the American Ornithologists' Union paid heed, and, in the *Check-list* of 1957, suggested that those who happen across this introduced species should limit the use of the word to the Gray Partridge. As for the other concerns, let us remember that the word has traveled extensively over a long period of time and has been used by many diverse peoples. The present correct spellings of several words are a crystallized mistake, for example, *brid* is now in the form of *bird,* causing no perturbation to schoolteachers. The Gr. *perdix* moved to L. *perdix* without alteration in spelling. Then it moved as a common Romantic word into all the languages derived from Latin except Rumanian. We can recognize it in Sp. and Por. *perdix,* and I. *pernice.* In Old French we find the word as *perdriz, -triz.* Here we find the second *r,* which the etymologists call intrusive, a polite way of saying that something has appeared unreasonably. In Modern French we have *perdrix,* the second *r* remaining but the final *z* reverting to *x.* The Middle English word appears as *pertriche* and *partrich.* In Yorkshire it came out not only *patrick* but *patrig.* The change from *-ch* to *-dge* in the final syllable was the last one making patrich finally partridge. We find this paralleled in knowledge, sausage, and other words. **Gray P.** gray from its coloring.

Parula. See Warbler, Parula; Warbler, Northern Parula; and Warbler, Tropical Parula; although the American Ornithologists' Union prefers "Parula" to stand without "Warbler."

Pauraque. This name is derived, according to Bent, "from a fancied resemblance to one of its notes." **Common P.** to differentiate it from other species to the south.

Peabody Bird. The White-throated Sparrow. For its song, "Peabody, Peabody, Peabody."

Peep. A general name for the smaller shorebirds. For their call notes.

Pelican. From F. *pelican,* from L. *pelicanus,* from Gr. *pelikan, pelikas;* "woodpecker" named for its pecking from Gr. *pelekus,* "axe." Gr. *pelekaw* means "I hew with an axe." In ancient times the word applied to birds notable for their bills, in addition to the woodpecker. W. Turner, writing about birds in 1544, used Pelecanus as a synonym for the Shovelard or Spoonbill. However, according to Swann, "The Pelican of Aristophanes is the Woodpecker, or joiner bird, which with its bill hewed out the gates of 'Cloud-Cuckoo Land.'" **Brown P.** AS. *brun,* "brown," as it is largely of this color. **White P.** as it is mostly white, now changed to **American White P.**

Peter Bird. Tufted Titmouse. For its song, "Peter, Peter, Peter."

Petrel. After mentioning that earlier variants of the word *pitteral* and *pittrel* are obscure, the *Oxford Dictionary of English Etymology* goes on to say that Dampier as early as 1703 ". . . has the spelling *petrel* and derives the name from that of St. Peter in the allusion to his 'walking upon the lake of Genneserath,' (Matt. XIV 30)." It is satisfying to pin down such an early allusion even if it raises another question: Was Dampier recording an allusion already given common acceptance, or did he originate it (and the spelling) himself? At any rate, his explanation of the origin of the name is now given credence, as the petrels when alighting on the water dangle their feet and hesitate to alight, seeming, like St. Peter, to doubt their ability to remain above its surface. William Dampier, who Swann feels quite certain is the Dampier referred to in the dictionary, was an English buccaneer and navigator. He was the pilot on the expedition that rescued Alexander Selkirk (Robinson Crusoe) from his lonely island, which was a minor incident on a voyage that made a profit of $200,000. It is interesting that F. *petrel* is derived from English, which is contrary to most derivations. If Dampier is correct, *petrel* is a diminutive of Peter. L. *petrus*, from Gr. *petros*, "a stone." Petrel has long been applied to some members of the family Procellariidae, as well as to all of the Hydrobatidae. Although the name apparently was first used for species in the latter family, paradoxically it recently has been restricted to some of the Procellariidae, and "storm-petrel" substituted for all those birds in the family Hydrobatidae. The storm-petrels occurring in North America are: **Ashy S.-P.** OE. *aesce*, "ash," for its uniform dull coloration. **Band-rumped S.-P.** for the white at the base of the tail. **Black S.-P.** for its dark plumage. **Forked-tailed S.-P.** AS. *forca*, cf. L. *furca*, "a fork"; AS. *taegl*, "a tail." For the shape of its tail. **Galapagos S.-P.** for the islands where it breeds but Wedge-rumped S.-P. now used. **Harcourt's S.-P.** for E. V. Harcourt (see Appendix), but Band-rumped S.-P. now used. **Leach's S.-P.** for William E.

Leach (see Appendix). **Least S.-P.** for its size. **Wedge-rumped S.-P.** for its large wedge-shaped white rump. **White-faced S.-P.** AS. *hwit*, "white"; F. *face*, from L. *facies*, "face." For the coloring of the head. **Wilson's S.-P.** for Alexander Wilson (see Appendix). The few "petrels" in our area are: **Black-capped P.** OE. *blac*, "black"; OE. *cap*, "a head covering," possibly from L. *caput*, "head." For the black top of the head. **Cape P.** for the Cape of Good Hope, from where type specimen came. **Mottled P.,** for the pattern of its plumage. **Scaled P.** ME. *scale*, from OF. *escale*, from HG *scala* akin to AS. *scalu*, "a shell, a scale." The word can be traced back to an Indo-European root and has derivatives in many languages such as G. *skallein*, "to stir up or to hoe." Our E. *shale, shell, skill* are related. The back of the bird in flight is somewhat scaly in appearance. Now replaced by Mottled P.

Pewee. From the note of the Eastern Wood-P. **Eastern Wood-P.** from its eastern range and habitat. **Western Wood-P.** from its western range and habitat.

Phainopepla. Derived from part of the scientific name of the bird. It seems rather a pity that the American Ornithologists' Union *Check-list* committee decided on this common name rather than either "Shining Fly-snapper" which Coues preferred, or "Silky Fly-snapper" which still has quite a vogue.

Phalarope. Borrowed from the scientific name. **Gray P.** so called by the British who prefer the name descriptive of the winter plumage rather than the American name, Red P. **Northern P.** from its northern breeding grounds, but now relegated to the synonymy of Red-necked P. **Red P.** for the color of the underparts in the breeding plumage. **Red-necked P.** taken from the reddish neck of the breeding plumage. **Wilson's P.** for Alexander Wilson (see Appendix).

Pheasant. F. *faisan*, "pheasant"; Gr. *phaisianos*, "pheasant," E. for the river Phasis, where the bird ranged. **Ring-necked P.** for the necklace of white feathers.

Phoebe. In imitation of the bird's call. **Black P.** for its dark plumage. **Eastern P.** for its range. **Say's P.** for Thomas Say (see Appendix).

Pigeon. F. *pigeon,* "a pigeon," from OF. *pijon,* "a young bird," from L. *pipio,* "to peep." Imitative as E. *peep, cheep.* **Band-tailed P.** alluding to the bands on the tail. **Passenger P.** "passenger" as used for this extinct bird has a special meaning, as in the phrase "bird of passage," "migratory." Cf. the special meaning in "passage of arms," implying an event, which the word retained from the original meaning, "tournament." L. *passare,* "to pass"; L. *passus,* "a step." **Red-billed P.** for the color of the bill. **White-crowned P.** from the white feathers on the top of its head.

Pintail. For the long pointed tail of the male of this duck. **Northern P.** for its Northern Hemisphere range.

Pipit. F. *pipit,* "a pipit," from L. *pipio,* "to chirp." **American P.** another name for the Water P. **Sprague's P.** after Isaac Sprague (see Appendix). **Water P.** for a European race which is usually found near water although the American is not. The American Ornithologists' Union committee prefers the name Water P. for the entire species.

Plover. OF. *plovier,* "plover," from L. *pluvarius, pluvialis,* "rainy"; L. *pluvia,* "rain." MacLeod lists several authorities with their explanations of the association of the bird's name with rain: "caught more easily in rainy weather, haunt rainy places, arrive in flocks in the rainy season, have markings on their upper plumage like raindrops, and foretell rain by their restlessness." None of these holds water. The German name *regenpfeifer,* "rain piper," suggests the bird sings in the rain. There seems to be no justification or known valid reason for the name. **American Golden-P.** for the color of its breeding plumage. Has been replaced by Lesser Golden-P. **Barnyard P.** for the Solitary Sandpiper, as it frequents barnyards. **Black-bellied P.** for its breeding plumage although the black on its underparts is not as extensive as in the Golden P. **Common Ringed P.** a substitution for the familiar Ringed P. **Gray P.** British name for the Black-bellied P. **Lesser Golden-P.** a new name for the American Golden P. **Mountain P.** from its breeding in mountains. **Piping P.** for its note. **Ringed P.** used at times for the Semipalmated P., but it is the name for a different European species which superficially resembles the American Semi-palmated P. **Semipalmated P.** L. *semi*, "half"; L. *palma*, "palm of the hand," for the partially webbed foot. **Snowy P.** for its pale plumage. **Thick-billed P.** a popular name for Wilson's P. **Upland P.** Bent says, "Let us be thankful that this gentle and lovely bird is no longer called Bartramian Sandpiper. It is a sandpiper truly enough, but one that has adopted the haunts and many of the habits of the plovers." In spite of this moving plea, the American Ornithologists' Union's *Thirty-second Supplement* to the *Check-list* feels that "to avoid misleading taxonomic implications, where a better name already has wide acceptance," the name should be changed to Upland Sandpiper. **Wilson's P.** for Alexander Wilson (see Appendix).

Poor Joe. A local name for the Great Blue Heron, probably for its lonely habit and unpleasant squawk.

Poorwill. Suggests the bird's call. **Common P.** for its presumed abundance relative to its Latin American counterparts.

Popinjay. Originally parrot. Cf. Sp. *papagavo*, "parrot." F. *papegoe*, "popinjay," had a double meaning which carried over to Middle English, "a target for archers or an over-dressed or noisy fop." Possibly the earliest target was a painted parrot on a stick, and then, as the target became any type of gaudily painted bird, the word continued to mean the target. As the popularity of archery declined, the meaning for an obtrusive fool has become the main one.

Prairie-chicken. See Chicken.

Preacher Bird. From the Red-eyed Vireo's reiteration of its song, which to some says: "First on the one hand . . . and then on the other" and to others: "Here I am, see me, up here."

Ptarmigan. From the Gaelic, *tarmachan*, "mountaineer?" or "White game?" Here, at least, we can pin down a misspelling. The *p* was added to the word by Sibbald in *Scotia Illustra*, 1684. He probably thought the word was of Greek origin, like *ptaer* or *ptarmike*, "yellow." Weekley says, "Earlier spelling *termagant* suggests possibly a nickname

based on some folklore belief." **Rock P.** from its habitat.
White-tailed P. the only ptarmigan with an all-white tail.
Willow P. from its predilection for the buds of the willow.

Puffin. E. *puff*, and *-in*, the diminutive suffix; literally "little puff" from the downy young or the puffed-up appearance of the mature bird. **Atlantic P.** the "new" name for **Common P**. **Horned P.** for the small stiff plume over the eye. **Tufted P.** for the tuft back of the eye during the breeding season.

Pyrrhuloxia. A reflection of the former generic name. (See *Pyrrhuloxia* under Scientific Names.)

Quail. OF. *quaille*, "quail." Cognate with quack, imitative of the call of the European species. A fairly popular name for the Bobwhite. **California Q.** a locality designation. **Gambel's Q.** for William Gambel (see Appendix). **Harlequin Q.** from its feather pattern (see Duck, Harlequin D.), but superceded by **Montezuma Q.** for the Aztec ruler. **Mountain Q.** for its habitat. **Scaled Q.** from the appearance of the feathering.

Rail. Probably a combination of French and Teutonic sources: F. *rale*, "a rail"; OF. *raale,* to make a scraping noise; L. *raelare*, "to scrape." **Black R.** for its color. **Clapper R.** E. *clap*, "a noise made by striking the hands together," from the call of the bird. **King R.** a compliment to its appearance, although it is very similar to the Clapper R. **Virginia R.** its range does not justify its name. **Yellow R.** for its yellow plumage.

Rain Bird. Another name for the American cuckoos. From an old superstition that its call foretold the coming of rain. A local name in England for the Green Woodpecker.

Raven. AS. *hraefn*, "a raven." Imitative of the bird's cry. **Chihuahuan R.** for the Mexican state of Chihuahua, replaces the familiar White-necked Raven. **Common R.** common only in the far north and west. **White-necked R.** for the scarcely visible ring of white neck feathers, but now used for an African species.

Razorbill. From the sharp-edged bill. Also, mainly in the past, used for the Puffin and Guillemot.

Redbird. Local name for the Cardinal.

Redbreast. Old name for Robin, especially in Britain.

Redhammer. The Red-shafted Flicker. For the pinkish red underwing and tail, and the tattoo it beats with its bill.

Redhead. From the color of this duck's head.

Redpoll. OE. *red,* for the color of the spot on its head. ME. *pol,* "head," as in taking a poll, i.e., counting heads. **Arctic R.** replaced by Hoary R. **Common R.** only in comparison with the Hoary R. **Hoary R.** AS. *har,* "hoar" or "white." For the whitish bird. **Hornemann's R.** for J. W. Hornemann (see Appendix), now also replaced by Hoary R.

Redstart. The American bird was so called for its resemblance to the European Redstart. AS. *read,* "red"; AS. *steort,* "tail." **American R.** as distinguished from the European. **Painted R.** in a different genus from the one above and alas, no red in its "start."

Reed-bird. A local name for the Bobolink, particularly in the Middle Atlantic states where it congregates in the reedy marshes during the fall migration.

Rice-bird. A local name for the Bobolink, particularly in the past on the southeast coast where it frequented the rice fields. This was Audubon's name for the bird.

Roadrunner. From its habit of running on the ground. **Greater R.** for it size when compared with other roadrunners.

Robert o' Lincoln. A name for the Bobolink suggested by the common name Bobolink, in turn suggested by the bird's song.

Robin. Wherever the English have settled they have tended to bestow the name Robin on any bird with a noticeable amount of red or russet in the plumage. If the russet is on the breast, the name is practically inevitable. The early settlers in America, who had more pressing concerns than the niceties of ornithological nomenclature, named the Robin because of its resemblance to the English bird with the orange-red face and breast. Gradually the name is becoming limited to this one species. In the past the Bluebird was also called Robin. The Towhee, alias Chewink, labored under the name of Ground Robin. Then, too, the Robin Snipe might be either the Knot or the Dowitcher. Calling the Baltimore Oriole the Golden Robin seems to be going a little too far. But things began to get out of control when the Cedar Waxwing was labeled the Canadian Robin, to say nothing of christening the Redbreasted Merganser the Sea Robin. Robin, a diminutive nickname of Robert, is of French origin. Both forms of the name were in common use near the beginning of the Middle English period. According to Weekley the name was originally HG. *Ruodperht* (G. *Ruprecht),* from HG. *hrode, ruod,* "fame," plus *berht,* "bright." The English have the sole responsibility for attaching the name Robin to the bird. It was first Redbreast, then the pet name Robin was added. Finally Redbreast was dropped. The process did not go as far with Jackdaw and Magpie. The *Dictionary of Word Origins* tells us, "the use of the bird's name, robin, in 'round robin,' a petition signed in a circular manner to avoid giving prominence to any one signature," had its origin on the brig *Catherine* at Gibralter in 1612. The crew was discontented but well aware that the captain had the right to enforce discipline by hanging to the yardarm whomever he decided was the chief dissenter. The first name signed to a petition was likely to be taken as sufficient evidence of leadership and justify the extreme penalty. To avoid this fate for any one individual the crew decided to append their names in the form of a circle. Thus all signatures were on an equal basis and the captain could scarcely hang the whole crew. The story goes that a statuette of a Robin on a circular base was close at hand. This was used to trace a circle which formed a guide for writing the signatures around it. This device to protect individual petitioners henceforth became known as a "round robin." Newton writing in 1894 says of the name in England, "Robin, a well-known nickname of the 'REDBREAST,' which in common use has almost supplanted the stock on which it was grafted." **American R.** this is now the name sanctioned by the American Ornithologists' Union as there are other birds in the world named Robin.

Rubythroat. The Ruby-throated Hummingbird. In the Old World Rubythroat refers to a small thrush.

Ruff, Reeve. Reeve most likely preceded ruff as the name for the bird. AS. *gerifa*, "one in authority," from which is derived *reeve*, "the chief officer of a town or district" and our modern word "sheriff." The bird was perhaps so named for the pugnacious-appearing display of the males at the onset of the breeding season. It is debatable whether the bird was named for the starched linen neckwear popular in Elizabethan times or the neckwear named for the bird. At any rate, "ruff" is generally used for the male bird and "reeve" for the female. Ruff is short for ruffle, which we still use to describe the raising of the feathers when it assumes a threatening posture. The ruff in the Elizabethan costume was open in front and widest and longest behind, while the bird's ruff is most evident in front and hardly noticeable behind the head.

Sanderling. AS. *sand*, "sand," from the habitat; *-er*, AS. and Germanic suffix, "one who has to do with," *-ling*, AS. diminutive suffix, often applied to animals, "little"; so literally the whole word means "the little one of the sand." Then, probably, from Ic. *sanderla*, a name for a shorebird.

Sandpiper. AS. *sand*, "sand"; AS. *pipe*, from LL. *pipa*, from L. *pipare*, "to chirp." We find this imitative word in I., Ic., Sp., Sw., *pipa*, G. *pfeife*, D. *pibe*, and in F. *pipe*. All are imitative of the cry of a young bird. E. suffix, *-er*, "one who." Thus we have "one who chirps on the sand." **Baird's S.** for Spencer F. Baird (see Appendix). **Bartramian** or **Bartram's S.** for William Bartram (see Appendix). Name for the Upland Plover used mainly by those whose scientific conscience rebels at calling a sandpiper a plover. **Buff-breasted S.** for the color of its breast. **Curlew S.** for its curlew-like bill. **Least S.** It is. **Pectoral S.** L. *pectus*, "breast"; not from the distinct shield of dark breast feathers but from the inflationary sac under this which gives resonance to the male's amatory outpourings. **Purple S.** for the purplish tone of its back. **Red-backed S.** formerly popular name for the Dunlin. **Rock S.** for its habitat. **Semipalmated S.** for its partially webbed feet. **Sharp-tailed S.** for its pointed tail. **Solitary S.** generally alone, never in large flocks. **Spoonbill S.** for the shape of its bill. **Spotted S.** for the spotted underparts in the breeding plumage. **Stilt S.** for its comparatively long legs. **Upland S.** as this bird is taxonomically a sandpiper, the American Ornithologists' Union now prefers to call it that rather than Upland Plover. **Western S.** more common in western North America than eastern. **White-rumped S.** for the obvious field mark.

Sapsucker. From the habit of drilling holes in the bark of trees and eating the sap and insects attracted thereto. **Red-breasted S.** for its red chest. **Yellow-bellied S.** for its yellowish underparts. **Williamson's S.** for Robert S. Williamson (see Appendix).

Sawbill. For the mergansers all of whose bills are serrated.

Saw-filer. A local name for Northern Saw-whet Owl.

Scaup. A Scottish variation of *scalp,* which meant not only the hairless top of a bald head but also a ledge which at times might be partially exposed above the surface of the water. *The Oxford Dictionary of English Etymology* states that *scaup* comes from *scaup bank* which provides a bed for shellfish on which the birds feed. MacLeod states that *scaup* originally meant a shell and that it is cognate with *scallop* and *scalp.* Possibly the old word for a shelf in the sea and a shellfish, being the same, is close enough in relation to the bird's habits that both played a part in giving it the name of scaup. The **Greater S.** is about an inch longer than the **Lesser S.**

Scoter. Probably a variation of coot, which is used by hunters for the scoters. In support of this MacLeod points out that *macreuse* in the north of France means a scoter, and in the south, a coot. It might also be connected with "*scot,*" a local name for the Guillemot and Razorbill. **Black S.** for its dark plumage. This is a much needed change from **Common S.** **Surf S.** from diving for shellfish in the surf. **Velvet S.** name for a European species now merged with New World White-winged S. **White-winged S.** for its white speculum.

Sea Pigeon. Local name for the Black Guillemot for its resemblance to the domestic pigeon.

Seedeater. OE. *saed,* "seed"; OE. *aet,* "eat." **White-collared S.** for the white band about the neck.

Sewick. The Least Flycatcher. For its song.

Shag. An accepted name for one of the cormorant family in Britain and used loosely in America for the Double-crested Cormorant. For the crest of feathers on the head which give it a shaggy appearance.

Shearwater. E. *shear*, "to cut close with a large pair of scissors"; E. *water*, "the element which makes up the sea." For the bird's manner of flight in skimming the water. **Audubon's S.** for John J. Audubon (see Appendix). **Buller's S.** for Sir Walter L. Buller (see Appendix). **Cory's S.** for Charles B. Cory (see Appendix). **Flesh-footed S.** for the color of its feet. Formerly called **Pale-footed S. Greater S.** for its large size. **Little S.** for its smallness. **Manx S.** for the Isle of Mann where it formerly bred in great numbers but has not done so since 1800. **New Zealand S.** former name for Buller's S., for the New Zealand islets where it breeds. **Pink-footed S.** for its flesh-colored feet. **Short-tailed S.** as this is the name used in its breeding region. Formerly called **Slender-billed S. Sooty S.** for its dark-brown color.

Sheldrake, Sheld Duck. A colloquial name for the merganser. *Sheld, shell,* E. dialect words for "dappled, variegated," applied to birds and to mammals which are particolored.

Shite poke. An attempt to render more delicate by a change in spelling a name for the bird derived from its habit of ejecting effluent when making a startled departure. In America applied indiscriminately to the Black-crowned Night Heron, the Green-backed Heron and the Bittern. *Poke,* now E. dialect, "bag", except when you buy a pig in one.

Shore Lark. Local name for the Horned Lark. Where it is found in winter.

Shoveler. From the shape of the large bill. AS. *scoff,* "shove."

Shrike. Turner first used the name for the bird in English in 1544, and states that he only saw it twice in England although more frequently in Germany. Possibly from AS. *scric,* "a shrieker," or OE. *scric,* "a thrush." It is evidently related to "shriek" as is S. *shrika,* "a jay." Turner seems to have been unaware that the name was probably in use for the Mistle Thrush. **Loggerhead S.** "loggerhead" is applied to animals with large heads and is similar to blockhead in derivation. Log is akin to Nor. *laag,* "a fallen tree," and Ic. *lag,* "a log." The bird's head is larger in proportion to its body than most birds' heads are. **Northern S.** for its more northern range. The English call the bird the Great Grey S.

Sickle Bill. A local name for the Long-billed Curlew.

Siskin. Closely related to the European Siskin. It gets its name from the Old World bird. Authorities differ as to its exact derivation in English as it may have been adopted from a number of sources of common origin; D. *sisgen* or *sidsken,* "a chirper"; S. *siska,* "a chirper"; Ic. *zieske, ziseke,* "a siskin"; Middle Dutch, *siseken.* Slavic forms of the word appear in Czech, *ciz,* and Russian, *chizh,* "siskin or small bird." **Pine S.** for its partiality for breeding in conifers.

Skimmer. Black S. for the color of the upper parts and the bird's method of procuring food by immersing its lower bill in the water while skimming over its surface. Pennant bestowed the name "The Black Skimmer" on the bird in 1773, evidently preferring this to Catesby's "cutwater."

Skua. A Faroese name for the bird. **Great S.** for its size. In the Old World "skua" is also used for those birds known in the Americas as "jaegers." Formerly **Brown S.**

Skylark. Whence come "the profuse strains of unpremeditated art." **Eurasian S.** the European bird introduced on Vancouver Island, British Columbia.

Snake Bird, Snake Killer. Local names for the Anhinga and the Roadrunner.

Snipe. AS. *snite,* "snipe," from Ic. *snipa,* "snipe," as a snipper, akin to modern *snip* and *snap.* **Common S.** more common in western Europe than the other two species of snipe found there, the Great S. and the Jack S. **Red-breasted S.** was the British name for the Dowitcher. We also have **Grass S.** for the Pectoral Sandpiper, **Robin S.** for the Knot, **Rock S.** for the Purple Sandpiper and **Sea S.** for the Phalaropes. **Wilson's S.** was an old name for the Common S. **Telltale S.** for the Yellowleg's readiness to sound its alarm notes.

Snow Bird. For the Dark-eyed Junco in its winter range.

Snowflake. Another name for the Snow Bunting.

Solitaire. For its elusive habits. F. *solitaire*, "alone." **Townsend's S.** after J. K. Townsend who found the first specimen near the Columbia River (see Appendix).

Sora. One of the few native American Indian bird names that has endured.

Sparrow. AS. *spearwa*, "sparrow," literally "flutterer," applied to any small bird. The word has an Indo-European base, *sper*, "flutter, quiver," and hence figuratively "to struggle, kick or jerk." Thus we have L. *parra*, "a bird of ill omen," and L. *spernere*, "to spurn"; Gr. *sporgiles*, "a sparrow," and Gr. *spairein*, "to struggle." E. *spavin* means lameness in a horse which has a bird-like hopping motion due to a swelling of a joint. Spur originally meant to spur a horse as a rider would seem to flutter his legs, and from there on to the word spurn, i.e., to kick against or reject. Newton points out, "Perhaps the earliest instance of nicknaming birds is to be found in Landland's Piers' 'The Plowman,' written soon after 1400, where the sparrow is called 'Philip.'" **American Tree S.** for its breeding habitat. "American" has been added recently to differentiate it from a European species. **Bachman's S.** named by Audubon for his friend John Bachman (see Appendix). **Baird's S.** for Spencer F. Baird (see Appendix). **Black-chinned S.** for its black throat. **Black-throated S.** for the black throat of the male. **Botteri's S.** for M. Botteri (see Appendix). **Brewer's S.** for Thomas M. Brewer (see Appendix). **Cape Sable S.** an obsolete name for a race of Seaside S. breeding on the coast of southern Florida. **Cassin's S.** for John Cassin (see Appendix). **Chipping S.** for its song of short quick notes. **Clay-colored S.,** as clay means fine grained earth and may be of various colors, the term is meaningless. **Dusky Seaside-S.** for its dark plumage. This is now a subspecies. **English S.** a popular name for the House S. **Eurasian Tree S.,** introduced from Europe but as yet confined to the area about St. Louis, Missouri. **Field S.** from its habitat. **Fox S.** for its reddish, fox-like color. **Golden-crowned S.** for its golden pate. **Grasshopper S.** from its song which resembles that of the insect.

Harris' S. for Edward Harris (see Appendix). **Henslow's S.** for John S. Henslow (see Appendix). **House S.,** AS. *hus,* "house"; from the bird's fondness for association with man's dwellings. **Ipswich S.** for Ipswich, Massachusetts, from where the first specimen came. It is now a subspecies of Savannah S. **Lark S.,** AS. *lawerc,* "lark," ME. *Laverock,* "a lark." Probably because of its musical notes. **LeConte's S.** for Dr. John LeConte (see Appendix). The name is a reflection of one of the previous trivial scientific names for this bird. Changes in scientific nomenclature particularly in such a large and complex family as the Fringillidae became necessary as new species were discovered and knowledge of them and their relation to each other accumulated. The first description was made by the English ornithologist John Latham in 1790 from a specimen from the interior of Georgia. He named it *Fringilla caudacuta* (L. "little finch with the sharp tail"). This placed it in the European genus *Fringilla* in company with the Chaffinch and the Brambling. As there was at that time no American genera, the bird was placed in one of the six genera of the European family Fringillidae. It was a lost species until Audubon rediscovered it in South Dakota in 1843. Thinking it a new species, he named it *Emberiza leconteii* placing it in the European genus with the bunting rather than the finches. This was possibly a slight improvement as there was not as yet any American classification. By 1872, the date of the publication of the first edition of Coues' *Key to North American Birds,* the British had added six genera and the Americans twenty-four genera to the family Fringillidae. Breaking away from the British nomenclature in this edition and in the three subsequent editions of his book, the bird was called *Coturniculus leconteii.* It then came to light that Gray in 1849 had called the genus *Ammodromus* and LeConte's S. joined the genus accompanying Henslow's S. So, conforming to the law of priority the name *Ammodromus leconteii* appeared in the first (1886) and second (1895) editions of the American Ornithologists' Union *Check-list.* Coues, who was chairman of the committee responsible for the *Check-*

list, changed the name in later editions of his *Key to North American Birds.* Previous to the publication of the third (1910) edition of the *Check-list,* it was felt that a group of which LeConte's S. was one should be reclassified. While casting about for a new name for the proposed new genus a bibliographical check proved rewarding as it was discovered that C. J. Maynard in 1895 had proposed the name *Passerherbulus* for the group. The Nomenclature Committee adopted this and the name appears in the third (1910) edition of the *Check-list* as *Passerherbulus lecontei,* the only casualty being the loss of the final *i.* Another difficulty arose. It was found that the bird that had been lost for over fifty years had a name that had been lost for over a hundred years. *Passerherbulus* could remain, but *lecontei,* according to the sacred law of priority, had to be dropped for the original *caudacuta,* with a change of gender to *caudacutus.* But there was already a *Passerherbulus caudacutus,* the Sharptailed S. Much to the satisfaction of the nomenclature committee, we can be sure, it was found that this bird really belonged in the genus *Ammospiza,* where it was placed, leaving LeConte's S. in undisputed possession of the name *Passerherbulus caudacutus* in the fourth (1931) and fifth (1957) editions of the *Check-list.* This state of nomenclatural quiescence lasted for forty-two years until shattered in the *Thirty-second Supplement* to the *Check-list (Auk;* vol. 90, no. 2). It is decided that, after all, LeConte's S. belongs to the genus *Ammospiza.* As there is already an *A. caudacuta* and it would not do to have two species so named, *leconteii* is revived, giving us *A. leconteii.* Later, in the sixth (1983) edition, *Ammospiza* is merged with *Ammodramus,* but fortunately *leconteii* survived. The common name which had remained only as a reflection of the scientific one now regains its former significance. The common name, which is not subject to the decisions of learned taxonomists, remains as a memento of the bird who not only was lost, but when found had proven to be very elusive. A cynic is supposed to have said that taxonomy is a branch of science concerned mainly with recording errors. **Lincoln's S.** for

Thomas Lincoln (see Appendix). **Olive S.** for the dull, olive-colored plumage. **Pine-woods S.** a popular name for Bachman's S. **Rufous-crowned S.** for its reddish crown. **Rufous-winged S.** for the reddish wings. **Sage S.** for its habitat. **Savannah S.** for Savannah, Georgia, where Alexander Wilson obtained his specimen, thus giving this bird the widest range between its scientific, *sandwichensis,* and common names. **Seaside S.** for its habitat in the coastal marshes. **Sharp-tailed S.** It has. **Song S.** for its habit of continuously singing its pleasant song. **Swamp S.** from its predilection for wetlands. **Marsh S.** would do just as well. **Vesper S.** from its habit of singing at dusk. **White-crowned S.** for the distinctive white crown. **White-throated S.** for its white throat.

Spoonbill. Referring to the wide, flat shape of the end of the bill. Formerly in England a name for the Shoveler. AS. *spon,* "a thin piece of wood." **Roseate S.** for the salmon shade of the plumage.

Sprig. A local name for the Pintail.

Stake Driver. A local name for the American Bittern. Suggested by its call.

Starling. AS. *stear, stearn,* and *sterlving,* "a starling," with the diminutive suffix -*ling.* In the west and north of England and in Ireland *stare* is still a term for the bird. In German the name of the bird is star and in Swedish stare. *Sterling* is possibly from the four birds on the silver coins of Edward the Confessor. It is thought by some that the name may mean "little star" suggested by the silhouette of the bird in flight. **European S.** for its origin.

Stilt. ME. *stilte,* "stilt," refers to the disproportionally long legs in which it is only outdone by the flamingo. **Black-necked S.** refers to the black on the back of the neck in contrast to the European bird.

Stork. OE. *storc,* "stork," supposed to refer to the bird's rigid habit. E. *stark* and *starch* are related. **Wood S.** as it nests in woods. This name is now preferred to Wood Ibis.

Storm-petrel. See Petrel.

Sugarbird. A local name for the Bananaquit.

Summer Redbird. For the Summer Tanager which is only a summer resident compared to the Cardinal, also called a red bird, which is almost non-migratory.

Surfbird. From its addiction to the rocky shoreline in winter.

Swallow. AS. *swalewe*, "swallow." **Bank S.** for its nesting sites. In Britain called the Sand Martin. **Barn S.** for its nesting sites. In Britain it is just plain Swallow. **Cave S.** for its nesting sites. **Cliff S.** for its nesting sites. **Rough-winged S.** from the recurved hooklets on the outer web of the first primary feather. This has recently been changed to **Northern Rough-winged S.** to differentiate it from a similar bird in Latin America. **Tree S.** for its nesting in holes in trees. **Violet-green S.** from the color of its upper back.

Swan. AS. *swan*, "swan." It was formerly often spelled swanne. The male is termed cob and the female, pen. G. *schwan* may go back with English in origin to an association with the musical note of such a species as the **Whooper S.** The Indo-European roots *swon, swen* are seen in Sa. *svanas*, "noise." L. *sonere*, "to sound," probably has the same derivation. **Mute S.** Mute is a misnomer as the bird is not silent though not as vocal as the two other swans known to the English, the Whooper S. and Bewick's S. Until about 1800 it was commonly called the Tame S. Eurasian **Bewick's S.** and the Whistling S. have been combined as the **Tundra S.** in the sixth edition of the American Ornithologists' Union *Check-list* (1983). **Trumpeter S.** from its trumpet-like call. **Whistling S.** so named from its call, although it has a nasal quality.

Swift. Aptly named as it is among the fastest flyers. **Black S.** for its dark plumage. **Chimney S.** from its roosts and nesting sites. **Vaux's S.** for William S. Vaux (see Appendix). **White-throated S.** for its white throat.

Tanager. From *tangara*, a kind of bird in Tupi, a South American Indian language. **Hepatic T.** L. *hepaticus*, "liver-colored," i.e., rusty red; this term was taken from the former scientific term which referred to the coppery color of the male's plumage. **Scarlet T.** from the bright crimson color of the body plumage of the male. **Summer T.** Catesby christened the bird Summer Red Bird possibly to differentiate it from the Cardinal, which he called the Red Bird, an all-year-round resident. **Western T.** for its range in western North America.

Tattler. For its rapid tinkling notes which supposedly give away the presence of the fowler to other birds. **Wandering T.** for its wide ranging, particularly over vast distances of water. Also used for the Yellowlegs and other sandpipers whose alarm notes alert other birds, to the hunter's dismay.

Teacher Bird. The Ovenbird which is said to call "Teacher, Teacher, Teacher."

Teal. Did not appear in English until the thirteenth or fourteenth century, although the authorities differ on this. All agree that the term is not Anglo-Saxon but that it is cognate with Du. *teling,* "a teal." **American Green-winged T.** This was formerly used for the New World Green-winged T. when it was believed that the Old World population, known variously as **Eurasian T.**, **European T.** or **Common T.**, was a distinct species. **Green-winged T.** for the green speculum. **Baikal T.** refers to its range around Lake Baikal, Siberia. **Blue-winged T.** for the bright blue speculum. **Cinnamon T.** for the cinnamon red of its head and underparts.

Teeter Bird. For the Spotted and to a lesser extent the Solitary Sandpiper. For their rocking habit.

Tern. ON. *taerne,* S. *tarna,* "tern." Most likely first applied to the Sandwich Tern, other terns being called sea swallows. **Aleutian T.** for its breeding range. **Arctic T.** for its breeding grounds. **Black T.** alluding to the dark breeding plumage. **Black Noddy T.** for its plumage and to differentiate it from the **Brown Noddy**, which used to be called simply **Noddy T.** The word "tern" is no longer used in conjunction with "noddy" and our two North American species are known as Black Noddy and Brown Noddy. **Bridled T.** for the pattern of the head plumage. **Cabot's T.** for Dr. Samuel Cabot (see Appendix). At the time Cabot originally described this tern, which he collected on the coast of Yucatán in 1847, the practice of recognizing and naming subspecies was not yet established. It did not become accepted until the end of the century. So this tern received both a scientific and common name. The common name Cabot's T., honoring the describer, came into wide use in this country. When it became clear that this bird was a subspecies of the Old World Sandwich T., the American Ornithologists' Union sanctioned the latter name in accordance with the convention of dropping subspecific common names. **Caspian T.** for the Caspian Sea, the site of the first specimen. **Common T.** widespread in North America and Europe. **Elegant T.** from the scientific term, *elegans*. **Forster's T.** for John R. Forster (see Appendix). **Gull-billed T.** from the shape of its bill. **Least T.** for its small size. **Noddy T.** E. *noddy,* "simpleton," an appropriate name given to the bird by sailors because it did not take alarm at their approach. **Roseate T.** for the faint tinge of pink color on its breast in breeding plumage. **Royal T.** for its impressive size and appearance. **Sandwich T.** for Sandwich, Kent, England, the site of the first specimen. **Sooty T.** for its dark plumage. **Trudeau's T.** as there is only one North American record for this South American bird, its authenticity has been repeatedly questioned. De Schauensee in *Species of Birds of South America and Their Distribution* (1966) says, "The type supposedly was taken on the coast of New Jersey, U.S.A., but the accuracy of the locality has been questioned." The American Ornithologists' Union *Check-lists* (1957, 1983) present the record as hypothetical and credit Audubon with taking the specimen instead of Trudeau. Audubon says in his *Ornithological Biography* (1839), "This beautiful tern, which has not hitherto been described, was procured at Great Egg Harbour, in New Jersey, by my much esteemed and talented friend, J. Trudeau, Esq. of Louisiana, to whom I have great pleasure in dedicating it. Nothing is known of its range, or even the particular habits in which it may differ from other species. The individual obtained was in the company of a few others of the same kind. I have received from Mr. Trudeau an intimation of the occurrence of several individuals [?also] on Long Island [, New York]." It seems that Trudeau sent the specimen to London where Audubon made the drawing in

1838. Unfortunately, there is no record of the date when Trudeau procured the bird; but most fortunately, the type specimen, which Audubon used for his description and painting of the bird, formerly at Vassar College, is now in the collection of the American Museum of Natural History, no. 156650. The label on it was not made by either Trudeau or Audubon. There is no question about the validity of the species. The only doubt is about the site of the record. It seems highly improbable that Trudeau obtained the bird in South America and then deliberately misled Audubon. **Wilson's T.** an old name for the Common T.

Thrasher. From E. *thrusher* from *thrush;* q.v., not connected with *thrash,* "to beat." **Bendire's T.** for Charles E. Bendire (see Appendix). **Brown T.** for its coloring. **California T.** for its range. **Crissal T.** for the rusty color of the under-tail coverts, the crissum; the only thrasher so marked. **Curve-billed T.** for the bill's shape. **LeConte's T.** for John L. LeConte (see Appendix). **Long-billed T.** reflection of the appropriately descriptive scientific term, *longirostre,* "long bill." **Sage T.** from its type of habitat.

Thrush. ME. *thrusch,* AS. *thryce,* "a thrush"; possibly allied to G. *trizo,* "to twitter." **Gray-cheeked T.** for the gray feathering behind the eye. **Hermit T.** from its solitary habits, especially in the winter. **Olive-backed T.** the accepted name for Swainson's T., for the very dull greenish tinge of the plumage of the back. **Swainson's T.** for William Swainson (see Appendix). **Varied T.** from the diversified plumage. **Wilson's T.** local name for the Veery. **Wood T.** from its habitat.

Thunder Pumper. The American Bittern. For its impressive vocalizing.

Tiercel. A falconer's term for the male peregrine or male goshawk considered to be a third smaller than the female.

Timber Doodle. More prosaically known as the American Woodcock.

Tip-up. For the Spotted and Solitary Sandpipers' see-saw habit.

Tit. ME. *tit-* "little"; doubtless short for titmouse. **Siberian T.**

for part of its range. "Boreal" would be better. Sometimes used for Tufted Titmouse. The British use this for all chickadee-like birds.

Titlark. A popular name for the Water Pipit.

Titmouse. Ic. *tittr*, anything small; AS. *mase*, a name used for small birds, e.g., AS. *fraecmase, colemase, spicmase*, all names of small birds. True plural should be titmouses, but due to confusion with mouse, it is titmice. **Black-crested T.** for the black tuft of feathers. L. *crista*, "a comb or tuft on a bird's head." This is now treated as a race of Tufted T. **Bridled T.** from the bridle-like pattern on the face. AS. *bridel*, "a bridle." **Plain T.** it has a crest, too, but not much color. **Tufted T.** E. *tuft* from F. *touffe*, "a lock of hair." For the crest of feathers.

Tomtit. Occasionally used for the Tufted Titmouse.

Towhee. Imitative, for the bird's call note, as is chewink which the American Ornithologists' Union *Check-list* ignores in the interest of conformity. **Abert's T.** for Major James W. Abert (see Appendix). **Brown T.** for the color of its plumage. **Green-tailed T.** a reflection of the scientific name, which ignores the fact that the dark green of the plumage is not confined to the tail. **Rufous-sided T.** for the plumage.

Trogon. Gr. *trogon*, "a gnawer." For the tooth-like edge of the bill. **Coppery-tailed T.** for the color of the male's tail, but now called **Elegant T.**, which it is.

Tropicbird. From E. *tropic*, the name of the lines bounding the Tropics where the sun appears to turn. Gr. *tropikos*, "relating to a turn." For the range of the birds. **Red-billed T.** AS. *bile*, "bill." For the bill's red color, which the following also has. **White-tailed T.** for the white tail, which the Red-billed T. also has. **Yellow-billed T.** is an old name for White-tailed T.

Turkey. Our wild turkey derives its name from the domestic turkey which is a descendent of turkeys brought alive from Mexico to Spain in 1630. *The Oxford Dictionary* says the name was first applied to the African bird (Guinea fowl) because it was brought from Guinea through Africa by the Portuguese, and later applied to the American bird. However, it is more generally agreed that the name turkey became attached to the bird from a widespread misconception of the country of its origin, Turkey. Ignorance as to the bird's place of origin is not confined to its reflection in English, as we find G. *calecutischer hahn,* literally "a cock of Calicut"; F. *coc d'Inde,* literally "a cock of India"; and the I. *gallo d'India,* "cock of India." One wonders whether or not some of the early settlers in America were a bit puzzled when they found the bird ahead of them.

Turnstone. From its penchant for turning over stones, shells and small bits in search of food. The name, according to Newton, appears to be first used by Willughby in 1676. **Black T.** for its dark appearance. **Ruddy T.** for its reddish color.

Veery. Probably imitative of the bird's song.

Verdin. Alexander Wetmore says it is "the French word for yellow head."

Vireo. L. *viridos,* "green." As some of the vireos have a greenish tinge in their plumage. William Turner in *A Short and Succinct History of the Principle Birds Noticed by Pliny and Aristotle* (1544), as translated by A. H. Evans (1905), says, "These are the words of Aristotle:—'The Vireo, which is entirely green, is singled out as easy to be caught, and clever for the business of life; but it flies badly and its color is unpleasing.' So far for Aristotle." In the Latin from which the above is translated the word "vireo" is present as it is in Evans' translation. The bird referred to is probably the Greenfinch, common in Europe. Despite this record of the name vireo for a bird in English in 1544, it never appears to have been accepted, not appearing in Swann who lists 5,000 names of British birds. In America the name has fared much better, being widely accepted. It probably is a reflection of the scientific name vireo, first used by Vieillot in 1807. **Bell's V.** for J. G. Bell (see Appendix). **Black-capped V.** almost a complete reflection of the scientific name, describing the dark plumage of the head. **Black-whiskered V.** its whisker marks are rather thin and modest but they are there. **Gray V.** for the gray plumage. **Hutton's V.** for William

Hutton (see Appendix). **Philadelphia V.** for the site of the type specimen. **Red-eyed V.** for the red eye of the mature bird. **Solitary V.** a reflection of the scientific name possibly both because of its preference during the breeding season for more secluded woodland areas than other vireos and also because it migrates earlier in the spring and later in the fall than the others. Perhaps poets will keep alive the name "blue-headed" which scientists in their striving for simplicity in nomenclature frown upon. **Warbling V.** Bent says, "Wherever we turn in the literature of the warbling vireo we find that the author, after commenting on the bird's inconspicuousness, speaks enthusiastically of its song, pointing out the differences from the songs of the other vireos, the length of the song period, and the charm of the smoothly flowing warble." So the bird is named for its most attractive feature. **White-eyed V.** for its white eyes. **Yellow-throated V.** for its yellow throat.

Vulture. L. *vultur,* "a vulture"; in old Latin it was *vulturus,* literally, "tearer," from *vuellere,* "to pluck or tear." **Black V.** for its black plumage. **Turkey V.** from its resemblance in appearance only to the bird which is honored at Thanksgiving.

Wagtail. For the pumping of the tail. **White W.** for the whitish plumage. **Yellow W.** for its yellow underparts.

Wake Up. Another name for the Flicker. For its loud and early calling.

Warbler. The word which means to sing with trills and quavers was first used for a genus (*Sylvia*) of birds by Pennant in 1773, although the birds are not all good singers. The word has become attached to the American Parulidae family which are not scientifically akin to the European warblers and have now been given the distinguishing name of wood warblers. **Arctic W.** for its northern breeding range. **Audubon's W.** for John J. Audubon (see Appendix). This has been dropped as a species but may be used for the western subspecies of Yellow-rumped W. **Bachman's W.** for John Bachman (see Appendix). **Bay-breasted W.** for its chestnut sides and throat. **Black-and-white W.** for its plumage.

Blackburnian W. Bent cites Bagg and Eliot as follows: "Some time in the later eighteenth century, a specimen (apparently female) was sent from New York to England, and there described and named for a Mrs. Blackburn [see Appendix] who collected stuffed birds and was a patron of ornithology." However, an earlier description came to light and took over the scientific name, although the popular name has remained. **Blackpoll W.** for its black cap. **Black-throated Blue W.** for its plumage. **Black-throated Gray W.** for the dark throat. **Black-throated Green W.** for the black throat and green of the male's plumage. **Blue-winged W.** from its plumage. **Canada W.** refers to the breeding range although it is not limited to Canada. **Cape May W.** named by Alexander Wilson for a specimen taken by his friend, George Ord, in Cape May County, New Jersey, in 1811. **Cerulean W.** for the sky blue plumage. **Chestnut-sided W.** from its appearance. **Colima W.** for the site in Mexico where it was first collected, Sierra Nevada de Colima, by W. B. Richardson in 1889. **Connecticut W.** named by Wilson for the state where he first found it. **Golden-cheeked W.** for the facial patches. **Golden-winged W.** for its bright yellow epaulets. **Grace's W.** for Grace D. Coues (see Appendix). **Hermit W.** possibly because it was thought to be rare when first found. **Hooded W.** for the ring of black feathers about the head suggesting a hood. **Kentucky W.** named by Wilson for the state where he found it abundant. **Kirtland's W.** for Jared P. Kirtland (see Appendix). **Lucy's W.** for Lucy Baird (see Appendix). **MacGillivray's W.** Both the scientific and common names were given by Audubon to honor his collaborator and friend, William MacGillivray (see Appendix). The original specimens collected by J. K. Townsend were given to Audubon for publication in his *Birds of America*. It seems that Audubon first confused the bird with the Mourning W. and then published it as MacGillivray's by which name it was known scientifically for years. As it has been shown that Townsend's description was published two months previous to Audubon's, MacGillivray has been replaced by *tolmiei* in the scientific name although not in the popular name. Possibly, Townsend was somewhat mollified to find that Audubon had named a bird Townsend's Solitaire as he had named Audubon's W. **Magnolia W.** so called by Wilson who shot the first specimen in a magnolia tree. **Mourning W.** so named by Wilson for whom the markings on the breast suggested the black clothes of grief for the dead. Bent and Forbush lament the name "for it seems as happy and active as most of the birds." Our only comment is, "Good grief." **Myrtle W.** from its fondness for the berries of the wax myrtle (*Myrica cerifers*). This has been dropped as a species but the name may be used for the eastern subspecies of Yellow-rumped W. **Nashville W.** named by Alexander Wilson, who discovered it near Nashville, Tennessee. **Necklace W.** for the Canada W.; for the ring of black spots on the throat. **Olive W.** from its coloration. **Olive-backed W.** for its plumage. As the species was enlarged the name was changed to **Tropical Parula W.**, although those who follow the A.O.U. will discard the "warbler" part of the name. **Orange-crowned W.** for the orange feathers in the crown. **Palm W.** as first describer probably found the bird in palm trees in Hispaniola. **Parula W.** from the scientific name meaning little titmouse. This is changed to **Northern Parula W. Pine W.** Both Wilson and Audubon called this bird the Pine Creeping W., which has given way to pine. It comes from the bird's habitat. **Prairie W.** The name is misleading as the bird is not found on prairies but in cut-over areas and in fairly open woods. **Prothonotary W.** a reflection of the scientific name, *Protonotaria*. **Red-faced W.** from the color of its face. **Swainson's W.** for William Swainson (see Appendix). **Tennessee W.** named by Alexander Wilson who discovered it on the banks of the Cumberland River in the state. **Townsend's W.** for John K. Townsend (see Appendix). **Virginia's W.** for Mrs. W. Anderson (see Appendix). **Wilson's W.** for Alexander Wilson (see Appendix). **Worm-eating W.**, a translation of the scientific name. **Yellow W.** for its coloration. **Yellow-rumped W.**, a former local name for Myrtle W., but now to be used to include both it and the former Auduto be used to include both it and the former Audubon's W. **Yellow-throated W.** for the yellow plumage of its throat.

Water Belcher. The American Bittern whose call has given him many colorful common names.

Waterouzel. See Ouzel.

Waterthrush. Although really a wood warbler, Forbush says it is well named as it is "disguised as a thrush" and is generally associated with water along the margins of streams and ponds. **Louisiana W.** the name implies it breeds to the south of the Northern W. While this is true, it breeds in the eastern United States except in the deep south. **Northern W.** from its northern breeding range.

Waterturkey. Another name for the Anhinga, as the bird looks somewhat like a small, thin turkey.

Wavy. Kortright tells us in *The Ducks, Geese and Swans of North America* that in the Canadian West the lesser snowgoose goes by the name of "wavy," a corruption of the Indian word "wa wa."

Waxwing. For the bright red coloring of the bare shafts of the tips of some of the secondary wing feathers which resembles the color of sealing wax. **Bohemian W.** Newton says it was "apparently first so-called by Stephens in 1817, having been before known as the 'Silk tail.'" The British, having only one species, called this bird the Waxwing. The reason for calling this species Bohemian is obscure. It cannot be a place name as Bohemia is outside both the breeding and winter range in Europe. **Cedar W.** for the bird's fondness for the berries of the evergreen commonly called cedar.

Wheatear. MacLeod says: "Two derivations have been given for this name. According to Ray's translation of Willughby the name was given 'because (in) the time of wheat harvest they (the birds) wax very fat.' Others, however, say that 'wheat' is derived from 'white,' and ear from a vulgar name for 'rump,' and certainly the bird's white rump is a very distinctive feature, which is reflected in the alternative name of 'whitetail.'" And others, with less circumlocution, contend that wheatear is a refined version of "white arse." **Northern W.** for its range.

Whimbrel. Whim is said to sound like the bird's call; *-rel* is a diminutive suffix. Peter Matthiessen in *Shore Birds of North America* says: "In North England, curlews and whimbels were called 'Gabriel's Hounds'; the name whimbrel comes from 'whimpernel' which, in the *Durham Household Book* of 1530, refers to a habit attributed to it of sound, like whimperings."

Whip-poor-will. Suggests the bird's call. Another species is **Ridgway's W.** for Robert Ridgway (see Appendix), now to be called Buff-collared Nightjar.

Whiskey Jack, Whiskey Jay. A popular name for the Gray Jay altered from Whiskey John from the American Indian (Algonquin) Whiskatjan.

Wigeon. From F. *vigeon,* "a whistling duck." Skeat suggests that it possibly comes from L. *vipio,* "a small crane." This was Pliny's name for a small crane. As Pliny's birds were not accurately described, this apparent change of meaning for the bird from a small crane to a duck is not implausible. **American W.** the species that is common in North America but casual in Europe. The common names for this and the following species seem sensible and are in contrast to the naming of the two teals which have comparable distributions. **Eurasian W.** the species that is common in Europe but casual in North America, formerly **European W.**

Willet. Imitative of the bird's call.

Woodcock. AS. *wudu-coc,* "woodcock." From its habitat. (For cock, see Chicken.) **American W.** as distinctive from the European as it is a different species from the **Eurasian W.,** which is much larger. Formerly **European W.**

Woodpecker. E. *wood* from AS. *wudu,* "wood." As wood means either timber or a growth of trees, the name applied to the bird may refer either to its habit of pecking wood or to its habitat in woods. E. *peck* from either AS. *pican,* "to peck," or from L. *picus,* "a woodpecker"; both have a common Indogermanic source, *spi-g.* Suffix *-er,* "one who." Thus a woodpecker is one that pecks wood or pecks in the woods. **Acorn W.** from its favorite food, more apt than the scientific name. **American Three-toed W.** an old name for the Three-toed W. **Ant W.** the Flicker, for its un-woodpeckerlike habit of procuring ants on the ground. **Arctic Three-toed W.** a former name for the Black-backed W. **Arizona W.** from its range. Now combined with another species and taking the name Strickland's W. **Black-backed Three-toed W.** rather full but apt, although now shortened to **Black-backed W. Downy W.** for its shaggy and hairy appearance, the name is a translation of the scientific one. **Gila W.** Gila, a river in Arizona in the vicinity of which the bird is found. **Golden-fronted W.** AS. *gold*, "gold," L. *frons*, "forehead." For the yellow forehead, as in the scientific name. **Golden-winged W.** a local name for the Flicker. **Hairy W.** for its rather hairy and shaggy appearance. It reflects the meaning of its scientific name. **Ivory-billed W.** for its large ivory-colored bill. **Ladder-backed W.** for its transverse stripes on the back, although several are so marked. **Lewis' W.** for Meriwether Lewis (see Appendix). **Northern Three-toed W.** for its range, but now "Northern" is omitted from the name. **Nuttall's W.** for Thomas Nuttall (see Appendix). **Pileated W.** from the scientific name meaning capped. **Red-bellied W.** alluding to a very slight pink on the belly. **Red-cockaded W.** cockade, "a knot of ribbon on a hat." From its resemblance to a cock's comb, because of red patches on the side of the head. **Red-headed W.** for its head plumage. **Strickland's W.** for H. E. Strickland (see Appendix). **Three-toed W.** another apt name but the old name of Northern Three-toed W. was even more helpful. **White-headed W.** for its outstanding white head.

Wren. AS. *wraenna*, "wren." **Bewick's W.** for Thomas Bewick (see Appendix). **Brown-throated W.** for its buffy throat, relegated to a race of House W. **Cactus W.** for its nesting sites. **Canyon W.** for its habitat in deep gorges. **Carolina W.** a loose term for its range. **House W.** AS. *hus*, "house"; as it stays about dwellings. **Long-billed Marsh W.** for its bill and habitat but, alas, the sixth edition of the A.O.U. *Check-list* uses only **Marsh W. Rock W.** as it is commonly found among the rocks. **Sedge W.** the "official" name for the former **Short-billed Marsh W.** comparing its bill with its co-dweller in the marshes. **Winter W.** for its winter range in mideastern and southern United States. Also found in Eurasia where it is the only wren and "winter" is omitted from the name.

Wrentit. "A little bird like a wren." (See Titmouse).

Yellowhammer. Another name for the Flicker. For its yellow underwing and habit of drumming on dead limbs.

Yellowlegs. From the color of the legs. **Greater Y.** the larger one. **Lesser Y.** smaller one.

Yellowthroat. From its bright yellow throat. As we have a Yellow-throated Warbler it is well to omit the word warbler from this bird's name as has happily been sanctioned by popular usage. **Common Y.** depending on location. **Gray-crowned Y.** only in the male.

The earth obey'd and straight
Op'ning her fertile womb teem'd at a birth
Innumerous living creatures, perfect forms,
Limb'd and full grown . . .
The grassy clods now calv'd; now half appear'd
The tawny lion, pawing to get free
His hinder parts, then springs as broken from bonds,
And rampant shakes his brindled mane;

John Milton, Paradise Lost, *VII*

I can entertain no doubt that the view that each species has
been independently created is erroneous. I am fully convinced
that species are not immutable; but that those belonging to what
are called the same genera are lineal descendents of some other
and generally extinct species, in the same manner as the ac-
knowledged varieties of any one species are the descendents of
that species.

Charles Darwin, The Origin of Species, *Introduction*

Scientific Names

For out of olde feldes, as men seith,
Cometh al this newe corn from yeer to yere;
And out of olde bokes, in good feith,
Cometh al this newe science that men lere.

Chaucer, The Parlement of Foules, *The Proem*

Construction of the Name

The scientific name of a bird has two parts: first, a group or
generic name, and second, a trivial or individual name. Somewhat the same scheme is used for the identification of individual persons. John Jones is a complete name made up of a
personal name, John, and a family name, Jones. The second
word in the scientific name is also called the specific term. This
may cause confusion if it is believed that this word alone names
the bird scientifically. Both words in the scientific designation
must be used to give a bird its correct scientific name, i.e., its
name as a species. A third term may be added to the group and
individual term to denote subspecific, or racial, status. This is
a refinement added to the original system of Linnaeus.

The generic term, the first one given, is a noun and is
capitalized. It means that any bird having this name in common
with another one has some characteristics which both share.

Thus *Passerina cyanea* (Indigo Bunting) and *Passerina amoena* (Lazuli Bunting) have enough features in common to be placed in the same group, and the generic name shows this relationship.

The specific term, the second one given, is usually an adjective modifying the first term although it may be a noun in apposition or in the genitive form. This second term indicates that this kind of bird has distinctive characteristics which it does not share with any other kind.

At the time of Linnaeus' invention of binomial nomenclature, Latin was the language of the learned. We still preserve the remnants of this means of communication in the Latin inflections used in scientific terms and generally call them Latin. Many of the words have Greek or Latin origins. Some come from other languages, while some commemorate a person or a geographic location. It is the privilege of the original describer to give the bird its scientific name. While Alexander Wilson often used place names, John Audubon was inclined to honor his friends and associates.

The name of the original describer using the binomial system follows the name of the bird. If the describer's name is in parentheses it means that the scientific name has been changed from when it was proposed. For example, the American Ornithologists' Union *Check-list* has *Troglodytes troglodytes* (Linnaeus). This means that the name has been changed from the name given by Linnaeus, *Motacilla troglodytes*. As the practice of taxonomists is to make as few changes as possible, only the generic name was changed, letting the specific name stand. The parentheses indicate that the bird is no longer retained in the genus where the original describer placed it.

The fact that most birds have had their names changed is not in any way an implication that the original describers were at fault, but rather that so much has been learned since their time that revisions in nomenclature are a necessary means for the incorporation of new knowledge into the system. In "Recent Advances in Systematics," *Bio-Science,* December 1968, Edward O. Wilson points out, "according to insulin structure, we find that the pig is closer to whales than it is to the cow, horse and sheep." This gives a hint of the continuing new implications for revisions of nomenclature that are coming from contemporary research. One of the chief virtues of the binomial system is that it is a resilient tool adaptable to the continuous growth of knowledge. It is pleasant to contemplate that this scientific system invented by Linnaeus a century before Darwin has so readily lent itself to the progress of science.

Origin and Development

The binomial system of nomenclature was first used for plants by Linnaeus in *Species Planatarium* in 1753. Five years later, in the tenth edition of his *Systema Naturae,* birds were first so classified. Before Linnaeus the scientific community identified plants and animals by means of descriptive phrases and clauses in Latin. While binomial terms were used occasionally, they were not developed into a comprehensive system which showed the relationship of one species to another. Linnaeus' system did this, and also replaced an unwieldy superfluity of words with a concise two-word term.

The acceptance of a single worldwide term for each species makes it possible for scientists, regardless of the language they use, to know the identity of any bird with which they are concerned. This is not to say, however, that there is complete and universal agreement. There are still some minor areas of confusion. For example, there are no firm criteria for delimiting genera because they are not, like species, biological entities. As a consequence there is more disagreement over how birds are grouped in genera than there is in deciding the limits of species.

Linnaeus' great contribution to biological nomenclature in classifying plants and animals as well as naming them became in a comparatively short time almost universally accepted. The value of his system lay not only in its contribution to systematizing the knowledge of his day, but also in its providing both for a revision of that knowledge and for the inclusion of new knowledge in the future. The development of a universally accepted set of rules as a guide for scientists of diverse nationalities for solving difficulties of nomenclature has been one of the major concerns of various international scientific congresses. A botanical congress concerned with botanical nomenclature met in Paris in 1867. In 1889, also in Paris, the International Zoological Congress first met. As a result of the deliberations of these bodies, a set of regulations was formulated in the hope that its acceptance would further the continuation of a common understanding and interpretation of systematics, which the binomial system had made possible in the first place. One can readily imagine how confusing the results would be without the formulation of precise and comprehensive rules. In practice, too much would depend on the personal and individual interpretation of every authority naming a new organism or changing the species status of an old one.

The Law of Priority

One of the most important contributions to the regulation of nomenclature was the formulation of the law of priority. Its basic provision is that each distinct living thing retain inviolate its original and unique binomial name as long as it is scientifically valid. If new data and interpretation should require the change of a species from one genus to another, the generic name would be changed but the specific name would remain. E.g., *Colymbus immer* Brünnich became *Gavia immer* (Brünnich).

The name given to a new species by its original describer stands if the publication in which it first appeared is considered adequate. And it stands in its initial form despite mistakes in the name of the color, place of geographic origin, misspelling, grammar or other error. It is practically inviolate. It must be remembered that the words given to name a species assume a new and special function and become technical terms. That some of them are etymologically incorrect has no bearing on their usefulness as technical scientific labels. A good example of the inviolate nature of an erroneous name can be seen on p. 162 (*Toxostoma dorsale*).

Categories

Taxonomy, according to Ernst Mayr, is "the theory and practice of classifying organisms." It may be thought of as the name for the rules of the game of classification. Linnaeus invented the first good set of rules. These rules worked well for putting the pieces (the species) into appropriate pigeonholes in accordance with the knowledge and concepts of the mid-eighteenth century. Linnaeus used only four categories: class, order, genus and species. He thought every species was created in a distinct form which clearly differentiated it from all others and that this form had been retained from the moment of creation and would continue unchanged into eternity. In justice to him we must say that in his later writings, as his increasing collection made evident variations in species, he had become aware that his original system was not comprehensive enough to include all the new data that were accumulating.

The system invented by Linnaeus rapidly gained wide acceptance. Organisms already known had their names changed into binomial ones, and those newly discovered were henceforth named in conformity with the Linnaean scheme. The ever-increasing number of species made the relationships among them progressively obscure. Larger and more comprehensive collections made it evident that there was much variation among specimens often of so minute a nature that it became increasingly difficult to justify species status for many specimens. In addition to the problem of insufficient and appropriate categories of the original system, there was difficulty because it viewed living things as unchanging over eons of time. This static species concept became increasingly inadequate and a handicap to correct classification.

A century after Linnaeus, Darwin, who tells us quite vividly how he pondered upon the variety among the finches of Galapagos, and Wallace, noting the variations among the mammals, birds and insects of the Malay Archipelago, realized at about the same time in the middle of the last century the inadequacy and falseness of the static concept as a basis for understanding living things. Mayr, in his *Systematics and the Origin of Species,* points out some "'good species' were found to be connected by intermediates or in which one species had slightly different attributes in different parts of its range. This showed clearly that a static species concept was no longer tenable and that it had to be replaced by a dynamic one. This change was hastened by the confusion caused by the species splitters." It is interesting that until the ruling of the United States Supreme Court in 1969, it was illegal in some sections of the United States for biology teachers to explain the relationships of living things by means of the dynamic (evolutionary) concept.

Subspecies—A Lower Category

Mayr points out that even before the publication of *The Origin of Species* by Darwin in 1859, Schlegel "was apparently the first author (from 1844 on) to use trinomials consistently (even though hesitatingly) for geographic subdivisions of species." This custom gradually became more widely accepted during the latter half of the nineteenth century and is now the common practice. A subspecies is considered to be a group of individuals with characteristics sufficiently distinctive to differentiate it from other groups (especially on a geographic basis) while at the same time having so much in common as to place it in the same species. The validity of a subspecies is the decision of the taxonomist and depends on the number of individuals with distinctive and like characteristics in a geographic area. This decision is difficult as a subspecies in nature is not always a clear-cut unit, and the dividing line between races frequently has to be arbitrary.

The Song Sparrow, *Melospiza melodia,* in the fifth edition (1957) of the American Ornithologists' Union *Check-list* is subdivided into thirty-one subspecies or races. Each subspecies is not given a common name in the *Check-list* as it would only be of limited local value. Each, however, does have a trinomial scientific name, the first two parts of which it has in common with other races within the species. The first word of the trinomial shows that all are in the same genus and the second that all are in the same species.

Although we are not including either the common or scientific subspecific names in this study, we are making one exception because it has such a good story behind it. It is *Troglodytes aedon parkmanii*, originally named as a species *Troglodytes parkmanii* by Audubon in 1835, before subspecies were used, for his friend and probable benefactor Dr. George Parkman, a prominent and wealthy member of one of Boston's most eminent families. His nephew was Francis Parkman, the historian. The generous doctor gave to Harvard University not only the ground on which to build its medical school, but also a chair of anatomy which the university named for him in appreciation. This chair was filled by Dr. Oliver Wendell Holmes whose lecture room was above the office of Dr. John White Webster, professor of chemistry and mineralogy. This gentleman, who had been helped financially by Dr. Parkman, found the erstwhile helpfulness of his benefactor turn to a nagging and annoying insistence for repayment after his dishonest manipulations came to light. He secretly sold a cabinet of minerals which were part of the security for his loan from Dr. Parkman. Dr. Parkman was last seen entering the building in which was the office of his debtor. Some of his anatomical remains were later found in a bricked-in vault below this office. After what was left of Parkman's false teeth were shown to fit the mold of his dentist, a first-degree conviction was a foregone conclusion. A belated confession failed to save Webster from the gallows. The Webster-Parkman tragedy which was long considered America's most celebrated murder case is fading while the name of an obscure little bird still carries with undiminished permanence the name of Parkman, whom it was meant to honor. So much for *Troglodytes aedon parkmanii*.

The Higher Categories

As the development of scientific ornithology necessitated the reorganization of the taxonomy of some species into subspecies, it also necessitated the reorganization of categories above the species level. The genera of Linnaeus were much less inclusive than those of today. In fact, his genera, which often included species that were based on rather minute morphological differences, became so numerous that their value for classification in showing relationships became questionable. To have value a genus should bring together both those species that are most alike in form and structure (morphologically) and also those that presumably have a common ancestry (phylogenetically).

One means of clarifying the taxonomic muddle was the addition of a new category above that of the genus, the family. This new pigeonhole was quite akin in its inclusiveness to the original one of the genus as it was first used by Linnaeus. It is now in universal use. All genera in the same family have characteristics in common of a grosser kind than those in the genera to which they belong. Moving in the same direction, all members of the same family have characteristics of a finer distinction than that of the next higher category, which is the order. Taxonomists have further refined classification by establishing sub- and super-stages for various categories. In the following table we can see how the Greater Scaup fits into the general taxonomic scheme of things.

Organization of Categories

Beginning with the highest category we shall move down to the smallest unit to which *Aythya marila,* the Greater Scaup, belongs.

Animal Kingdom. The Greater Scaup is one of over a million species of animals and not a vegetable or a mineral.

Phylum Chordata. The bird belongs in this phylum of a little over one hundred thousand species that have spinal chords.

Subphylum Vertebrata. Birds are subdivided into this classification of animals that have a backbone protecting the spinal chord. There are seven vertebrate classes.

Class Aves. Here we find the nine thousand species of heavier-than-air machines which fly through the air, with the exception of a few such as the Ostrich and the Kiwi. Adaptation to flight has evolved in them special characteristics such as feathers, wings, and light-weight bones.

Order Anseriformes. The ordinal names of birds end in

iformes. Alexander Wetmore in his *Revised Classification of Birds* lists twenty-seven orders of living birds and seven extinct orders.

Suborder Anseres. This contains the ducks, geese, and swans, eliminating the screamers.

Family Anatidae. Family names end in *idae*. Although it is the only family in its suborder, it is divided into several subfamilies; one each for the swans, geese, whistling ducks, surface feeding ducks, diving ducks, ruddy and masked ducks, and mergansers. Just why there could not be several families instead of subfamilies illustrates the difficulties faced by taxonomists in deciding where to place birds. In this case it seems that they felt that the differences among the groups were too small to justify family status, but still sufficient to place them in a lower category as a subfamily.

Subfamily Aythyinae. Subfamily names end in *inae*. The diving ducks are placed here.

Genus Aythya Boie. This is the first category followed by the name of a person. It signifies that he was the one who named and described the genus. There are a dozen species in this genus, which is quite a drop from the one million in the first category.

Species Aythya marila (Linnaeus). This is the Greater Scaup. The parentheses around the name of Linnaeus indicates that he was the first to describe the bird in the binomial system but the species has been shifted to another genus from where placed originally.

Subspecies Aythya marila mariloides (Vigors). As there is a difference between the American and the European Greater Scaup which is too minor to justify placing each in a separate species but still worthy of note, a third word is added signifying that it is a subspecies. Vigor's name within parentheses indicates that in his original description of the bird it was placed in another genus.

Authority for Nomenclature

The American Ornithologists' Union is the recognized authority responsible for the nomenclature of American birds. The work is delegated to a committee of experts who not only check on the material to be published but submit the sections to collaborators throughout the United States and Canada who have specialized knowledge about a family or an area. "The continuous flow of new information on avian relationships and distribution renders any check-list instantly obsolete in at least some respects, and the need for revision and addition inevitably increases through time." This quotation is from the preface to the sixth edition of the *Check-list of North American Birds* published in 1983. Previous editions were published in 1886, 1895, 1910, 1931, and 1957. Changes in status or other revisions of the *Check-list* are published in *The Auk,* the journal of the American Ornithologists' Union, from time to time between *Check-lists* and serve to keep nomenclature up to date. In contrast to earlier *Check-lists* which covered species and subspecies found in North America north of Mexico, including Greenland, Bermuda, and Baja California, the latest edition extends its coverage south to Panama, the West Indies, and Hawaii, and excludes Greenland. Subspecies are not treated in this volume, but coverage is promised in a future publication.

List of Scientific Names

Acanthis Borkhausen. Gr. *acanthis,* "a bird fond of thistles, the linnet." The genus is sometimes merged with *Carduelis,* as in the A.O.U. *Check-list* (1983).

Accipiter Brisson. L. *accipiter,* "hawk," from L. *ad,* "after"; L. *capito,* "take." **A. cooperii** (Bonaparte): COOPER'S HAWK for William Cooper (see Appendix). **A. gentilis** (Linnaeus): NORTHERN GOSHAWK; LL. *gentilis,* "noble." L. *gentilis* meant belonging to the same clan, from L. *gens* "tribe or clan." From this the descendants of the word have come to mean those qualities which at one time were considered the special attributes of the well born. They were qualities to be admired and by medieval times could be readily applied to a bird which was courageous, domesticated and much ad-

mired: the Goshawk. The L. *gens* from which we inherit, gentle, gentile, genus was derived from an Indo-European root which was also the progenitor of E. *king* and E. *kin*. The word *gentilis* was a term used by falconers who divided their birds into two classes. The members of the first class were the long- and pointed-winged falcons. They were called "noble" for their spectacular plunging after prey. In the second class were the rounder- and shorter-winged hawks. As their catching of prey was less entertaining they were called "ignoble." An exception was made for the Goshawk which in spite of its physical affinity to the round-winged hawks was a thrilling hunter and by courtesy was admitted into the "noble" class of falcons. Albertus Magnus described it as "the most noble kind of all falcons." The word *gentilis* was often applied only to the female. In naming the bird *Falco gentilis* Linnaeus implies that it was one of the "noble" hawks traditionally reserved for the pleasure of the nobility in the sport of falconry. This does not seem to be the case. Grossman and Hamlet say, "By the Twelfth Century even the citizens of London—the merchant, the baker and the candlestick maker kept sparrowhawks (accipiters) and goshawks, 'the short-winged hawks.' Gyrfalcons and Peregrines, 'the long-winged hawks,' were . . . reserved . . . for . . . the nobility." The Eurasian Sparrowhawk and the Goshawk, "the birds of the yeoman and the priest. And last of all, at the bottom of the social ladder, reserved for knaves, servants and children, was the pliable, brave little Old World Kestrel." Linnaeus' *Falco gentilis* was, according to Swann, an immature Goshawk based on a description Albin published in 1738. Brisson in 1760 removed the accipiters from the falcons, thus giving them a new generic name. Linnaeus' name, in parentheses, indicates a change was made, substituting *Accipter* for *Falco*.
A. striatus Vieillot: SHARP-SHINNED HAWK; L. *striatus,* "striped," for the streaks on the underside.

Actitis Illiger. Gr. *aktites,* "a dweller on the sea coast." **A. macularia** (Linnaeus): SPOTTED SANDPIPER; L. *macula,* "spot," for the spots on the underparts in the breeding season.

Aechmophorus Coues. ML. term coined by Coues. Gr. *aichme,* "spear"; Gr. *phoreus,* "bearer"; for the spear-like bill. **A. occidentalis** (Lawrence): WESTERN GREBE; L. *occidentalis,* "western," for its range in western North America.

Aegolius Kaup. Gr. *aigolios,* "a kind of owl," mentioned by Aristotle. Remotely from the resemblance of its notes to the bleating of a goat. Gr. *aigos,* "a goat." **A. acadicus** (Gmelin): NORTHERN SAW-WHET OWL; L. *acadicus,* "of Acadia," for Nova Scotia where the first specimen was found. **A. funereus** (Linnaeus): BOREAL OWL; L. *funereus,* "mournful," as its call has been likened to the "slow tolling of a soft but high-pitched bell."; cf. E. *funereal.*

Aeronautes Hartert. Gr. *aer,* "air"; Gr. *nautes,* "a sailor." **A. saxatalis** (Woodhouse): WHITE-THROATED SWIFT; L. *saxatilis,* "rock-dweller," from its habitat.

Aethia Merrem. Gr. *aithya,* "a sea bird." **A. cristatella** (Pallas): CRESTED AUKLET; L. *cristatellus,* diminutive of *cristatus,* "crested." **A. pusilla** (Pallas): LEAST AUKLET; L. *pusillus,* "very small," apt term as it is the least in size being 5¼ inches in length. **A. pygmaea** (Gmelin): WHISKERED AUKLET; L. *pygmaea,* "dwarfish," from Gr. *pygmaioi,* "mythical dwarfs whose height was the length of a *pygme,*" i.e., from the elbow to the knuckles of the closed fist (13 to 14 inches). Gr. *pygme* also meant fist as did L. *pugnus,* the base of E. *pugnacious* and *pugilist.* Close to the length of the *pygme* was the L. *cubitus,* "cubit," the length from the elbow to the end of the middle finger (18 to 22 inches). Happily for the translators of the King James version of the bible, the length of the cubit and the length of the Hebrew *ammah* is the same. They were thus saved arithmetical calculation when they could write, "Goliath of Gath whose height was six cubits and a span."

The Pygmies, according to Homer, were forced in bloody battles to defend their fields of grain in their homeland near the sources of the Nile every winter when the migrating cranes threatened to devastate them.

Agelaius Vieillot. Gr. *agelaios,* "flocking." **A. phoeniceus** (Linnaeus): RED-WINGED BLACKBIRD; Gr. *phoinikeos,* L. *phoeniceus,* "red," the color introduced into Greece by the Phoenicians. This is the Tyrian (Tyre, the Phoenician city) dye used in robes of state. It was violet-purple and was obtained from shellfish. **A. tricolor** (Audubon): TRI-COLORED BLACKBIRD; L. *tricolor,* "three-colored," red, white, and black in the plumage.

Aimophila Swainson. Gr. *aima,* "blood"; Gr. *phila,* "fond of." Swainson is credited with naming this genus in 1837, its lone species being *A. aestivalis.* The four other species of the same genus were first described later. It would appear that Swainson made a separate genus for one species and then gave the genus a singularly inappropriate name. "What's so blood-loving about a sparrow?" **A. aestivalis** (Lichtenstein): BACHMAN'S SPARROW; L. *aestivalis,* "summery," L. *aestas,* "summer." **A. botterii** (Sclater): BOT-TERI'S SPARROW for M. Botteri (see Appendix). **A. carpalis** (Coues): RUFOUS-WINGED SPARROW; L. *carpalis,* "having to do with the wrist," L. *carpus,* "wrist." It is the bend of the wing, or wrist, that is rufous-brown. **A. cassinii** (Wood-house): CASSIN'S SPARROW for John Cassin (see Appendix). **A. ruficeps** (Cassin): RUFOUS-CROWNED SPARROW; L. *ruficeps,* "red-headed," for the red crown.

Aix Boie. Gr. *aix,* "a kind of waterfowl." **A. sponsa** (Linnaeus): WOOD DUCK; L. *sponsa,* "betrothed," i.e., dressed for a wedding, from the bird's attractive appearance.

Ajaia Reichenbach. Ajaia is a South American native name for the spoonbill, also spelled "ajaja". **A. ajaja** (Linnaeus): ROSEATE SPOONBILL.

Alauda Linnaeus. L. *alauda,* "lark," possibly from Celtic *al,* "high"; *aud,* "song." **A. arvensis** Linnaeus: EURASIAN SKY-LARK; L. *arvensis,* "of the cultivated field," alluding to its habitat.

Alca Linnaeus. S. and Ic. *alka,* "auk." **A. torda** Linnaeus:

RAZORBILL; *torda,* name of the bird in the Gottland province of Sweden.

Alectoris Kaup. Gr. *alektor,* "a cock." **A. chukar** (Gray): CHUKAR, a range name for one of its geographical races.

Alle Link. S. *alle,* "the dovekie." **A. alle** (Linnaeus): DOVEKIE or LITTLE AUK.

Amazilia Lesson. *Amazilia,* a barbarism, which is a lexicographer's term for a word of no known derivation or meaning. **A. violiceps** (Gould): VIOLET-CROWNED HUMMINGBIRD; L. *violoceus,* "violet-colored"; L. *cephalicus,* "head," as the bird has a conspicuous violet crown. **A. yucatanenis** (Cabot): BUFF-BELLIED HUMMINGBIRD; ML. *yucatanensis,* "of Yucatán," locality of original specimen.

Ammodramus Swainson. Gr. *ammos,* "sand"; Gr. *dramein,* "to run," not particularly apt. **A. bairdii** (Audubon): BAIRD'S SPARROW for Spencer F. Baird (see Appendix). **A. caudacutus** (Gmelin): SHARP-TAILED SPARROW; L. *cauda,* "tail"; L. *acuta,* "sharp," descriptive of the tail. **A. henslowii** (Audubon): HENSLOW'S SPARROW for John S. Henslow (see Appendix). **A. leconteii** (Audubon): LECONTE'S SPARROW for Dr. John LeConte (see Appendix). **A. maritimus** (Wilson): SEASIDE SPARROW; L. *maritima,* "seaside," for the bird's habitat. **A. mirabilis** (Howell): CAPE SABLE SPARROW; L. *mirabilis,* "marvelous." Here the poet got ahead of the scientist as the bird is a very pretty little sand finch. Now a subspecies of *A. maritimus.* **A. nigrescens** (Ridgway): DUSKY SEASIDE SPARROW; L. *nigrescens,* "dusky," for the dark plumage. Also now a subspecies of *A. maritimus.* **A. savannarum** (Gmelin): GRASSHOPPER SPARROW; L. *savannarum,* "of the meadows," as the bird frequents a grassy habitat.

Ammospiza Oberholser. Gr. *amme,* "sand"; Gr. *spiza,* "a finch." The genus is now merged within *Ammodramus.*

Amphispiza Coues. Gr. *amphi,* "on both sides"; Gr. *spiza,* "a finch"; "alluding to the close relation of the genus to those about it" according to Coues. **A. belli** (Cassin): SAGE SPARROW; for John G. Bell (see Appendix). **A. bilineata** (Cas-

sin): BLACK-THROATED SPARROW; L. *bilineata*, "two-lined,"
alluding to the stripes on the head.

Anas Linnaeus. L. *anas*, "a duck." **A. acuta** Linnaeus: NORTH-
ERN PINTAIL; L. *acutus*, "sharp," in reference to the tail. **A.
americana** Gmelin: AMERICAN WIGEON; ML. *americana*,
"American," for its range. **A. crecca carolinensis** Gmelin:
AMERICAN GREEN-WINGED TEAL; ML. *carolinensis*, "of
Carolina." This is a subspecies of *A. crecca* (see below). It
was originally described as being from Carolina to Hudson's
Bay. This was shortened to the first geographical area. **A.
clypeata** Linnaeus: NORTHERN SHOVELER; L. *clypeata*,
"furnished with a shield." Possibly for the reddish patches
on the sides of the male. **A. crecca** Linnaeus: GREEN-
WINGED TEAL. The Gr. *krex* means a long-legged bird,
which does not fit. Macleod suggests it is a coined word that
"probably represents the bird's incessant calling; cf. the
onomatopoeic Gr. *kreko*, 'cause a string to sound by striking
it.'" **A. cyanoptera** Vieillot: CINNAMON TEAL; Gr. *chy-
aneous*, "dark blue"; Gr. *pteron*, "wing"; referring to the
blue patch on the wing which is easily observed in flight.
A. diazi Ridgway: MEXICAN DUCK; for Agustín Díaz (see
Appendix). Currently treated as a race of the Mallard. **A.
discors** (Linnaeus): BLUE-WINGED TEAL; L. *discors*, "dis-
cordant," according to most authorities in reference to the
bird's harsh call. The difficulty with this is that the call of
the bird is not harsh. Bent, in *Life Histories of American
Wildfowl*, pt. II, p. 118, says, "About the vocal powers of
this teal there is very little to be said. Dawson (1903) has
covered the ground very well in the following words, 'In
addition to the whistling of the wings, the teals have a soft
whistling note, only remotely related to the typical anatidine
quack, and it is uttered either in apprehension or encouragement.'" While the male peeps, the female has a soft quack.
Contrary to MacLeod, Jorday and Eaton suggest that the
derivation may be *disc* from Gr. *discos*, "a disc," and L. *os,
oris*, "pertaining to the mouth." Thus *discors* may mean
"disc about the mouth" and refers to the well-known field

mark of the bird, the oral disc. **A. formosa** Georgi: BAIKAL TEAL; ML. *formosa*, Latinized form referring to the island of Formosa, one of the places in its winter range. **A. fulvigula** Ridgway: MOTTLED DUCK; L. *fulvus*, "reddish-yellow"; L. *gula*, "the throat." **A. penelope** Linnaeus: EUROPEAN WIGEON or EURASIAN WIGEON. Coues, Eaton and others suggest that *penelope* is a mistake for *penelops*, a kind of goose mentioned by Aristotle and Pliny. But Linnaeus may not have erred too much in using the name of a goose for a wigeon. Conrad Gessner (1516–1565), the German-Swiss naturalist, cites an old legend that Penelope was thrown into the sea by her parents (no reason given) and rescued by sea birds (species not cited) whose name she was given. At any rate Penelope survived to win renown as the virtuous and patient model of Greek propriety who waited twenty years for her husband, Ulysses, to return from the Trojan War, and who used weaving as a device to forestall her suitors. As Gr. *penelope* means "weaver," we may surmise that our bird was named for a skill, a woman, or a sea bird that just possibly may have been a wigeon. **A. platyrhynchos** Linnaeus: MALLARD; Gr. *platus*, "broad"; Gr. *rhynchos*, "bill." **A. rubripes** Brewster: BLACK DUCK; L. *ruber*, "red"; L. *pes*, "foot." **A. strepera** Linnaeus: GADWALL; L. *streperus*, "noisy."

Anhinga Brisson. A South American native (Tupi) name for the Water Turkey. **A. anhinga** (Linnaeus): ANHINGA.

Anous Stephens. Gr. *anous*, "stupid," referring to the bird's failure to take alarm. **A. minutus** Boie: BLACK NODDY; L. *minutus*, "little." **A. stolidus** (Linnaeus): BROWN NODDY; L. *stolidus*, "stupid," so the stupid, stupid bird also gets it over again in (see) Noddy.

Anser Brisson. L. *anser*, "goose." **A. albifrons** (Scopoli): GREATER WHITE-FRONTED GOOSE; L. *albus*, "white"; L. *frons*, "forehead," for the white forehead of the adult.

Anthus Bechstein. Gr. *anthos*, "a kind of bird." It received its name from a youth who changed into a bird after being killed by his father's horses. **A. spinoletta** (Linnaeus): WATER PIPIT; ML. *spinoletta*, a mistake for I. *spipoletta*, "water pipit." **A. spragueii** (Audubon): SPRAGUE'S PIPIT for Isaac Sprague (see Appendix).

Aphelocoma Cabinis. Gr. *aphelos*, "smooth"; Gr. *koms*, "hair"; as there is no crest. **A. coerulescens** (Bosc): SCRUB JAY; L. *caeruleus*, "dark blue," for the plumage. **A. ultramarina** (Bonaparte): GRAY-BREASTED JAY; L. *ultra*, "beyond"; L. *marina*, "marine"; deeper blue in color than the sea.

Aphriza Audubon. Gr. *aphros*, "sea foam"; Gr. *zoa*, "to live." **A. virgata** (Gmelin): SURFBIRD; L. *virgatus*, "striped."

Aquila Brisson. L. *aquila*, "eagle," perhaps related to L. *aquilus*, "dark brown," hence a dun-colored bird; *aquilus* is from *aqua*, "water." E. *aquiline*, "like an eagle," used in describing a human nose hooked like an eagle's beak. **A. chrysaetos** (Linnaeus): GOLDEN EAGLE; Gr. *aetos*, "eagle"; Gr. *chrysos*, "golden." The bird was called *chrysaetos* by Aelian, a Roman who wrote in Greek in the third century A.D.

Aramus Vieillot. Unknown origin. **A. guarauna** (Linnaeus): LIMPKIN; Guarauna is the name of a tribe inhabiting the delta of the Orinoco in Venezuela, hence, a locality name for the bird that does likewise.

Archilochus Reichenbach. Gr. *arch*, a prefix meaning "chief"; Gr. *lochos*, "a body of people," here meaning "first among the birds." Naming the hummingbirds has caused the systematists difficulty. Unique to the New World, their first describers had no background for their scientific classification. Hindsight shows us that the problem was further compounded by the fact that most hummingbirds have their range in the western part of the country. As new species were discovered one by one the relationship of each to the as yet unknown ones was impossible to determine. The consequence of this was that the original names had to be changed when fuller knowledge of the hummingbird made a more valid classification possible. Wilson knew only the Rubythroat and Audubon included only four in his *Birds of America*. Baird in 1858 named seven. Coues could name only ten in 1872, although he was able to list eighteen in 1890. The A.O.U. *Check-list* of 1957 names eighteen, all but one having its original name revised. Since then two more species of hummingbirds have been recorded in the United States. **A. alexandri** (Bourcier and Mulsant): BLACK-CHINNED HUMMINGBIRD for Dr. Alexandre (see Appendix). **A. colubris** (Linnaeus): RUBY-THROATED HUMMINGBIRD; L. *colubris*, "a serpent," so inappropriate that a misspelling by Linnaeus is more likely. The word is from F. *colibre*, "hummingbird."

Ardea Linnaeus. L. *ardea*, "heron." **A. herodias** (Linnaeus): GREAT BLUE HERON; Gr. *herodios*, "a heron."

Arenaria Brisson. L. *arenaria*, "having to do with sand," from L. *arena*, "sand." **A. interpres** (Linnaeus): RUDDY TURNSTONE; L. *interpres*, "interpreter, go-between" or, in this case, "tell-tale," for its notes of alarm that warn other birds. Coues says that the name was given in error by Linnaeus who misunderstood the native name "tolk" used for the Redshank on the island of Gottland in the early 1700s. The "tolk" does alarm other birds more than the Turnstone. **A. melanocephala** (Vigors): BLACK TURNSTONE; Gr. *melas*, "black"; Gr. *cephalos*, "head"; for its dark head.

Arremonops Ridgway. Gr. *arremon*, "silent," a name of a South American genus, and Gr. *opsis*, "appearance," for the resemblance to the southern genus. **A. rufivirgatus** (Lawrence): OLIVE SPARROW; L. *rufus*, "reddish"; L. *virgata*, "striped"; for the inconspicuous reddish stripes on the head. It is more easily identified in the field by its notes which sound like a ping-pong ball bouncing on a hard surface.

Asio Brisson. L. *asio*, "a kind of horned owl." **A. flammeus** (Pontoppidan): SHORT-EARED OWL; L. *flammeus*, "flame-colored," for its tawny plumage. **A. otus** (Linnaeus): LONG-EARED OWL; Gr. *otos*, "an eared owl."

Asyndesmus Coues. Gr. *a*, "without"; Gr. *syn*, "together"; Gr. *desmos*, "a band." Coues, who made this name, says it alludes "to loosened texture of feathers in certain parts." Now merged with *Melanerpes*.

Athene Boie. Gr. *Athene*, goddess of wisdom. **A. cunicularia** (Molina): BURROWING OWL; L. *cunicularius*, "a miner or burrower," from L. *cuniculus*, "a rabbit."

Auriparus Baird. L. *aurum,* "gold," for the yellow head. L. *parus,* "a titmouse." **A. flaviceps** (Sundevall): VERDIN; L. *flaviceps,* "yellow head."

Aythya Boie. This one really aroused Coues' dander. He said, "I am willing to follow the A.O.U. in adopting the genus, but not in violating plain rules for the transliteration from the Greek to the Latin, which give us neither *Aithya* Boie, nor *Aithya* Kaup, nor *Aithyia* Bp., nor anything but *Æthyia.*" Gr. *aythya,* "a kind of waterbird," in Homer's *Odyssey* and Aristotle's *Natural History.* **A. affinis** (Eyton): LESSER SCAUP; L. *affinis,* "related," i.e., to the species above. **A. americana** (Eyton): RED-HEAD; L. *americana,* "American." **A. collaris** (Donovan): RING-NECKED DUCK; L. *collaris,* "collared," referring to the ringed neck. **A. marila** (Linnaeus): GREATER SCAUP; probably Gr. *marile,* "charcoal." **A. valisineria** (Wilson): CANVASBACK; *valisineria* should be spelled *vallisneria* as it is spelled by Coues and Eaton. It refers to one of the main foods of the bird, *Vallisneria americana,* the wild or water celery. The plant was named in honor of an eminent Italian physician and naturalist, Antonio Vallisneri or Vallisnieri (1661–1730). While it is debatable as to whether the botanists or the ornithologists are the worse spellers, the ornithologists go way ahead on this one. Wilson in discussing the bird's food says, "The plant is said to be a species of valisineria." He thus admits his inability to be more definite.

Bartramia Lesson. In honor of William Bartram (see Appendix). **B. longicauda** (Bechstein): UPLAND SANDPIPER; L. *longus,* "long"; L. *caudus,* "tail."

Bombycilla Vieillot. A coined word from L. or Gr. *bombyx,* "silk"; ML. *cilla,* which through error was taken to mean "tail." *Cilla* is the last part of L. *motacilla,* "wagtail." This word according to MacLeod is most likely derived from L. *motax, motacis,* "mover," and L. *illa,* the feminine diminutive suffix. Thus the word means "little mover." Varro, the Roman scholar, explained the word which he used, "The bird owes its name to the fact that it is always moving its tail (*caudam*); and this clearly gave rise to the idea that *mota,* the first part of the word, meant 'moving'; *cilla,* the second part of the name, meant 'tail.'" It is obvious, however, that if there had been such a word as *cilla,* Varro would have said in his explanation of *motacilla* that the bird moves its *cilla* and not its *cauda.* **B. cedrorum** Vieillot: CEDAR WAXWING; L. *cedrorum,* "of the cedars," from the bird's partiality to this tree. **B. garrulus** (Linnaeus): BOHEMIAN WAXWING; L. *garrula,* "chattering," as its crest makes it resemble the European Jay known as *garrulous,* which is quite noisy. Cf. E. *garrulous.*

Bonasa Stephens. L. *bonasum,* Gr. *bonasos,* "the aurochs, a wild ox," the drumming of the bird being likened to the bellowing of a bull. It is suggested that consideration be given to L. *bonus,* "good," plus L. *assum,* "a roast." **B. umbellus** (Linnaeus): RUFFED GROUSE; L. *umbellus,* "a sunshade," alluding to the neck tufts.

Botaurus Stephens. ML. *botaurus,* "a bittern," from either ME. *boter* or F. *butor* probably derived from L. *butio,* "a bittern." Both the French and English names may be imitative of the bird's call. MacLeod says: "Possibly *Botaurus* was also intended to suggest a derivation from two old L. words *bos,* 'ox,' and *taurus,* 'bull'; in allusion to the bittern's old L. name *taurus,* which according to Pliny (X, 57) had its origin in the bird's imitating a bull's bellowing." At any rate, in this case we have the correct tie-up of the bird's name with its vocalizing. **B. lentiginosus** (Rackett): AMERICAN BITTERN; L. *lentiginosus,* "freckled," from L. *lent,* "a lentil," referring to the freckled or lentil-shaped spotting of the bird's upper parts.

Brachyramphus Brandt. Gr. *brachus,* "short"; Gr. *rhamphos,* "beak," from Gr. *ramphis,* "a hook"; quite appropriate. **B. brevirostris** (Vigors): KITTLITZ'S MURRELET; L. *brevis,* "short"; L. *rostrum,* "beak." As all the murrelets and their relatives have small bills, the name does not imply special distinction for this bird. E. *rostrum,* "a platform used by speakers," comes from L. *rostra,* "beaks." The Romans used the word rostrum for the pointed bronze ram on the prow of a war galley as its shape resembled the beak of a bird. In classical times before the use of gunpowder, the most effective ship in naval combat was the war galley. Propelled by banks of oars, it had great speed and maneuverability compared to cargo ships, which relied mainly on sail. On the prow of the war galley was a heavy pointed ram mounted slightly above water level. This ram easily penetrated the side of a wooden ship. The Romans in 338 B.C. sent the consul Maenius to remove the menace to their trading ships by the pirates at Antium, now Anzio. He was victorious and brought back as mementos the rostra, "beaks," of six of the destroyed pirate galleys. These were hung on the platform used by speakers in the forum, which was from that time on called the *rostra*. **B. marmoratus** (Gmelin): MARBLED MURRELET; L. *marmoratus*, "marbled," from its underparts in breeding plumage.

Branta Scopoli. ML. *branta*, coined from English *brant* from AS. *bernan*, *brennan*, "to burn," with reference to the charred or burnt appearance of the bird's plumage, particularly around the neck. Also possibly a corruption of Gr. *brentha*, "an unknown water bird." **B. bernicla** (Linnaeus): BRANT; Nor. *bernicla*, "barnacle"; the Latinized form of ME. *bernekka* was first Latinized as *bernaca* by Giraldus Cambrensis who originally "put forth the tale" about 1175 that the bird hatched from the shellfish of the name *bernaca*, "barnacle." Although repeating the tale, Turner, writing in 1544, remarks "that no one has seen the Bernicle's nest or egg as evidence of this spontaneous generation" as Swann points out. Disregarding this doubt, Gerard, in his *Herbal* of 1597, states, "As it groweth greater, it openeth the shell by degrees till at length it is all come forth and hangeth only by the bill; in short space after, it cometh to full maturity and falleth into the sea, where it gathereth feathers." The *Oxford Dictionary* says, "All the evidence shows that the name was originally applied to the bird which had the marvelous origin, not to the shell which produced it." This leaves the derivation of the name of the bird unresolved; but no matter which came first, the chicken or the egg, in the legend, barnacles are whitish and the bird does have a burnt coloration. **B. canadensis** (Linnaeus): CANADA GOOSE; M. *canadensis*, "Canadian," referring to the bird's main summer range. **B. leucopsis** (Bechstein): BARNACLE GOOSE; Gr. *leukos*, "white"; Gr. *ophis*, "face." **B. nigricans** (Lawrence): BLACK BRANT; L. *nigricans*, "black." Now considered the same species as the Brant and *nigricans* is relegated to a subspecies.

Bubo Dumerill. L. *bubo*, "the great horned owl," cognate with Gr. *buas*, "the great horned owl" from Gr. *buzo*, "to hoot," **B. virginianus** (Gmelin): GREAT HORNED OWL; ML. *virginianus*, "Virginian." Considering the extent of its range, *americanus* would be more appropriate.

Bubulcus Bonaparte. L. *bubulus*, "concerning cattle"; L. *cus*, "suffix denoting belonging to." **B. ibis** (Linnaeus): CATTLE EGRET; L. *ibis* from Gr. *ibis*, who borrowed the word from the ancient Egyptians' *ibis*. The Egyptians also called the bird *hab*. Both the glossy and sacred ibis have been identified from mummies. The sacred ibis was sacred to Thoth, one of the greatest gods in the Egyptian pantheon, who was the patron of learning. The birds are frequently portrayed in Egyptian hieroglyphics. Just why Linnaeus named this straight-billed egret an ibis is puzzling.

Bucephala Baird. Gr. *bous*, "ox or bull," plus Gr. *kephale*, "head"; for the shape of the head and not for the famous horse of Alexander. **B. albeola** (Linnaeus): BUFFLEHEAD; L. *albus*, "white"; L. *-olus*, diminutive suffix; "little white head," which is appropriate as the predominant color is white. **B. clangula** (Linnaeus): COMMON GOLDENEYE; L. *clangula*, diminutive of *clangor*, "noise," referring to the little noise of the whirring wings. **B. islandica** (Gmelin): BARROW'S GOLDENEYE; ML. *islandica*, "of Iceland," one of the bird's breeding localities.

Buteo Lacepede. L. *buteo*, "a hawk," probably akin to E. *buzzard*. **B. albicaudatus** Vieillot: WHITE-TAILED HAWK; L. *albus*, "white"; L. *caudatus*, "tailed." **B. albonotatus** Kaup: ZONE-TAILED HAWK; L. *albus*, "white"; L. *notatus*, "marked." **B. brachyurus** Vieillot: SHORT-TAILED HAWK; Gr. *brachys*, "short"; Gr. *ours*, "tail." **B. jamaicensis**

(Gmelin): RED-TAILED HAWK; ML. *jamaicensis*, "of Jamaica," site of original specimen. **B. jamaicensis harlani** (Audubon): HARLAN'S HAWK for Dr. R. Harlan (see Appendix). **B. lagopus** (Pontoppidan): ROUGH-LEGGED HAWK; Gr. *lagos*, "a hare"; Gr. *pous*, "foot"; probably in reference to the feathered shanks. **B. lineatus** (Gmelin): RED-SHOULDERED HAWK; L. *lineatus*, "striped," most likely for the black and white stripes on the wings seen from above. **B. nitidus** (Latham): GRAY HAWK; L. *nitidus*, "bright, shining." While lighter in color than most buteos, the common name more aptly portrays its color. **B. platypterus** (Vieillot): BROAD-WINGED HAWK; Gr. *platys*, "broad"; Gr. *pteron*, "wing." **B. regalis** (Gray): FERRUGINOUS HAWK; L. *regalis*, "royal." **B. swainsoni** Bonaparte: SWAINSON'S HAWK for William Swainson (see Appendix).

Buteogallus Lesson. L. *buteo*, "a hawk"; L. *gallus*, "a domestic cock"; roughly "a chicken hawk." **B. anthracinus** (Deppe): COMMON BLACK-HAWK; L. *anthracinus*, "coal black," from Gr. *anthrax*, "coal."

Butorides Blyth. *Butorides* is etymologically uncertain. It is a coined ML. word, probably allied to L. *butio*, "bittern," and Gr. *eidos*, "resembling." **B. striatus** (Linnaeus): GREEN-BACKED HERON; L. *striatus*, "striped," for the streaks on its back. The population of North America used to be separated as **B. virescens** (Linnaeus): GREEN HERON; L. *virescens*, "growing or becoming green." Possibly it is losing its green, of which the bird has very little.

Calamospiza Bonaparte. Gr. *calamos*, L. *calamus*, "a reed"; Gr. *spiza*, "a finch." **C. melanocorys** Stejneger: LARK BUNTING; Gr. *melanos*, "black," for the predominant color of the male's plumage. Gr. *corys*, "a lark," possibly for its singing on the wing like the European Skylark.

Calcarius Bechstein. L. *calcar*, "a heel," in reference to the enlarged hind claw of the genus. **C. lapponicus** (Linnaeus): LAPLAND LONGSPUR; L. *lapponicus*, "of Lapponia," Lapland. Breeds in the Arctic and sub-Arctic regions of the Northern Hemisphere. Possibly Linnaeus saw it on his trip to Lapland. At any rate, it was the site of the type specimen.

C. mccownii (Lawrence): MCCOWN'S LONGSPUR for J. P. McCown (see Appendix). **C. ornatus** (Townsend): CHEST-NUT-COLLARED LONGSPUR; L. *ornatus,* "adorned," for its striking plumage. **C. pictus** (Swainson): SMITH'S LONG-SPUR; L. *pictus,* "painted," for the gay summer plumage of the male.

Calidris Merrem. Gr. *calidris,* "a gray speckled sandpiper." The genera *Crocethia, Eurentes,* and *Erolia* are now merged in *Calidris* (1973). **C. acuminata** (Horsfield): SHARP-TAILED SANDPIPER; L. *acuminata,* "sharp-pointed," for the pointed tail. **C. alba** (Pallas): SANDERLING; L. *alba,* "white," for the light colored winter plumage. **C. alpina** (Linnaeus): DUNLIN or RED-BACKED SANDPIPER; L. *alpina,* "alpine," for its breeding in an alpine-like climate which may be on the Arctic tundra as well as in the mountains. **C. bairdii** (Coues): BAIRD'S SANDPIPER for Spencer F. Baird (see Appendix). **C. canutus** (Linnaeus): RED KNOT; ML. *canutus,* "King Canute," said to be named for Canute be-cause (1) the birds and the king both came from Denmark, (2) the species when broiled was his favorite food, (3) the birds frequent the scene of his famous rebuke. The story is that Canute, bored by the outrageous flattery of his cour-tiers, commanded the tide to stay its advance. Its disregard of his edict suggested that the courtiers, too, be realistic. Swann gives Camden (1607) responsibility for originating the tale. Coues says, "Named for King Canute by Linnaeus, who accepted the dubious tradition that connected this bird with a story of the Danish King Knut, Cnut, Canut, etc. The name appears in the poems of Michael Drayton (1563–1631) and Knotts are named in mss. of the sixteenth century. Sir T. Browne has Gnatts or Knots, c. 1672. Other forms are Gnat, Knat, Knet, etc." More likely Linnaeus thought the tale interesting and gave it no more credence than the mythological stories which inspired his naming of some birds. **C. ferruginea** (Pontoppidan): CURLEW SANDPIPER; L. *ferruginea,* "rusty red," for the color of the underparts. **C. fuscicollis** (Vieillot): WHITE-RUMPED SANDPIPER; L. *fuscus,* "dusky"; L. *collum,* "neck." As the bird does not have a dark neck, the name is misleading. **C. himantopus** (Bonaparte): STILT SANDPIPER; Gr. *himantopus*, "a leather strap or thong"; Gr. *pous*, "foot"; for the resemblance of the long legs to thongs. **C. maritima** (Brünnich): PURPLE SANDPIPER; L. *maritima*, "belonging to the sea." It is partial to the rocky sea coasts. **C. mauri** (Cabanis): WESTERN SANDPIPER; for Ernesto Mauri (see Appendix). **C. melanotos** (Vieillot): PECTORAL SANDPIPER; Gr. *melas*, "black"; Gr. *notos*, "the back." As the bird does not have a black back, it looks like more carelessness on the part of Vieillot. **C. minutilla** (Vieillot): LEAST SANDPIPER; L. *minutilla*, "very small," apt name for the smallest sandpiper. **C. ptilocnemis** (Coues): ROCK SANDPIPER; Gr. *ptilon*, "feather"; Gr. *cnemis*, "a greave," the shin armor of a Greek foot soldier comparable to the shin guard of an American baseball catcher. The term refers to the feathering on the leg from the knee to the heel. **C. pusilla** (Linnaeus): SEMIPALMATED SANDPIPER; L. *pusillos*, "very small."

Callipepla Wagler. Gr. *kallos*, "a beauty"; Gr. *peplos*, "a robe"; hence "beautifully dressed," **C. californica** (Shaw): CALIFORNIA QUAIL; ML. *californicus*, "of California," for the range. **C. gambeli** (Gambel): GAMBEL'S QUAIL; for William Gambel (see Appendix). **C. squamata** (Vigors): SCALED QUAIL; L. *squamatus*, "scaled," as the plumage suggests.

Calonectris Mathews and Iredale. Gr. *calos*, "beautiful"; Gr. *nectris*, "swimmer"; apt though generally seen on the wing rather than in the water. **C. diomedea** (Scopoli): CORY'S SHEARWATER; for Diomedes whose companions were changed into birds after the ship returning them from the Trojan War was lost.

Calothorax Gray. Gr. *calos*, "beautiful"; Gr. *thorax*, "chest"; not too accurate as it is the throat and not the chest that has color. **C. lucifer** (Swainson): LUCIFER HUMMINGBIRD; L. *lucifer*, "light bearer," like a small torch sailing in the air.

Calypte Gould. Gr. *Calypte*, "a proper name of unknown significance." **C. anna** (Lesson): ANNA'S HUMMINGBIRD for Anna, Duchess of Rivoli (see Appendix). **C. costae** (Bourcier): COSTA'S HUMMINGBIRD for Marquis de Costa (see Appendix).

Campephilus Gray. Gr. *campa*, "a caterpillar"; Gr. *philos*, "loving." **C. principalis** (Linnaeus): IVORY-BILLED WOOD-PECKER; L. *principalis*, "principal," hence principal caterpillar lover or grub lover.

Camptorhynchus Bonaparte. Gr. *kamptos*, "bent"; Gr. *rhynchos*, "beak"; **C. labradorius** (Gmelin): LABRADOR DUCK; LL. *labradorium*, "of Labrador," for the bird's range.

Camptostoma Sclater. Gr. *kamptos*, "bent"; Gr. *stoma*, "mouth"; referring to the fact that the bill is compressed and not depressed as is usual in the other members of the Tyrannidae. **C. imberbe** Sclater: NORTHERN BEARDLESS-TYRANNULET or BEARDLESS FLYCATCHER; L. *imberbis*, "beardless," as it does not have the hairlike feathers at the base of the bill common to the other flycatchers.

Campylorhynchus Spix. Gr. *campylos*, "curved"; Gr. *rhynchos*, "beak." **C. brunneicapillus** (Lafresnaye): CACTUS WREN; L. *brunneus*, "brown"; L. *capillus*, "hair"; for its brownish plumage.

Canachites Stejneger. Gr. *kanacheo*, "to make a noise, to crow." The genus is now combined with *Dendragapus* and bears the latter name.

Capella Frenzel. L. *caper*, "goat"; L. *-ella*, a feminine diminutive; "little female goat," from the resemblance of the sound made particularly in the breeding season by the male bird to the bleating of a goat. MacLeod points out that a Scottish name is "heather-bleater." The A.O.U. *Check-list* (1983) treats *Capella* as a synonym of *Gallinago*.

Caprimulgus Linnaeus. L. *caprimulgus*, "goat milker." The Romans got the traditional superstition though not the name from the Greeks, Gr. *aigothelas*, "goat milker," from Gr. *aix*, (genitive, *aigos*), "goat"; Gr. *thelazo*, "to suckle." Aristotle evidently accepted the belief of the shepherds when he stated, "Flying to the udders of she-goats, it sucks them, and thus gets its name." **C. carolinensis** Gmelin: CHUCK-

WILL'S WIDOW; ML. *carolinensis,* "of Carolina"; L. *Carolus,* "Charles"; from the area where Catesby obtained the bird, named from the colony of the English king. **C. ridgwayi** (Nelson): RIDGWAY'S WHIP-POOR-WILL, for Robert Ridgway (see Appendix) or BUFF-COLLARED NIGHTJAR. **C. vociferus** Wilson: WHIP-POOR-WILL; L. *vociferus,* "noisy" literally "voice-carrying."

Caracara Merrem. Probably a South American native name for the bird, derived from its call, a low rattle. **C. cheriway** (Jacquin): CRESTED CARACARA. Coues says that cheriway is probably a South American native name. In the latest (1983) A.O.U. *Check-list* this caracara is known as *Polyborus plancus.*

Cardellina Bonaparte. Possibly from L. *carduelis,* "some kind of finch." **C. rubifrons** (Giraud): RED-FACED WARBLER; L. *ruber,* "red"; L. *frons,* "forehead"; not only the forehead but the whole face and neck are red.

Cardinalis Bonaparte. L. *cardinalis,* "important," from L. *cardo,* "the hinge of a door," which came to mean figuratively "important," something upon which an object or an idea hinged or depended. A cardinal is an important church official upon whose decisions matters of administration and policy depend. His robe and hat are red. Hence the name of the bird whose plumage is the same color. **C. cardinalis** (Linnaeus): CARDINAL.

Carduelis Brisson. L. *carduelis,* "goldfinch"; L. *carduus,* "thistle," the bird's favorite food. **C. carduelis** (Linnaeus): EUROPEAN GOLDFINCH. **C. flammea** (Linnaeus): COMMON REDPOLL, L. *flammea,* "flame-colored," for its plumage. **C. hornemanni** Holböll: HOARY REDPOLL; for J. W. Hornemann (see Appendix). **C. lawrencei** Cassin: LAWRENCE'S GOLDFINCH; for G. N. Lawrence (see Appendix). **C. pinus** (Wilson): PINE SISKIN; L. *pinus,* "pine," as the bird favors conifers for breeding. **C. psaltria** (Say): LESSER GOLDFINCH; Gr. *psaltria,* "a lutist," for the bird's musical song. **C. sinuatus** Bonaparte: PYRRHULOXIA; L. *sinuata* "bent," for the bill, from L. *sinus,* "a fold, bosom, or bay." A look at the profile of the bill may suggest what Bonaparte had in mind. **C. tristis** (Linnaeus): AMERICAN GOLDFINCH; L. *tristis,* "sad." Coues says the term is for the bird's note. Linnaeus in naming the bird changed it from the one given by Catesby which did not suggest sadness. As the call is not mournful it is difficult to understand the reason for Linnaeus' choice.

Carpodacus Kaup. Gr. *carpos,* "fruit"; Gr. *dacos,* "biting." Seemingly a questionable name for a genus of seed-eating birds, but they are seasonally fruit eaters. **C. cassinii** Baird: CASSIN'S FINCH for John Cassin (see Appendix). **C. mexicanus** (Müller): HOUSE FINCH; ML. *mexicanus,* "of Mexico." To Müller, who first described the bird in 1776, Mexico, the site of his specimens, meant "Valley of Mexico." He could not have known that the term did not signify the major portion of the bird's range, which is to the north. **C. purpureus** (Gmelin): PURPLE FINCH; L. *purpureus,* "crimson" or other reddish color, from Gr. *porphura,* "a shellfish," from which the Tyrean purple dye was obtained (see *Agelaius phoeniceus*). To the Romans the word meant either the color or the cloth dyed with it. So in the classical sense the color is correct for the plumage of the male bird. Now the E. *purple,* which originated in the Latin, means a color obtained from mixing red and blue (OE. *purpur*) and means a color less reddish.

Casmerodius Gloger. Gr. *chasma,* "open mouth"; Gr. *herodios,* "a heron." As there is nothing open-mouthed about the egret, the name seems nonsensical. Almost certainly Gloger erred in spelling the name with an "a"; it should have been an "o," giving "cosmerodius," based on Gr. *kosmos,* "decoration." A "decorated heron" for an egret is appropriate. **C. albus** (Linnaeus): GREAT EGRET; L. *albus,* "white."

Cassidix Lesson. L. *cassidis,* "helmet." The application of this term to the bird is obscure. *Cassidix* is now combined with *Quiscalus,* with the latter name prevailing.

Catharacta Brünnich. Gr. *kathartes,* "a purifier"; Gr. *akta,* "the sea shore"; from its scavenging for food at sea rather than along the shore. **C. skua** Brünnich: SKUA, GREAT SKUA, or BROWN SKUA; Faroese name for the bird.

Cathartes Illiger. Gr. *kathartes,* "a purifier." **C. aura** (Linnaeus): TURKEY VULTURE. Jordan says *aura* is a South American name for the bird.

Catharus Bonaparte. Gr. *catharos,* "pure." Just how this applies to the genus is obscure. **C. fuscescens** (Stephens): VEERY; L. *fuscus,* "dark"; L. *-escens,* a qualifying suffix, "slightly." **C. guttatus** (Pallas): HERMIT THRUSH; L. *gutta,* "a drop," hence a drop-like spot, for the spotted breast. **C. minimus** (Lafresnaye): GRAY-CHEEKED THRUSH; L. *minimus,* "least"; seems inapplicable as this bird is if anything slightly larger than its closest relatives. **C. ustulatus** (Nuttall): SWAINSON'S THRUSH; L. *ustulata,* "singed," for its brownish color.

Catherpes Baird. Gr. *catherpes,* "a creeper." **C. mexicanus** (Swainson): CANYON WREN; ML. *mexicanus,* "Mexican," as the type specimen was obtained in Mexico.

Catoptrophorus Bonaparte. Gr. *katoptron,* "mirror"; Gr. *phero,* "to bear"; mirror bearing alluding to the white patches in the wings. **C. semipalmatus** (Gmelin): WILLET; *semipalmatus* for the partially webbed feet (see *Charadrius semipalmatus*).

Centrocercus Swainson. Gr. *kentron,* "a point"; Gr. *kerkos,* "tail." **C. urophasianus** (Bonaparte): SAGE GROUSE; Gr. *oura,* "tail"; Gr. *phasianos,* "pheasant"; so we have the pointed-tailed pheasant tail.

Centurus Swainson. Gr. *kentron,* "a prickle"; Gr. *oura,* "tail"; for the stiff feathers in the tail. The genus is now combined with *Melanerpes,* which is the older name.

Cepphus Pallas. Gr. *kepphos,* "a kind of sea bird." **C. columba** Pallas: PIGEON GUILLEMOT; L. *columba,* "a pigeon," from the size and shape of the bird. **C. grylle** (Linnaeus): BLACK GUILLEMOT; S. *grylle,* the name for the bird in Gothland, an island in the Baltic.

Cerorhinca Bonaparte. Gr. *keros,* "a horn"; *rhyncos,* "beak"; which is rhinoceros backwards. **C. monocerata** (Pallas):

RHINOCEROS AUKLET; Gr. *monos,* "single"; *keros,* "horn"; this gives us the single-horned beak.

Certhia Linnaeus. L. *certhius,* "a creeper." **C. familiaris** Linnaeus: BROWN CREEPER or TREE CREEPER. L. *familiaris,* "domestic, homelike," hence friendly. The latest A.O.U. *Check-list* (1983) separates the American bird (*americana*) from the Old World species (*familiaris*).

Ceryle Boie. Gr. *kerylos,* "a sea bird," "the kingfisher." **C. alcyon** (Linnaeus): BELTED KINGFISHER; Gr. *alkyon,* "the kingfisher," after Alcyon who so grieved after her drowned husband, Ceryx, that the gods changed them both into kingfishers. Pliny says: "They breed in winter, at the season called the halcyon days, wherein the sea is calm." **C. torquata** (Linnaeus): RINGED KINGFISHER; L. *torquatus,* "wearing a necklace," for its white collar.

Chaetura Stephens. Gr. *chaite,* "a bristle"; Gr. *oura,* "tail." **C. pelagica** (Linnaeus): CHIMNEY SWIFT; Gr. *pelagios,* "marine." In commenting on the use of *pelagica* for this land bird, Coues says, "In 1758 Linnaeus named it *Hirundo Pelagica,* but in 1766 he changed the specific term to *pelasgia.* The *Pelasgi* were anciently a nomadic tribe, and the implication of the term in ornithology is supposed to be the bird's migration, without any reference to the sea." Coues goes on to say that L. *pelasgius* from a Greek form means Grecian or Hellenic and that *Pelasgia,* the noun, is the name of a district of Thessaly. Coues used *pelasgica* for a time, but finally went back to *pelagica,* the term used by the American Ornithologists' Union. Possibly Linnaeus made a slip in spelling and tried to retrieve it. Coues in reverting to the original spelling evidently realized the futility of his brief endeavor. This was fortunate as his interpretation of *pelasgic* is questionable. L. *pelasgia* meant the Peloponnesus after *Pelasgos,* the mythical progenitor of the natives living there. A name once given to a species has the primary function of identifying that animal regardless of initial error or subsequent refinement of meaning. **C. vauxi** (Townsend): VAUX'S SWIFT for William S. Vaux (see Appendix).

Chamaea Gamber. Gr. *chamai,* "on the ground." **C. fasciata**

(Gambel): WRENTIT; L. *fasciata*, "striped," from L. *fascis*, "a bundle of faggots." Seems to refer to both bird's fondness for staying close in the underbrush and the striped underparts.

Charadrius Linnaeus. Gr. *charadrios*, L. *charadrius*, "a plover," from Gr. *charadra*, "a gully," from the nesting site. **C. alexandrinus** Linnaeus: SNOWY PLOVER; named for Alexandria, since the first specimen came from that city in Egypt. **C. melodus** Ord: PIPING PLOVER; L. *melodus*, "a melody," from the notes of the bird. **C. montanus** Townsend: MOUNTAIN PLOVER; L. *montanus*, "of the mountains," although it is found mostly in the high plains. **C. morinellus** Linnaeus: EURASIAN DOTTEREL; ML. *morinellus*, "little fool," a coined word made by adding a Latin diminutive suffix to the Gr. *moros*, "stupid," cf. E. *moron*. Swann quotes Ray as saying "it is a very foolish bird, and is taken in the night time, by the light of a candle, by imitating the gestures of the fowler, for if he stretches out an arm, the bird also stretches out a wing, if he a foot the bird likewise a foot, in brief, whatever the fowler does, the bird does the same, and so being intent upon the man's gestures it is deceived, and covered with the net spread for it." A grain of salt is also useful. **C. semipalmatus** Bonaparte: SEMIPALMATED PLOVER; L. *semi*, "half"; L. *palma*, "palm of the hand"; literally half-webbed, referring to the feet. **C. vociferus** Linnaeus: KILLDEER; L. *vociferus*, "vociferous," from its loud call. **C. wilsonia** Ord: WILSON'S PLOVER for Alexander Wilson (see Appendix).

Chen Boie. Gr. *chen*, "goose." **C. caerulescens** (Linnaeus): SNOW GOOSE; L. *caerulescens*, "bluish." **C. canagica** (Sevastianov): EMPEROR GOOSE; ML. *canagica*, "Kanaga Island," one of the Aleutians where the original specimen was obtained. **C. hyperborea** (Pallas): BLUE GOOSE; Gr. *hyperboreus*, "far north." As *C. hyperborea* is now considered the white morph of a polymorphic species whose dark morph (BLUE GOOSE) has been known as *C. caerulescens*, the name for both becomes *C. caerulescens* as this term has priority being used for the blue morph by Linnaeus in 1758, while *C. hyperborea* was not used for the white morph till 1769. **C. rossii** (Cassin): ROSS' GOOSE for Bernard R. Ross (see Appendix).

Chlidonias Rafinesque. Should be spelled chelidonias. Gr. *chelidon*, "a swallow," ML. *-ias*, suffix, "denoting or characteristic of." **C. niger** (Linnaeus): BLACK TERN; L. *niger*, "black," from the breeding plumage.

Chloroceryle Kaup. Gr. *chloros*, "greenish"; Gr. *kerylos*, "kingfisher." **C. americana** (Gmelin): GREEN KINGFISHER; ML. *americana*, "American."

Chlorura Sclater. Gr. *chloros*, "green"; Gr. *oura*, "tail." Not only the tail but the wings and back are a dark green, while the Greek word means light green. The genus is no longer recognized and the single species is placed in *Pipilo*.

Chondestes Swainson. Gr. *chondros*, "a grain, grit, a lump of salt"; Gr. *odestes*, "an eater." Swainson certainly abbreviated this one. He probably meant seed eater. **C. grammacus** (Say): LARK SPARROW; Gr. *grammicus*, "marked with a line, streaked," from Gr. *gramme*, "a line, writing," to indicate the line on the head. We agree with Coues that the term is "badly selected and badly spelled."

Chordeiles Swainson. Gr. *choros*, most likely "a circular dance" hence "a moving about"; Gr. *deile*, "evening"; alluding to the bird's spectacular flight and call when hawking for insects at that time of day. **C. acutipennis** (Hermann): LESSER NIGHTHAWK; L. *acutus*, "sharp"; L. *penna*, "a feather"; alluding to the sharp pointed wings. **C. minor** (Forster): COMMON NIGHTHAWK; L. *minor*, "smaller." When described in 1771, it was so called as it was then smaller than the only other bird in the same family known at that time, the Nightjar of Europe.

Cinclus Borkhausen. Gr. *kinklos*, "a bird," mentioned by Aristotle; possibly the Water Ousel or Wagtail. **C. mexicanus** Swainson: AMERICAN DIPPER; ML. *mexicanus*, "Mexican," from the range of a subspecies.

Circus Lacépède. L. *circus*, from Gr. *kirkos*, "a kind of hawk"; from its circling in the air; mentioned by Aristotle who most likely did not mean a harrier which infrequently circles. **C.**

cyaneus (Linnaeus): MARSH HAWK or NORTHERN HARRIER; Gr. *kyaneous*, "dark blue" referring to the blue of the male's back.

Cistothorus Cabanis. Gr. *cistos*, "a shrub"; Gr. *thouros*, "leaping" or "running through." **C. palustris** (Wilson): MARSH WREN or LONG-BILLED MARSH-WREN; L. *palustris*, "marshy." **C. platensis** (Latham): SEDGE WREN or SHORT-BILLED MARSH-WREN; L. *platensis*, "from Río La Plata," the locality from which came the specimen bearing the name.

Clangula Leach. ML. *clangula*, "noise," from Gr. *klange*," "a noise or sound." **C. hyemalis** (Linnaeus): OLDSQUAW; L. *hiemalis*, "wintry." Earlier ornithologists were for a time confused by the different plumages which they thought belonged to two species, naming one *hyemalis* and the other *glacialis*.

Coccothraustes Brisson. Gr. *kokkos*, "kernal"; Gr. *thrauo*, "shatter;" in reference to its crushing fruit pits. **C. vespertinus** (Cooper): EVENING GROSBEAK; L. *vespertina*, derived from the Greek and having the same double meaning as the bird's former genus, *Hesperiphona* (which see), i.e., "evening" or "western."

Coccyzus Vieillot. Gr. *kokkux*, "a cuckoo." **C. americanus** (Linnaeus): YELLOW-BILLED CUCKOO; ML. *americanus*, "American," as are some of the others in the same genus. **C. erythropthalmus** (Wilson): BLACK-BILLED CUCKOO; Gr. *erythros*, "red"; Gr. *ophthalmos*, "eye"; which it is not, as the red is confined to the eyelids. **C. minor** (Gmelin): MANGROVE CUCKOO; L. *minor*, "smaller" although it is about the same size as the other cuckoos.

Coereba Vieillot. Brazilian name of a small bird. **C. flaveola** (Linnaeus): BANANAQUIT or HONEYCREEPER; L. *flavus*, "yellow," for the plumage.

Colaptes Vigors. Gr. *kolapto*, "to peck with the bill, chisel." **C. auratus** (Linnaeus): NORTHERN or COMMON FLICKER; L. *auratus*, "golden." The former is the name for the enlarged species and includes the former **C. auratus, C. cafer,** and **C. chrysoides**. **C. auratus cafer** (Gmelin): RED-SHAFTED FLICKER. Following is Coues' reaction to the term *cafer:*

"With every disposition to follow the dogma and ritual of the A.O.U., I cannot bring myself to call this bird *C. cafer,* for no better reason than because *Picus cafer* Gm. 1788 was mistaken for a bird of the Cape of Good Hope! Say what we please in our canons, there *is* something in a name after all, and 'the letter of the law killeth' when wrenched from its spirit, in defiance of science and common sense. Individually I cannot incur the penalty of deliberately using for a North American bird a name only applicable to one from South Africa. The fact that *Cafer* is a sort of Latin for Caffraria or Caffrarian makes its use in this connection as bad as 'Hottentot Woodpecker' or 'Zulu Flicker' would be; and how would such a combination sound in plain English?" The original specimen described by Gmelin in 1778 came from the Bay of Good Hope, Nootka Sound, Vancouver Island, British Columbia. So Gmelin confused the Bay and the Cape of Good Hope. Coues chose the name *C. mexicanus* in his writings, but the A.O.U. *Check-list* Committee in deference to the law of priority retained *cafer.* **C. auratus chrysoides** (Malherbe): GILDED FLICKER; Gr. *chrysos,* "gold"; Gr. *eidos,* "resembling."

Colinus Goldfuss. Sp. *colin,* from "zolin," meaning a partridge, in Nahuatl, a Central American Indian tongue. **C. virginianus** (Linnaeus): NORTHERN BOBWHITE; ML. *virginianus,* "of Virginia."

Columba Linnaeus. L. *columba,* "a dove, pigeon." **C. fasciata** Say: BAND-TAILED PIGEON; L. *fascia,* "a band"; ML. *-ata,* "a suffix signifying an adjective"; for the striking band of the tail. **C. flavirostris** Wagler: RED-BILLED PIGEON; L. *flavis,* "yellow"; L. *rostrum,* "bill." Not a very good name as the bill is red with only a yellow tip. **C. leucocephala** Linnaeus: WHITE-CROWNED PIGEON; Gr. *leucos,* "white"; Gr. *cephala,* "head." **C. livia** Gmelin: ROCK DOVE; L. *lividus,* "to be bluish," for the bird's bluish-gray color.

Columbina Spix. L. *columba,* "a dove, pigeon." **C. inca** (Lesson): INCA DOVE. This dove is not a native of Peru, the home of the Incas. It is a native of Mexico, home of the Aztecs. If Lesson thought he was using a place name, it might have been more accurate to have used the name of country where the bird lives. **C. passerina** (Linnaeus): COMMON GROUND DOVE; L. *passerina*, "sparrow-like." We have now the end product of the changes in nomenclature which gives us "sparrow-like, domestic hen-like pigeon." It may be an improvement in scientific accuracy even if the bird does not look like either a hen or a sparrow. Gone into limbo is Catesby's *Turtur minimus guttatus*, "the little spotted dove" and Baird's *Chamaepelia passerina*, "sparrow-like ground dove."

Contopus Cabanis. Gr. *kontos*, "short"; Gr. *pous*, "foot"; as its feet are very small. **C. borealis** (Swainson). OLIVE-SIDED FLYCATCHER; L. *borealis*, "northern," for its breeding range in the northern coniferous woods. **C. pertinax** Cabanis and Heine: GREATER PEWEE or COUES' FLYCATCHER; L. *pertinax*, "closer to," meaning (closely) allied to the Olive-sided Flycatcher. **C. sordidulus** Sclater: WESTERN WOOD-PEWEE; L. *sordius*, "dirty, foul," L. *ulus*, diminutive suffix; hence "the dirty little one." Possibly so called out of exasperation of the systematist who had to distinguish it from *C. virens*, **C. virens** (Linnaeus): EASTERN WOOD-PEWEE; L. *virens*, "greenish."

Conuropsis Salvadori. ML. *conuropsis*, coined to mean "resembling *Conurus*," another genus of parakeet. **C. carolinensis** (Linnaeus): CAROLINA PARAKEET; ML. *carolinensis*, "of Carolina," suggesting a southern range.

Coragyps Geoffroy. Gr. *korax*, "raven"; Gr. *gyps*, "vulture"; the griffon-vulture of Homer. **C. atratus** (Bechstein): BLACK VULTURE; L. *atratus*, "clothed in black as for mourning."

Corvus Linnaeus. L. *corvus*, "a crow." **C. brachyrhynchos** Brehm: AMERICAN or COMMON CROW; Gr. *brachys*, "short"; Gr. *rhynchos*, "beak"; which it is, compared to a raven's. **C. caurinus** Baird: NORTHWESTERN CROW; L. *caurinus*, "northwestern," from L. *caurus*, "the northwest wind." **C. corax** Linnaeus: COMMON RAVEN; Gr. *korax*, "raven," imitative of the call, cognate with Gr. *krazo*, "to croak." **C. cryptoleucus** Couch: CHIHUAHUAN RAVEN, formerly

WHITE-NECKED RAVEN; Gr. *cryptos*, "hidden," which is very apt as the Gr. *leucos*, "white," of the neck is rarely seen in the field. **C. ossifragus** Wilson: FISH CROW; L. *ossifragus*, "bone breaker," puzzling as a name for the bird (see Osprey).

Coturnicops Gray. L. *coturnix*, "quail"; Gr. *opsis*, "appearance"; thus looking like a quail. **C. novaboracensis** (Gmelin): YELLOW RAIL; ML. *noveboracum*, "New York"; L. *-ensis*, a suffix meaning "belonging to"; a poor place name as the bird is rare in New York. L. *novus*, "new"; L. *Eboracum*, the Roman name for York, England.

Crex Bechstein. Gr. *krex*, the name used by Aristotle for a long-legged bird and by Herodotus for a bird the size of an ibis; name imitates call. **C. crex** (Linnaeus): CORN CRAKE, a better imitation of its call is when both words are used.

Crotophaga Linnaeus. Gr. *kroton*, "a bug"; Gr. *phagos*, "eating." **C. ani** Linnaeus: SMOOTH-BILLED ANI; Tupi Indian (Brazil) *ani*, "ani." **C. sulcirostris** Swainson: GROOVE-BILLED ANI; L. *sulcus*, "furrow"; L. *rostrum*, "bill."

Cyanocitta Strickland. Gr. *cyanos*, "blue"; Gr. *kitta*, "a jay." **C. cristata** (Linnaeus): BLUE JAY; L. *cristata*, "crested." **C. stelleri** (Gmelin): STELLER'S JAY after George Wilhelm Steller (see Appendix).

Cyanocorax Boie. Gr. *cyanos*, "blue"; Gr. *corax*, "a croaker, the raven." **C. yncas** (Boddaert): GREEN JAY; *yncas*, same as Inca, the name of the chief of the aboriginal natives of Peru. The species' name is based on a specimen from Peru.

Cyclorrhynchus Kaup. Gr. *kyklos*, "circle"; Gr. *rhynchos*, "beak." **C. psittacula** (Pallas): PARAKEET AUKLET; L. *psittaculus*, "a little parrot."

Cygnus Bechstein. L. *cygnus*, "swan," from Gr. *kyknos*, "swan." **C. buccinator** Richardson: TRUMPETER SWAN; L. *bucinator*, "a trumpeter." **C. columbianus** (Ord): WHISTLING or TUNDRA SWAN; ML. *columbianus*, refers to the great narrows of the Columbia River where Lewis and Clark obtained the specimen described by Ord. **C. cygnus** (Linnaeus): WHOOPER SWAN; derivation the same as the generic name. **C. olor** (Gmelin): MUTE SWAN; L. *olor*, "swan." *Olor* was used by Pliny and according to MacLeod "appears to be of Celtic origin."

Cynanthus Swainson. Gr. *kyon*, kynos, "a dog"; Gr. *anthos*, "flower"; possibly for the bird "hounding" flowers as it feeds on their nectar. **C. latirostris** Swainson: BROAD-BILLED HUMMINGBIRD; L. *latus*, "wide"; L. *rostrum*, "beak."

Cypseloides Streubel. Gr. *kypselos*, L. *cypselus*, "the European Swift"; Gr. *eidos*, "resembling." **C. niger** (Gmelin): BLACK SWIFT; L. *niger*, "black," from the dark plumage.

Cyrtonyx Gould. Gr. *kyrtos*, "curved"; Gr. *onyx*, "claw." **C. montezumae** (Vigors): MONTEZUMA or HARLEQUIN QUAIL; after Montezuma, the Aztec emperor of Mexico at the time of the Spanish conquest. The name is a Nahutl word meaning "angry chief." A gastric disturbance which affects some visitors to Mexico is known as Montezuma's revenge.

Daption Stephens. Gr. *dapte*, "devour"; L. *-ion*, suffix meaning "having to do with." The name may be explained by this quote from Murphy's *Oceanic Birds of South America*, "Cape Pigeons are eager devourers of garbage and it would not be unnatural if bands of the birds sometimes pursued vessels a considerable distance." **D. capense** (Linnaeus): CAPE PETREL; ML. *capensis*, "of the Cape," referring to the Cape of Good Hope in the area of which the type specimen was obtained.

Dendragapus Elliott. Gr. *dendron*, "a tree"; Gr. *agape*, "love"; tree-loving. **D. canadensis** (Linnaeus): SPRUCE GROUSE; ML. *canadensis*, "Canadian," found mostly in Canada. **D. obscurus** (Say): BLUE GROUSE; L. *obscurus*, "dark," from its coloration.

Dendrocopos Kock. Gr. *dendron*, "a tree"; Gr. *kopis*, "a dagger." The genus has been combined with *Picoides*.

Dendrocygna Swainson. Gr. *dendron*, "a tree"; Gr. *kyknos*, L. *cygnus*, "swan." **D. autumnalis** (Linnaeus): BLACK-BELLIED WHISTLING-DUCK or BLACK-BELLIED TREE-DUCK; L. *autumnalis*, "autumnal." The reason for the name is unknown. **D. bicolor** (Vieillot): FULVUS WHISTLING-DUCK or FULVUS TREE-DUCK; L. *bi*, "two"; L. *color*, "color."

Dendroica Gray. Gr. *dendron*, "a tree"; Gr. *oicos*, "inhabit";

tree-dweller. **D. coronata auduboni** (Townsend): AUDU-BON'S WARBLER in honor of J. J. Audubon (see Appendix). Changed to subspecies of yellow-rumped warbler, 1973. **D. caerulescens** (Gmelin): BLACK-THROATED BLUE WARBLER; L. *caerulescens*, "becoming blue." **D. castanea** (Wilson): BAY-BREASTED WARBLER; L. *castanea*, "a chestnut," for the color of the breast. **D. cerulea** (Wilson): CERULEAN WAR-BLER; L. *ceruleus*, "sky blue." **D. chrysoparia** Sclater and Salvin: GOLDEN-CHEEKED WARBLER; Gr. *chrysos*, "golden"; Gr. *pareia*, "cheek." **D. coronata** (Linnaeus): YELLOW-RUMPED WARBLER; L. *coronata*, "crowned," for the yellow crown. Myrtle Warbler is still available for the subspecies. **D. discolor** (Vieillot): PRAIRIE WARBLER; L. *discolor*, "of different colors." **D. dominica** (Linnaeus): YELLOW-THROATED WARBLER; ML. *dominica*, "St. Domingo," now Hispaniola where this bird was first found. **D. fusca** (Müller): BLACKBURNIAN WARBLER; L. *fuscus*, "dark." **D. graciae** Baird: GRACE'S WARBLER to honor Grace D. Coues, sister of Elliott Coues (see Appendix). **D. kirtlandii** (Baird): KIRTLAND'S WARBLER for Dr. J. P. Kirtland (see Appendix). **D. magnolia** (Wilson): MAGNOLIA WARBLER; E. *magnolia*, so named by Wilson, who shot a specimen in a magnolia tree. **D. nigrescens** (Townsend): BLACK-THROATED GRAY WARBLER; L. *nigrescens*, "becoming black." **D. occidentalis** (Townsend): HERMIT WARBLER; L. *occidentalis*, "western," from the bird's range. **D. palma-rum** (Gmelin): PALM WARBLER; L. *palmarum*, "of the palms," from its frequenting the palm trees of Hispaniola, whence it was first known. **D. pensylvanica** (Linnaeus): CHESTNUT-SIDED WARBLER; *pen*, a misspelling for Pennsyl-vania as the first specimen came from Philadelphia, Penn-sylvania. L. *sylva*, "woods"; L. *pensylvanic*, "Penn's Woods," from the probable site of the original specimen near Philadelphia, Pennsylvania. **D. petechia** (Linnaeus): YELLOW WARBLER; ML. *petechia*, I. *pettechia*, "purplish spot"; Gr. *pittakia*, "patch." E. *petechiae* is a medical term for reddish or purplish spots that appear as a rash on the skin. Evidently the russet-red streaks on the breast of the male suggested a rash to the original describer. **D. pinus** (Wilson): PINE WARBLER; L. *pinus*, "a pine tree," from its habitat. **D. striata** (Forster): BLACKPOLL WARBLER; L. *striata*, "striped." **D. tigrina** (Gmelin): CAPE MAY WARBLER; L. *tigrina*, "striped like a tiger," with the black stripes on its yellow breast. **D. townsendi** (Townsend): TOWNSEND'S WARBLER for J. K. Townsend (see Appendix). **D. virens** (Gmelin): BLACK-THROATED GREEN WARBLER; L. *virens*, "growing green."

Dichromanassa Ridgway. Gr. *di*, "two"; Gr. *chroma*, "colored"; Gr. *anassa*, "a lady, a queen." Merged with *Egretta*, which see.

Diomedea Linnaeus. Diomedes, king of Aetolia and later of Argos, was a Greek hero of the Trojan War, second only to Achilles in renown. He disappeared and possibly was buried on one of the islands in the Adriatic called after him, the Diomedae. Here, according to Ovid, his companions were changed into birds. William Beebe in "Galapagos, World's End" has this to say about the name, "'Instead of the cross, the albatross about my neck was hung.' Intellectually, man's relation with the albatross has been less spectacular but of equal interest. Linnaeus, 168 years ago, first played taxonomic Adam to the albatross, calling it *Diomedea exulans*. Its godfather was probably, therefore, the famous hero of the seige of Troy, but the Grecian etymology provides a much more poetic and appropriate derivation, and it is pleasant to think of the albatross, whether winging over foam crests or at home on its little isle, as being over Diomedea or God-counseled. In its specific appellation Linnaeus was also happy, for to the ordinary observer the wandering albatross is truly exulans 'homeless,' banished apparently from all connection with solid land." **D. albatrus** Pallas: SHORT-TAILED ALBATROSS (see Albatross). **D. cauta** (Gould): SHY or WHITE-CAPPED ALBATROSS; L. *cautus*, "beware," possibly in deference to the sailor's superstition concerning the dire consequences for harming the bird. **D. chlororhynchos** Gmelin: YELLOW-NOSED ALBATROSS; Gr. *chloros*, "greenish yellow"; Gr. *rhynchos*, "beak." **D. im-**

mutabilis Rothschild: LAYSAN ALBATROSS; L. *immutabilis,* "never changing." **D. melanophris** Temminck: BLACK-BROWED ALBATROSS; Gr. *melan,* "black"; Gr. *ophris,* "eyebrow." **D. nigripes** Audubon: BLACK-FOOTED ALBATROSS; L. *niger,* "black"; L. *pes,* "foot."

Dolichonyx Swainson. Gr. *dolichos,* "long"; Gr. *onux,* "claw"; for the very large claws. **D. oryzivorus** (Linnaeus): BOB-LINK; Gr. and L. *oryza,* "rice"; L. *voro,* "devour"; from the bird's fondness for the grain.

Dryocopus Boie. Gr. *drys,* "a tree"; Gr. *kopis,* "a cleaver or dagger." **D. pileatus** (Linnaeus): PILEATED WOODPECKER; L. *pileatus,* "capped"; L. *pileum,* "a cap"; for the bird's conspicuous red and black crest.

Dumetella S.D.W. The only systematist not identified by name in the A.O.U. *Check-list.* L. *dumus,* "a thorn bush"; L. *-ella,* diminutive suffix giving us "little one of the thorn bush." **D. carolinensis** (Linnaeus): GRAY CATBIRD or CAT-BIRD; ML. *carolinensis,* "of Carolina," for the region called Carolina by Marc Catesby.

Ectopistes Swainson. Gr. *ectopistes,* "a wanderer," which Coues says is very appropriate. **E. migratorius** (Linnaeus): PASSENGER PIGEON; L. *migratorius,* "migratory."

Egretta Forster. F. *aigrette,* "egret." **E. caerulea** (Linnaeus): LITTLE BLUE HERON, L. *caeruleus,* "dark-colored, dark blue." **E. rufescens** (Gmelin): REDDISH EGRET; L. *rufescens,* "reddish." **E. thula** (Molina): SNOWY EGRET. Thula is a Chilean name for the bird used by Molina (1740–1839), a Chilean naturalist, who first described the species in 1782. **E. tricolor** (Müller): TRICOLORED HERON or LOUISIANA HERON; L. *tri,* "three"; L. *color,* "hue."

Elanoides Vieillot. Gr. *elanos,* "a kite," plus Gr. *oideos,* a suffix meaning "resembling." Thus we have "like a kite" for the meaning of the genus. **E. forficatus** (Linnaeus): AMER-ICAN SWALLOW-TAILED KITE or SWALLOW-TAILED KITE; L. *forficatus,* "deeply forked."

Elanus Savigny. L. *elanus,* "a kite." **E. caeruleus** (Desfontaines): BLACK-SHOULDERED KITE; L. *caerulea,* "blue." **E. leucurus** (Vieillot): WHITE-TAILED KITE; Gr. leukouros, "white tailed." The latter has been combined with the former and now bears its scientific and vernacular names.

Empidonax Cabanis. Gr. *empis* (genitive, *empidos*), "a gnat"; Gr. *anax*, "king"; the genitive is used so we understand the term as "king of the gnats." **E. alnorum** Brewster: ALDER FLYCATCHER; L. *alnorum*, "of the alders" for the bird's habitat. This is a new species made by dividing *E. traillii*. **E. difficilis** Baird: WESTERN FLYCATCHER; L. *difficilis*, "difficult, undoable," to which Coues says "very appropriate," because of its close resemblance to *E. flaviventris*. The notes and range are more helpful in identifying it than its plumage. **E. flaviventris** (Baird and Baird): YELLOW-BELLIED FLYCATCHER; L. *flavus*, "yellow"; L. *ventrus*, "the belly." **E. fulvifrons** (Giraud): BUFF-BREASTED FLYCATCHER; L. *fulvus*, "tawny"; L. *frons*, "forehead," to be interpreted here as the English meaning of front. For the buffy underparts. **E. hammondii** (Xántus de Vesey): HAMMOND'S FLYCATCHER; for William A. Hammond (see Appendix). **E. minimus** (Baird and Baird): LEAST FLYCATCHER; L. *minimus*, "least." **E. oberholseri** Phillips: DUSKY FLYCATCHER; for Dr. Harry C. Oberholser (see Appendix). **E. traillii** (Audubon): WILLOW FLYCATCHER; for Thomas S. Traill (see Appendix). When circumstances prevent species identification (by hearing the song in spring), Traill's Flycatcher "remains available for the complex." **E. virescens** (Vieillot): ACADIAN FLYCATCHER; L. *virescens*, "growing green." Possibly the color suggested to Vieillot that of some fruit ripening into greenness but still having a long way to go. **E. wrightii** Baird: GRAY FLYCATCHER; for Charles Wright (see Appendix).

Endomychura Oberholser. Gr. *ende*, "wanting, in need of"; Gr. *mychos*, "hidden"; Gr. *oura*, "tail." As the tails of the birds in this family are small. The genus is now merged with *Synthliboramphus*.

Eremophila Boie. Gr. *eremos*, "lonely"; Gr. *phileo*, "love"; hence loving solitude, although they gather in flocks in winter. **E. alpestris** (Linnaeus): HORNED LARK; ML. *alpestris*, "alpine." Holarctic in distribution from mountains to deserts, although breeding in mountains is not limited to such a habitat.

Eudocimus Wagler. Gr. *eudokimos,* "famous, in good standing." Wagler quite correctly removed these birds from the genus *Scolopax,* where they had been placed in company with the European Woodcock, and put them into a new genus, *Eudomicus,* which is in an entirely different scientific order. It seems he could not resist naming the genus after his accomplishment in placing the bird in a scientific classification in good standing. **E. albus** (Linnaeus): WHITE IBIS; L. *albus,* "white." **E. ruber** (Linnaeus): SCARLET IBIS; L. *ruber,* "red."

Eudromias Brehm. Gr. *eu,* "good"; Gr. *dromos,* "running"; from its habit of making short quick runs in search of food. The genus is no longer recognized and the Dotterel is now placed in *Charadrius.*

Eugenes Gould. Gr. *eugenes,* "well born," and by implication, attractive in appearance. **E. fulgens** (Swainson): MAGNIFICENT HUMMINGBIRD or RIVOLI'S HUMMINGBIRD; L. *fulgens,* "glittering."

Euphagus Cassin. Gr. *eu,* "good"; Gr. *phago,* "to eat"; literally "good to eat." This should not lead to confusion with "the four and twenty blackbirds" of nursery-rhyme renown which belong to the genus *Turdus* of the Old World. **E. carolinus** (Müller): RUSTY BLACKBIRD; referring to the Carolinas where the first specimens were found; L. *Carolus,* after Charles II of England. **E. cyanocephalus** (Wagler): BREWER'S BLACKBIRD; Gr. *cyanos,* L. *cyanus,* "blue"; Gr. *cephale,* "head"; as the plumage of the head is dark blue in contrast with the greenish cast of the body.

Eurynorhynchus Nilsson. Gr. *euryno,* "to make wide"; Gr. *rhynchos,* "a beak"; refers to the broad beak. **E. pygmeus** (Linnaeus): SPOONBILL SANDPIPER; Gr. *pygmios,* "dwarfish," from Gr. *pygme,* "first"; cf. Tomthumb, literally the little wide-beak.

Falco Linnaeus. LL. *falco,* "falcon," from L. *falx,* "sickle," after the shape of the talons and the beak. **F. columbarius** Linnaeus: MERLIN or PIGEON HAWK; L. *columbarius,* "a pigeon keeper," but in ML. "pidgeon," an adjective, from L. *columba,* "a dove," plus *-arius* "pertaining to." Referring to the bird's reputation as an occasional pigeon snatcher. **F. femoralis** Temminck: APLOMADO FALCON; ML. *femoralis,* "pertaining to the thighs," refers to the bright coloring of the upper legs. **F. mexicanus** Schlegel: PRAIRIE FALCON; ML. *mexicanus,* "Mexican." **F. peregrinus** Tunstall: PEREGRINE FALCON; L. *per,* a prefix meaning "through," and L. *ager, agri,* "field," plus L. *-inus,* a suffix meaning "pertaining to the nature of"; on the base of these the Romans evolved the L. *peregrinus,* "foreign, wandering." Albertus Magnus (c. 1206–1280) gives two reasons for the bird's name: (1) that it constantly moves from one place to another; (2) that its nest can never be discovered." J. Ray writing in 1713 says it "took its name either from passing from one country to another, or because it is not known where it builds." The medieval falconers, Ingersoll says, "so named 'the bird' because the young were not taken like 'eyas' from the nest, but caught in their passage from the breeding place." **F. rusticolus** Linnaeus: GYRFALCON; *rusticolus* is Linnaean Latin. It should be *rusticulus,* a diminutive of *rusticus,* "a rustic," according to MacLeod. Probably for the bird's habitat in the remote tundra. **F. sparverius** Linnaeus: AMERICAN KESTREL or SPARROW HAWK; L. *sparverius,* "pertaining to a sparrow," a rather unfortunate term as it implies that the bird preys preeminently on sparrows. **F. tinnunculus** Linnaeus: EURASIAN KESTREL; L. *tinnunculus,* "most likely the Kestrel," from L. *tinnulus,* "ringing," as the bird's notes suggest a ringing bell.

Florida Baird. Named for the state. The genus is now included in *Egretta.*

Fratercula Brisson. ML. *fraterculus,* "friar," diminutive of L. *frater,* "brother"; hence "little brother." MacLeod suggests, "perhaps with reference to the bird's habit, when rising from the sea, of clasping its feet as though in prayer." More likely it was the similarity of the bird's pattern to a monk's cowl. **F. arctica** (Linnaeus): COMMON PUFFIN or ATLANTIC PUFFIN; L. *arctucus;* "arctic," from Gr. *arktikos,* "of the bear," "northern," from the constellations in the northern sky which the Greeks called the Greater and Lesser Bear, but which we know as the Big and Little Dipper. **F. cirrhata** (Pallas): TUFTED PUFFIN; L. *cirratus,* "curled," literally "curly locks." The spelling *cirrh* is due to the mistaken notion that there was a Greek word with such a stem. **F. corniculata** (Naumann): HORNED PUFFIN; L. *cornu,* "horn"; L. *cula,* diminutive suffix for the horn-like beak.

Fregata Lacépède. Now we have the Italian word for frigate spelled correctly by the French naturalist, Conte de Lacépède. **F. magnificens** Mathews: MAGNIFICENT FRIGATE-BIRD; L. *magnus,* "great," L. *facio,* "make."

Fulica Linnaeus. L. *fulica,* "a coot," perhaps from L. *fuligo,* "soot," from the bird's color. **F. americana** (Gmelin): AMERICAN COOT; ML. *americana,* "of America," to differentiate it from the European species.

Fulmarus Stephens. See Fulmar, the common name, of which this is the Latinized form. **F. glacialis** (Linnaeus): NORTHERN FULMAR or FULMAR; L. *glacialis,* "frozen, full of ice," descriptive of the habitat.

Gallinago Brisson, 1760. Coined from L. *gallina,* "a hen." The use of "go" as a suffix is more puzzling than the reason for making the goat a female in the first suffix, giving us the little goatlike hen or vice versa. **G. gallinago** (Linnaeus): COMMON SNIPE.

Gallinula Brisson. L. *gallinula,* "hen." **G. chloropus** (Linnaeus): COMMON GALLINULE or COMMON MOORHEN; Gr. *chloros,* "green"; Gr. *pus,* "foot."

Gavia Forster. L. *gavia,* "gull." Turner identifies the bird as the "se cob or see-gell," which could mean any gull without reference to a particular species, in the same way we use the term today. Some modern dictionaries give the meaning of *gavia* as "sea-mew." As obsolete *mew* meant gull we come up with the same translation. The choice of the generic term *Gavia* for the loons was made by Forster in 1789 and has held sway in American ornithological nomenclature. Just why he chose the Latin word for gull for the loons eludes us. The genus was originally named *Colymbus* by

Linnaeus in 1758. It is from Gr. *kolymbis,* "a diving bird." *Columbus* was formerly used as a generic term for some species of grebes, but has now been superseded. **G. adamsii** (Gray): YELLOW-BILLED LOON; in honor of Edward Adams (see Appendix). **G. arctica** (Linnaeus): ARCTIC LOON or, sometimes, PACIFIC LOON; Gr. *arktikos,* "northern," from Gr. *arktos,* "bear"; the name given to the constellations in the northern sky and hence meaning northern. **Gavia immer** (Brünnich): COMMON LOON; E. *immer,* "diver," was a common name for the bird, possibly from L. *immersus,* "to plunge into." Related to S. *immer* and *emmer* and Ic. *himbrimi,* "the common loon." **G. stellata** (Pontoppidan): RED-THROATED LOON; L. *stellata,* "starred," referring to the spotty appearance of the back of the bird in winter.

Gelochelidon Brehm. Gr. *gelos,* "laughter"; Gr. *chelidon,* "a swallow"; literally "laughing swallow." The explanation as to why Alfred Edmund Brehm, when he felt it incumbent upon himself to change the name of the genus from *Hydrochelidon,* substituted *gelos* for *hydro* seems to be that he thought the bird had a call resembling human laughter, which the European subspecies of GULL-BILLED TERN possibly does. The American form, however, is given to short nasal honkings which suggest derisive disapproval generally heard at such nonliterary pursuits as baseball games where it is termed in the parlance of the diamond "the raspberry" or the "the Bronx cheer." While it is certain that Herr Brehm, the German zoologist and author of "Das Leben der Vögel," never attended a ball game, it is not certain that he ever heard the bird call. The species is now placed with the other terns in the genus *Sterna.*

Geococcyx Wagler. Gr. *ge,* "the earth, land"; Gr. *kokkux,* "cuckoo"; literally "land cuckoo." **G. californianus** (Lesson): GREATER ROADRUNNER or ROADRUNNER; ML. *californianus* "of California," although found throughout southwestern United States and Mexico.

Geothlypis Cabanis. Gr. *ge,* "the earth"; Gr. *thlypis,* "a kind of finch." **G. trichas** (Linnaeus): COMMON YELLOWTHROAT; Gr. *trichas,* "a thrush." We have to rate Linnaeus low on this one. **G. poliocephala** Baird: GRAY-CROWNED YELLOW-THROAT or GROUND CHAT; Gr. *polios,* "gray"; Gr. *cephale,* "head"; for the gray head of the male.

Glaucidium Boie. Gr. *glaukidion,* diminutive of "glaring" in reference to the eyes, hence Gr. *glaux,* "an owl," sacred to Athene. **G. brasilianum** (Gmelin): FERRUGINOUS PYGMY-OWL; ML. *brasilianum,* "Brazilian," one of the areas where the bird is found. **G. gnoma** Wagler: NORTHERN PYGMY-OWL; L. *gnoma,* "a spirit or sprite"; cf. Gr. *gnome,* "intelligence," tied up with the idea of the owl being wise. This association of the owl with wisdom has come down from classical times. Athene, the goddess of wisdom, was prayerfully referred to as "glaucopis Athene" which may be translated as "gleaming eyed" or "owl-eyed Athene."

Grus Pallas. L. *grus,* "crane." The Latin word is derived from an Indo-European root, *g(w)er,* "to cry out." The ancestral word, perhaps imitative, spawned in its long history. Gr. *geranos,* "a crane"; Gr. *gerus,* "speech"; L. *garrulus,* "chattering," and via AS. our crane, crow, croon, and care. **G. americana** (Linnaeus): WHOOPING CRANE; ML. *americana,* "of America." **G. canadensis** (Linnaeus): SANDHILL CRANE; ML. *canadensis,* "of Canada."

Guiraca Swainson. Coues says: "A Mexican or South American name of some bird." **G. caerulea** (Linnaeus): BLUE GROSBEAK; L. *caerulea,* "blue."

Gymnogyps Lesson. Gr. *gymnos,* "naked," in reference to the naked head; Gr. *gyps,* "vulture." **G. californianus** (Shaw): CALIFORNIA CONDOR; ML. *californianus,* "of California," area where remaining birds are found.

Gymnorhinus Wied. Gr. *gymnos,* "naked"; Gr. *rhinos,* "nose"; as the nostrils are large and more exposed than those of most birds. **G. cyanocephalus** Wied: PINYON JAY; Gr. *cyanos,* "blue"; Gr. *cephale,* "head"; for the plumage.

Haematopus Linnaeus. Gr. *haima* (genitive *haimatos*), "blood," referring to the color; Gr. *pous,* "foot"; hence blood-red foot. **H. bachmani** Audubon: BLACK OYSTER-CATCHER; named by Audubon after his friend, the Reverend John Bachman (see Appendix). **H. palliatus** Temminck:

AMERICAN OYSTERCATCHER; L. *palliatus*, "wearing a cloak," from the dark feathering of the back.

Haliaeetus Savigny. Gr. *haliaetos*, "the osprey," literally sea eagle from Gr. *hals, halos*, "the sea"; Gr. *aetos*, "eagle." The Greeks wrote the word with an accent mark over the *e*. This signified that the letter had a sound of its own and was not part of a diphthong. Coues, in translating the word, put a dieresis over the *e* in the Greek word signifying the same. Savigny, when he separated this genus from the falcons, evidently transliterated the *e* in the Greek word into a diphthong *ae*, an error. The old A.O.U. *Check-lists* followed this. As diphthongs became passé, the fifth edition of the A.O.U. *Check-List* transliterated the *ae* diphthong into the letters *a* and *e*. Thus orthography has reinforced a spelling error which the law of priority perpetuates. **H. leucocephalus** (Linnaeus): BALD EAGLE; Gr. *leukos*, "white"; Gr. *kephalos*, "head"; for the white plumage of the head.

Halocyptena Coues. Gr. *hals*, "the sea"; Gr. *okus*, "swift"; Gr. *ptenos*, "winged." The genus is now merged with *Oceanodroma*.

Helmitheros Rafinesque. A misspelling of Gr. *helminthos*, "a bug"; Gr. *theran*, "to hunt"; hence a bug-hunter. **H. vermivorus** (Gmelin): WORM-EATING WARBLER; L. *vermis*, "a worm"; L. *voro*, "eat."

Hesperiphona Bonaparte. Gr. *hesperis, hesperios*, two related meanings: (1) of place, "western," where the sun goes down; (2) of time, "evening," at sunset. As a plural noun we have *Hesperides*, "the Daughters of the Night" who dwelt on the western edge of the world. Gr. *phone*, "voice or sound." This can be interpreted as either the song of the west or the song of the evening. The genus has been merged with *Coccothraustes*.

Heteroscelus Baird. Gr. *heteros*, "different"; Gr. *skelis*, "a leg"; i.e., different in the leg from all other sandpipers in regard to the covering with small scales. **H. incanus** (Gmelin): WANDERING TATTLER; L. *incanus*, "gray," coloring of upper parts.

Himantopus Brisson. Gr. *himantopous*, "a kind of water bird";

Gr. *himantos*, "strap"; Gr. *pous*, "foot"; for the resemblance of the leg to a thong. **H. mexicanus** (Müller): BLACK-NECKED STILT; ML. *mexicanus*, "of Mexico," originally described from a Mexican bird.

Hirundo Linnaeus. L. *hirundo*, "a swallow." **H. fulva** Vieillot: CAVE SWALLOW; L. *fulvus*, "tawny," for the buffy breast. **H. pyrrhonota** Vieillot: CLIFF SWALLOW; Gr. *pyrrhos*, flame-colored; Gr. *notos*, "back"; for the orange rump. **H. rustica** Linnaeus: BARN SWALLOW; L. *rustica*, "rustic," as compared with the House Martin which is more urban where both birds occur in Europe.

Histrionicus Lesson. L. *histrionicus*, "histrionic," from L. *histrio*, "a stage player," referring to its plumage as though dressed up to play a part. The common name suggests the same thing. **H. histrionicus** (Linnaeus): HARLEQUIN DUCK, just some more of the same.

Hydranassa Baird. Gr. *hydor*, "water"; Gr. *anassa*, "queen." This genus has been merged with *Egretta*.

Hydroprogne Kaup. Gr. *hydor*. "water"; Gr. *Prokne*, who was changed into a swallow (see the story of Pandion), hence "water swallow." *Hydroprogne* is now considered to be a synonym of *Sterna*.

Hylocharis Boie. Gr. *hyle*, "a wood"; Gr. *charis*, "beauty." **H. leucotis** (Vieillot): WHITE-EARED HUMMINGBIRD; Gr. *leukos*, "white"; Gr. *ous, otos*, "ear."

Hylocichla Baird. Gr. *hyle*, "forest"; Gr. *cichla*, "a thrush." **H. mustelina** (Gmelin): WOOD THRUSH; L. *mustelina*, "weasel-like," i.e., tawny in color; L. *mustela*, "a weasel."

Icteria Vieillot. Gr. *ikteros*, "the jaundice," hence yellow. **I. virens** (Linnaeus): YELLOW-BREASTED CHAT; L. *virens*, "green."

Icterus Brisson. Gr. *ikteros*, "jaundice," hence yellowish, and also a greenish-yellow bird, the oriole, which was supposed to cure the disease when it was seen. **I. cucullatus** Swainson: HOODED ORIOLE; L. *cucullatus*, wearing the *cuculla*, "a hood." It doesn't. **I. galbula** (Linnaeus): NORTHERN ORIOLE or BALTIMORE ORIOLE; L. *galbula*, "a small yellow bird." The name for the species is Northern Oriole and in-cludes both the Baltimore and Bullock Orioles. **I. galbula bullockii** (Swainson): BULLOCK'S ORIOLE for William Bul-lock (see Appendix). It is now considered conspecific with *I. galbula*. **I. graduacauda** Lesson: AUDUBON'S ORIOLE or BLACK-HEADED ORIOLE; L. *gradus*, "a step"; L. *cauda*, "tail"; the label "graduated tail" is not obvious nor is the tail distinctive as is the head. It would have been more helpful if the original describer of the bird had concentrated on the other end of it. **I. gularis** (Wagler): ALTAMIRA ORIOLE or LICHTENSTEIN'S ORIOLE; L. *gula*, "throat," for the black throat, although this is a feature of all orioles. **I. parisorum** Bonaparte: SCOTT'S ORIOLE; for the Paris brothers (see Ap-pendix). **I. pectoralis** (Wagler): SPOT-BREASTED ORIOLE; L. *pectoralis*, "pertaining to the breast." We now have the part of the anatomy which is distinctive in appearance, but not the reason for the name. It could not have been in the interest of brevity, as *maculata pectoralis* would be *anatis jusculum* (duck soup) to any scientist. **I. spurius** (Linnaeus): OR-CHARD ORIOLE; L. *spurius*, "spurious," an undeserved name implying an inferior relationship to the Baltimore Oriole, which was also reflected in a former common name "Bas-tard Baltimore Oriole." Alexander Wilson pointed out that the name resulted from an error in identifying the female Baltimore Oriole as the male of this species.

Ictinia Vieillot. Gr. *iktinos*, "a kite." **I. "misisippiensis"** (Wil-son): MISSISSIPPI KITE. The reason for Wilson's spelling is puzzling as the article on the bird in his *American Orni-thology* is entitled "The Mississippi Kite." This spelling of the common name from which the scientific one is derived assures us that the schoolteacher knew how to spell the word. Why drop the double *s* and keep the double *p?* The misspelling irritated Elliott (note the double *l* and *t*) Coues who among other things was a high-handed and aggressive champion of conservative orthography. In his *Key to North American Birds*, 1872, he has *mississippiensis*, as has the first and second edition of the A.O.U. *Check-list* of whose committee Coues was a member. Coues was not on the committee for the third edition, but no change was made. The fourth and fifth editions went back to Wilson's original spelling out of deference to the law of priority, but the sixth edition (1983) reverts to *mississippiensis*. Coues, by the way, may have noted the correction in spelling in Thomas H. Brewer's edition (1840) of Wilson's *American Ornithology*.

Iridoprocne Coues. Gr. *iridos*, "of the rainbow," referring to the color; Gr. *Prokne*, who was changed into a "swallow." For the gruesome details, see *Pandion*. The genus *Iridoprocne* has been replaced by *Tachycineta*.

Ixobrychus Billberg. Gr. *ixos*, "the mistletoe berry, the mistletoe plant or the bird lime made from the berry"; Gr. *brycho*, "to eat, to eat noisily with a belching accompaniment and to roar or bellow." Jordan translates *ixes* as "reed." Eaton gives us Gr. *ixos*, "birdlime," and Gr. *bryxaomai*, "to bellow." MacLeod says, "Billberg who invented the name in 1828 translates *ixos* by L. *arundo*, 'reed,' and *brycho* by L. *fremo*, 'to roar or boom': with reference presumably to the old belief that the (common) bittern produced its 'boom' by plunging its bill into a reed and blowing through it." Billberg's Greek is questionable although we surmise his meaning. One wonders whether he ever heard the series of soft coos of the Least Bittern. **I. exilis** (Gmelin): LEAST BITTERN; L. *exilis*, "small."

Ixoreus Bonaparte. Gr. *ixos*, "mistletoe"; Gr. *oreos*, "mountain." Although the American bird is not partial to a diet of mistletoe, the plant has been associated from the time of Aristotle with a European thrush which breeds in mountains. **I. naevius** (Gmelin): VARIED THRUSH; L. *naevius*, "spotted or varied," as its plumage is striking for a thrush.

Jacana Brisson. A native Brazilian name for the bird. **J. spinosa** (Linnaeus): NORTHERN JACANA; L. *spina*, "thorn"; L. *osus*, "carrying"; for the spur at the bend of the wing.

Junco Wagler. L. *juncus*, "a rush." A singularly inappropriate name for a genus whose habitat is not among the reeds. *J. aikeni*, *J. hyemalis*, and *J. oreganus* are now considered conspecific with consequent changes below. **J. hyemalis**

(Linnaeus): DARK-EYED JUNCO; L. *hyemalis*, "winter." Linnaeus based the name on Catesby who was familiar only with the bird as a winter visitor. This is now the species name. **J. hyemalis aikeni** Ridgway: WHITE-WINGED JUNCO; for C. E. Aiken (see Appendix). **J. caniceps** (Woodhouse): GRAY-HEADED JUNCO; L. *caniceps*, "gray-headed," for the head color. **J. hyemalis hyemalis**. Formerly of species status with retention of the name SLATE-COLORED JUNCO. **J. hyemalis oreganus** (Townsend): OREGON JUNCO, a place name. **J. phaeonotus** Wagler: MEXICAN JUNCO; Gr. *phaios*, "dun-colored"; Gr. *notos*, "back"; although the back is more reddish chestnut than gray brown. This species now includes the former **J. bairdii** and as enlarged becomes the YELLOW-EYED JUNCO.

Lagopus Brisson. Gr. *lagopus*, "hare-footed," for the feathering on the tarsi suggesting a resemblance to a rabbit's foot. **L. lagopus** (Linnaeus): WILLOW PTARMIGAN. **L. leucurus** (Richardson): WHITE-TAILED PTARMIGAN; Gr. *leukos*, "white"; Gr. *oura*, "tail"; the only ptarmigan without any black in the tail. **L. mutus** (Montin): ROCK PTARMIGAN; L. *mutus*, "silent," probably for the low call.

Lampornis Swainson. Gr. *lampas*, "a lamp"; Gr. *ornis*, "a bird." **L. clemenciae** (Lesson): BLUE-THROATED HUMMINGBIRD; for Clemence Lesson (see Appendix).

Lanius Linnaeus. L. *lanius*, "a butcher," from its hanging its prey on thorns. **L. excubitor** Linnaeus: NORTHERN SHRIKE or GREAT GRAY SHRIKE; L. *excubitor*, "a sentinel," from L. *ex*, "out"; L. *cubo*, "to lie down"; literally, "one who lies down out of doors." MacLeod points out, "for once Linnaeus explains his meaning. 'Accipitres adventates observat et aviculis indicat,' 'it looks out for the approach of hawks and warns little birds.'" No comment from this side of the Atlantic which has the same species as Europe. **L. ludovicianus** Linnaeus: LOGGERHEAD SHRIKE; ML. *ludovicianus*, "of Louisiana." Linnaeus' specimen probably a subspecies found in the southern United States.

Larus Linnaeus. Gr. *laros*, L. *larus*, "a gull." **L. argentatus** Pontoppidan: HERRING GULL; L. *argentatus*, "silvery," originally "plated with silver." **L. atricilla** Linnaeus: LAUGHING GULL; L. *ater,* "black"; ML. *cilla,* "tail"; rather a poor term as only the immature have a black band on the tail. **L. californicus** Lawrence: CALIFORNIA GULL; ML. *californicus,* "of California," where the first specimen was obtained. **L. canus** Linnaeus: MEW GULL; L. *canus,* "grayish-white," from the plumage. **L. delawarensis** Ord: RING-BILLED GULL; "of the Delaware" referring to the river below Philadelphia where it was first found. **L. glaucescens** Naumann: GLAUCOUS-WINGED GULL; L. *-escens,* "somewhat like," referring to the Glaucous Gull which it resembles except for darker primaries. **L. glaucoides** Meyer: ICELAND GULL; Gr. *glaukos,* "silvery"; Gr. *-oides,* suffix meaning "like." The name means "like the Glaucous Gull" which formerly had the scientific name *L. glaucus.* Although smaller, it resembles it. **L. heermanni** Cassin: HEERMANN'S GULL; for A. L. Heermann (see Appendix). **L. hyperboreus** Gunnerus: GLAUCOUS GULL; Gr. *hyperboreos,* "beyond the north wind," the extreme north, named for Boreas, the god of the north wind. Poor Boreas met with no encouragement from the nymph, Orithyia, as his inability to breathe gently, let alone sigh, did not fit her maidenly idea of a lover. So, being a Greek god, and not overly patient, he carried her off. Things did not work out too badly as the union was blessed with two superb winged warriors, Zetes and Calais, who on the Argonautic foray did a good job on those monstrous birds, the Harpies. **L. marinus** Linnaeus: GREAT BLACK-BACKED GULL; L. *marinus,* "marine." **L. minutus** Pallas: LITTLE GULL; L. *minutus,* "very small," and it is for a gull. **L. occidentalis** Audubon: WESTERN GULL; L. *occidentalis,* "western." **L. philadelphia** (Ord): BONAPARTE'S GULL; for Philadelphia, the city near which the type specimen was found. **L. pipixcan** Wagler: FRANKLIN'S GULL; *pipixcan,* an Aztec word whose meaning Wagler did not reveal if he knew it. **L. ridibundus** (Linnaeus): COMMON BLACK-HEADED GULL; L. *rid,* "laugh"; L. *abundo,* "overflow." W. H. Hudson says "his notes . . . often sound like laughter"; hence laughing gull and the species name *ridibundus.* **L. thayeri**

Brooks: THAYER'S GULL, for John Eliot Thayer (see Appendix).

Laterallus Gray. L. *lateo*, "lurk or hide"; ML. *rallus*, "a rail"; from F. *rale*, "a rail," which also means "a rattle in the throat" and possibly suggested the name of the bird for its rattle-like calls in the marsh, where the bird is more often heard than seen. **L. jamaicensis** (Gmelin): BLACK RAIL; ML. *jamaicensis*, "of Jamaica," first specimen possibly a winter migrant.

Leptotila Swainson. Gr. *leptos*, "thin"; Gr. *ptilon*, "feather"; from the shape of the first primary for which Coues called them "pinwing doves." **L. verreauxi** Bonaparte: WHITE-TIPPED DOVE or WHITE-FRONTED DOVE; for the Verreaux brothers (see Appendix).

Leucosticte Swainson. Gr. *leucos*, "white"; Gr. *sticte*, "varied"; for the muted white plumage. **L. arctoa** (Pallas): ROSY FINCH; Gr. *arcto*, "the north" for its distribution. The following three names have been applied to geographical entities in North America and were treated as distinct species. They all have recently been merged with *arctoa*, which also occurs in northern Asia, and are considered subspecies. **L. atrata** Ridgway: BLACK ROSY FINCH; L. *atrata*, "blackened," for the dominant color of the male's plumage. **L. australis** Ridgway: BROWN-CAPPED ROSY FINCH; L. *australis*, "southern," for its range, which is to the south of the other rosy finches. **L. tephrocotis** (Swainson): GRAY-CROWNED ROSY FINCH; Gr. *tephros*, "gray"; Gr. *kotis*, "top and back of the head."

Limnodromus Wied. Gr. *limne*, "marsh"; Gr. *dromos*, "running." Although not given to running, the birds are marsh feeders. **L. griseus** (Gmelin): SHORT-BILLED DOWITCHER; ML. *griseus*, "gray," coined from HG. *gris* or F. *gris*, "gray." Restored to species status after 1950 explorations supplied more accurate knowledge of the breeding range. **L. scolopaceus** (Say): LONG-BILLED DOWITCHER; Gr. *scolopax*, "the woodcock," of Aristotle, from Gr. *skolops*, "anything pointed," for the bill. So "a woodcock that courses about the marsh" is apt enough.

Limnothlypis Stone. Gr. *limne,* "a marsh"; Gr. *thlypis,* "a kind of finch." **L. swainsonii** (Audubon): SWAINSON'S WARBLER for William Swainson (see Appendix).

Limosa Brisson. L. *limosa,* "muddy," from the habitat. **L. fedoa** (Linnaeus): MARBLED GODWIT. The origin of *fedoa* is unknown. Coues says, "The word goes back to Turner (1544) 'Anglorum goduuittam, sive fedoam,' and has been variously applied to godwits and some other birds before and since Linnaeus named this species, *Scolopax fedoa* in 1758." Newton regards it as a Latinized form of some English name of the European godwit, "now apparently lost beyond recovery." **L. haemastica** (Linnaeus): HUDSONIAN GODWIT; Gr. *haimastidos,* "blood-red," for the color of the breast in breeding plumage. **L. lapponica** (Linnaeus): BAR-TAILED GODWIT; ML. *lapponica,* "of Lapland," one of its breeding areas and the site of the type specimen.

Lobipes Cuvier. L. *lobus,* "lobe"; L. *pes,* "foot." The genus is currently included within *Phalaropus.*

Lophodytes Reichenbach. Gr. *lophos,* "crest"; Gr. *dytes,* "a diver." **L. cucullatus** (Linnaeus): HOODED MERGANSER; L. *cucullata,* "hooded."

Lophortyx Bonaparte. Gr. *lophos,* "a crest"; Gr. *ortyx,* "a quail." *Lophortyx* is now merged with *Callipepla.*

Loxia Linnaeus. Gr. *loxos,* "crooked," for the shape of the bill. **L. curvirostra** Linnaeus: RED CROSSBILL; L. *curvirostra,* "curved bill," for the shape of the bill, which must have impressed Linnaeus to name it the crooked curved bill in two languages. **L. leucoptera** Gmelin: WHITE-WINGED CROSSBILL; Gr. *leucos,* "white"; Gr. *pteron,* "wing"; for the white wing bars.

Lunda Pallas. Scandinavian, *lunde,* "a puffin." Possibly the island of Lundy in the Bristol Channel is named after this bird. Unfortunately, the genus is now treated as a synonym of *Fratercula.*

Megaceryle Kaup. Gr. *megas,* "great"; Gr. *kerylos,* "a sea bird," "the kingfisher." This is another genus that has been merged, in this instance with *Ceryle.*

Melanerpes Swainson. Gr. *melas,* "black"; Gr. *herpes,* "a creeper." **M. aurifrons** (Wagler): GOLDEN-FRONTED WOOD-PECKER; L. *aurus*, "gold"; L. *frons*, "forehead"; for its bright yellow forehead. **M. carolinus** (Linnaeus): RED-BELLIED WOODPECKER; ML. *carolinus*, "of Carolina." **M. erythrocephalus** (Linnaeus): RED-HEADED WOODPECKER; Gr. *erythros*, "red"; Gr. *cephale*, "head." **M. formicivorus** (Swainson): ACORN WOODPECKER; L. *formica*, "an ant"; L. *voro*, "devour." Acorn-devourer might be more appropriate although ants are also part of the bird's diet. **M. lewis** (Gray): LEWIS' WOODPECKER for Meriwether Lewis (see Appendix). **M. uropygialis** (Baird): GILA WOODPECKER; Gr. *ouropygion*, "the rump," which, being banded, is a field mark for this species.

Melanitta Boie. Gr. *melas*, "black"; *nitta*, appears to be a mis-spelling for Gr. *netta*, "duck." **M. deglandi** (Bonaparte): WHITE-WINGED SCOTER; for C. D. Degland (see Appendix). Now considered a New World subspecies of *M. fusca*, but the American vernacular name is applied to the species as a whole. **M. fusca** (Linnaeus): VELVET SCOTER; L. *fuscus*, "dark." **M. nigra** (Linnaeus): BLACK SCOTER; L. *nigra*, "black," for the color of the plumage. **M. perspicillata** (Linnaeus): SURF SCOTER; L. *perspicillata*, "conspicuous."

Meleagris Linnaeus. Gr. and L. *meleagris*, "a Guinea-fowl," apparently from the vague resemblance of the American tur-key to the African Guinea-fowl. **M. gallopavo** Linnaeus: TURKEY; L. *gallus*, "a cock"; L. *pavo*, "a pea fowl"; thus we have an American bird named for both an African and an Asiatic bird.

Melospiza Baird. Gr. *melos*, "song"; Gr. *spiza*, "a finch." **M. georgiana** (Latham): SWAMP SPARROW; ML. *georgiana*, "of Georgia," for King George II of England. The type speci-men was collected in Georgia in 1790. **M. lincolnii** (Au-dubon): LINCOLN'S SPARROW for Thomas Lincoln (see Appendix). **M. melodia** (Wilson): SONG SPARROW; Gr. and L. *melodia*, "a pleasant song," the taxonomists' favorite with thirty-one subspecies so far described. California, where the aim seems to be to have one for each county, is in the lead with thirteen subspecies.

Mergus Linnaeus. L. *mergus*, "a diver," name of a bird mentioned by Pliny. **M. merganser** Linnaeus: COMMON MERGANSER; LL. *mergus*, "diver"; L. *anser*, "goose." **M. serrator** Linnaeus: RED-BREASTED MERGANSER; L. *serrator*, "a sawer," referring to the serrated bill.

Micrathene Coues. Gr. *micros*, "small"; Gr. *Athene*, "the goddess of wisdom," to whom the owl was sacred. **M. whitneyi** (Cooper): ELF OWL; for Josiah Dwight Whitney (see Appendix).

Micropalama Baird. Gr. *mikros*, "small"; Gr. *palame*, "a web"; for small webs between front toes. The genus has been merged with *Calidris*.

Mimus Boie. L. *mimus*, "a mimic." **M. polyglottos** (Linnaeus): NORTHERN MOCKINGBIRD; Gr. *poly*, "many"; Gr. *glotta*, "tongue"; alluding to the bird's varied mimicry.

Mniotilta Vieillot. Gr. *mnion*, "moss"; Gr. *tiltos*, "plucked"; possibly due to the erroneous idea that moss is used habitually in the nest. **M. varia** (Linnaeus): BLACK-AND-WHITE WARBLER; L. *varia*, "varied," for the plumage.

Molothrus Swainson. Gr. *molothrus*, an error for *molobros*, "a parasite or greedy person." **M. aeneus** (Wagler): BRONZED COWBIRD; L. *aeneus*, "brassy," for the sheen of its plumage. **M. ater** (Boddaert): BROWN-HEADED COWBIRD or COMMON COWBIRD; L. *ater*, "black," for the color of the plumage.

Morus Vieillot. Gr. *moros*, "stupid." The genus has been replaced by *Sula*.

Motacilla Linnaeus. L. *motus*, "moving"; ML. *cilla*, "tail"; see Bombycilla. **M. alba** Linnaeus: WHITE WAGTAIL; L. *alba*, "white," for the predominantly white plumage. **M. flava** Linnaeus: YELLOW WAGTAIL; L. *flavus*, "yellow," for the yellow underparts.

Muscivora Lacépède. L. *musca*, "a fly"; L. *voro*, "eat." *Muscivora* is now treated as a synonym of *Tyrannus*.

Myadestes Swainson. Gr. *myia*, Attic Gr. *mya*, "a fly"; Gr. *edestes*, "anteater." **M. townsendi** (Audubon): TOWNSEND'S SOLITAIRE; for John K. Townsend (see Appendix).

Mycteria Linnaeus. Gr. *mykter*, "a nose." **M. americana** Linnaeus: WOOD STORK, formerly WOOD IBIS; ML. *americana*, "American," i.e., Western Hemisphere.

Myiarchus Cabanis. Gr. *myia*, "a fly"; Gr. *archos*, "a ruler." **M. cinerascens** (Lawrence): ASH-THROATED FLYCATCHER; L. *cinerascens*, "ashy." **M. crinitus** (Linnaeus): GREAT CRESTED FLYCATCHER; L. *crinitus*, "hairy," which can be stretched a bit to mean "crested." **M. tuberculifer** (d'Orbigny and Lafresnaye): DUSKY-CAPPED FLYCATCHER or OLIVACEOUS FLYCATCHER; L. *tuberculum*, diminutive of *tuber*, "a lump" (a knob); L. *fero*, "to bear or carry." After studying the name of this bird from every side, the best we can come up with is "a carrier of little lumps." A carrier of a little knob most likely refers to the bird's small crest. **M. tyrannulus** (Müller): BROWN-CRESTED FLYCATCHER or WIED'S CRESTED FLYCATCHER; ML. *tyrannulus*, "little tyrant."

Myioborus Baird. Gr. *myia*, "a fly"; Gr. *borus*, "devouring"; thus a fly-eater. **M. pictus** (Swainson): PAINTED REDSTART; L. *pictus*, "painted."

Myiodynastes Bonaparte. Gr. *myia*, "a fly"; Gr. *dynastes*, "a ruler." **M. luteiventris** Sclater: SULPHUR-BELLIED FLY-CATCHER; L. *luteus*, "yellow"; L. *venter*, "belly"; for the light gray-olive underparts which are heavily streaked.

Myiopsitta Bonaparte. Gr. *myia*, "a fly"; Gr. *psittake*, "a parrot." **M. monachus** (Boddaert): MONK PARAKEET; Gr. *monachos*, "solitary," to L. *monas, monacis*, "a monk." Originally applied to the solitary religious hermit, the word changed its meaning to apply to members of religious communities and possibly to this bird, as it flies about in small flocks and nests in colonies. Or, its hooded head may suggest a monk.

Nucifraga Brisson. L. *nux, nucis*, "nut"; L. *frango*, "break." **N. columbiana**, (Wilson): CLARK'S NUTCRACKER; ML. *columbiana*, for the Columbia River area, as the bird was first discovered along the Clearwater River which flows into the Columbia.

Numenius Brisson. Gr. *neos*, "new"; Gr. *mene*, "moon"; for the resemblance of the shape of the bill to the new moon.

N. americanus Bechstein: LONG-BILLED CURLEW; ML. *americanus,* "of America." **N. borealis** (Forster): ESKIMO CURLEW; L. *borealis,* "northern." **N. phaeopus** (Linnaeus): WHIMBREL or HUDSONIAN CURLEW; Gr. *phaios,* "dusky"; Gr. *pous,* "foot"; for the grayish feet and legs. **N. tahitiensis** (Gmelin): BRISTLE-THIGHED CURLEW; ML. *tahitiensis,* "of Tahiti," where it was first found by Sir James Banks, a naturalist who accompanied Captain James Cook round the world (1768–1771).

Nuttallornis Ridgway. For Thomas Nuttall (see Appendix); Gr. *ornis,* "bird." The genus is now merged with *Contopus.*

Nyctanassa Stejneger. Gr. *nyctos,* "night"; Gr. *anassa,* "a lady, a queen." *Nyctanassa* has been combined with *Nycticorax.*

Nyctea Stephens. Gr. *nycteus,* "nocturnal." Most owls are, but not this one. **N. scandiaca** (Linnaeus): SNOWY OWL; L. *scandia,* an ancient name for the southern end of Sweden, although the breeding range is in the north in both hemispheres.

Nycticorax Forster. Gr. *nyx, nyctos,* "night"; Gr. *corax,* "a crow." **N. nycticorax** (Linnaeus): BLACK-CROWNED NIGHT-HERON. The repetition of the name is the responsibility of Forster and not Linnaeus, who first termed the bird *Ardea nycticorax.* The bird's squawk in the darkness overhead very likely suggested the name to Linnaeus. **N. violacea** (Linnaeus): YELLOW-CROWNED NIGHT-HERON; L. *viola,* "the violet," for the color of the bird's back, which is stretching it a bit as the bird has an overall gray appearance.

Nyctidromus Gould. Gr. *nyx, nyctos,* "night"; Gr. *dromos,* "running or coursing"; i.e., a night flyer. **N. albicollis** (Gmelin): COMMON PAURAQUE; L. *albus,* "white"; L. *collum,* "neck"; for the white collar of feathers.

Oceanites Keyserling and Blasius. The Oceanides or Oceanites were, according to the Greeks, sea nymphs, the daughters of Oceanus and Tethys. According to Apollodorus they numbered three thousand, while Hesiod could count only forty-one. Both, however, agree that they spent their lives at sea, as, for the most part, do the petrels. **O. oceanicus** (Kuhl): WILSON'S STORM-PETREL;

Gr. *Oceanes* (see above and *Oceanodroma*).

Oceanodroma Reichenbach. L. *oceanus*, from Gr. *Okeanos*, "the ocean"; the name, according to Homer, of the great river that encompasses the earth and also the name of the god who rules this domain. Gr. *droma*, "running or coursing." **O. castro** (Harcourt): BAND-RUMPED STORM-PETREL, HARCOURT'S STORM-PETREL, or MADEIRA STORM-PETREL; from *Roque* (rook) de *castro*, the bird's name, according to Harcourt, in the Deserta Islands, Madeira. He first described the bird in his *Sketch of Madeira*, 1851. **O. furcata** (Gmelin): FORK-TAILED STORM-PETREL; L. *furcatus*, "forked," for the shape of the tail. **O. homochroa** (Coues): ASHY STORM-PETREL; Gr. *homos*, "same"; Gr. *chroa*, "color"; for the uniform coloration. **O. leucorhoa** (Vieillot): LEACH'S STORM-PETREL; Gr. *leukos*, "white"; Gr. *orrhos*, "the rump"; for the white upper tail coverts. **O. melania** (Bonaparte): BLACK STORM-PETREL; Gr. *melania*, "black," for its plumage. **O. microsoma** (Coues): LEAST STORM-PETREL; Gr. *mikros*, "small"; Gr. *soma*, "body"; appropriate for the smallest storm-petrel. **O. tethys** (Bonaparte): GALAPAGOS STORM-PETREL or WEDGE-RUMPED STORM-PETREL; Gr. *Tethys*, wife of Okeanos, who rules the sea with her husband.

Oenanthe Vieillot. Gr. *oinanthe*, "a bird," possibly the wheatear and also the name of "a kind of plant." It seems that the bird appeared at the time of the plant's blossoming. Gr. *oinas*, "wild pigeon"; Gr. *anthos*, "flower"; to the Greeks the bird seems to have been called "the flower bird." **O. oenanthe** (Linnaeus): NORTHERN WHEATEAR.

Olor Wagler. L. *olor*, "swan." The genus has been removed to *Cygnus*.

Oporornis Baird. Gr. *opera*, "end of summer"; Gr. *ornis*, "bird." **O. agilis** (Wilson): CONNECTICUT WARBLER; L. *agilis*, "active." **O. formosus** (Wilson): KENTUCKY WARBLER; L. *formosus*, "beautiful." **O. philadelphia** (Wilson): MOURNING WARBLER; for the city near which Wilson found the bird. **O. tolmiei** (Townsend): MACGILLIVRAY'S WARBLER; for W. F. Tolmie (see Appendix).

Oreortyx Baird. Gr. *oros, orees,* "mountain"; Gr. *ortyx,* "quail." **O. pictus** (Douglas): MOUNTAIN QUAIL; L. *pictus,* "painted," as its plumage appears to be the work of an artist in color.

Oreoscoptes Baird. Gr. *oros,* "a mountain"; Gr. *scoptes,* "a mimic." **O. montanus** (Townsend): SAGE THRASHER; L. *montanus,* "mountain." Although found in the high plains of the Rocky Mountains, it is essentially a desert bird.

Ortalis (Merram). Gr. *ortalis,* "a young bird." **O. vetula** (Wagler): PLAIN CHACHALACA; L. *vetula,* "a little old woman," most likely in reference to the bird's constant calling.

Otus Pennant. Gr. *otos,* "an eared owl." Let us quote Aristotle: "The Otus is like a Noctua (Night Owl), furnished with little tufts sticking out near the ears, whence it has got its name, as though one should say eared." Gr. *ous, otos,* "ear." **O. asio** (Linnaeus): EASTERN SCREECH-OWL; L. *asio,* "a king of horned owl." **O. flammeolus** (Kaup): FLAMMULATED OWL; L. *flammeus,* "flame-colored," plus the diminutive suffix *-eus* for its reddish color. **O. kennicottii** (Elliot): WESTERN SCREECH-OWL; for Robert Kennicott (see Appendix). **O. trichopsis** (Wagler): WHISKERED SCREECH-OWL; Gr. *thrix, trichos,* "hair"; Gr. *opsis,* "appearance"; for its long whiskers.

Oxyura Bonaparte. Gr. *oxys,* "sharp"; Gr. *oura,* "tail." **O. dominica** (Linnaeus): MASKED DUCK; ML. *dominica;* Dominican Republic where the first specimen was found. **O. jamaicensis** (Gmelin): RUDDY DUCK; ML. *jamaicensis,* "of Jamaica," the source of the bird originally described by Latham as the Jamaican Shoveler in 1785.

Pachyramphus Gray. Gr. *pachys,* "thick" or "stout"; Gr. *rhamphos,* "hooked" or "curved beak"; hence a thick, curved beak. Moderately descriptive. **P. aglaiae** (Lafresnaye): ROSE-THROATED BECARD; Gr. *aglais,* "brightness, splendor" associated with one of the three Greek Graces; an apt description of this attractive bird.

Pagophila Kaup. Gr. *pagos,* "frost"; Gr. *phileo,* "love"; hence frost lover for its main range in the north. **P. eburnia** (Phipps): IVORY GULL; L. *eburneus,* "ivory-colored," for the white adult plumage.

Pandion Savigny. The law of priority in nomenclature has an embarrassing side effect, to wit, it perpetuates not only initial errors of a minor sort as in spelling, but also embalms errors of fact and fancy. For example, Savigny quite justifiably moved the osprey from the genus *Falco* where Linnaeus had placed it to a new genus of his own creation which, in a flight of mythological exuberance, he called *Pandion.* If he had checked the delightful Greek myth, he would have found birds in it but that Pandion was not directly involved. Pandion, the king of Athens, had two daughters, Procne and Philomel. The former married Tereus, king of Thrace. After a son, Itylus, was born, Tereus decided that Philomel was the more attractive sister but was given pause by his awareness of the Pandion family's high regard for the sanctity of marriage and also their rather fervid clannishness. Not wishing to go to extremes, he cut out his wife's tongue and let it be known that she was dead. After an appropriate interval of mourning, he married Philomel. But he had underestimated Procne. Although she could not speak, she, like most of the Greek girls, could weave. So she wove the story into a web which was given to Philomel. The two sisters did not cry and mope, but went into action which they considered adequately vengeful. They served, properly roasted and seasoned, the baby, Itylus, as part of a full-course dinner to Tereus, the father and erring husband. Although the gods, given to indulge in phallic frolics themselves, were quite tolerant with human amatory escapades, they were angry with the lengths to which this family group had gone. For penance, they transformed Procne into a swallow and Philomel into a nightingale. This in itself would not have been so bad except for the fact that they had continuously to lament their sin while being pursued by Tereus in the form of a hawk. The chase was to last eternally. Thus it seems that Savigny made two errors. First, if he wished to commemorate the mythological hawk, he should have named his new genus *Tereus*, as it was he who was metamorphosed and not Pandion. Second, it is rather stretching things a bit ornithologically to have an osprey that preys on fish chasing a swallow and a nightingale. Another version of this story is that Philomel was the sister who had her tongue removed. This is obviously the wrong version as Philomel in being changed into a nightingale could not possibly be a good singer without a tongue. She could only twitter like a swallow. Having faith in the god's omniscience, which surely included a familiarity with the songs of birds, we can be certain that the first version of the myth is the authentic one. Gr. *Pandion* possibly from Gr. *pan,* "all"; Gr. *dio(n),* "god." **P. haliaetus** (Linnaeus): OSPREY; here we have the correct spelling. See *Haliaeetus.*

Parabuteo Ridgway. Gr. *para,* "beside," a prefix meaning near or parallel, plus L. *buteo,* "a kind of hawk." The meaning here is that this genus is closely related to the genus, *Buteo.* **P. unicinctus** (Temminck): HARRIS' HAWK; L. *uni-* "once"; L. *cinctus,* "girdled"; possibly referring to the single broad band on the tail.

Parula Bonaparte. L. *parus,* "a titmouse"; L. *-ula,* "little," a diminutive suffix, hence "little titmouse." **P. americana** (Linnaeus): NORTHERN PARULA or PARULA WARBLER; ML. *americana,* "American." **P. pitiayuma** (Vieillot): TROPICAL PARULA or OLIVE-BACKED WARBLER; *pitiayumi,* possibly a South American word for the fiber used in the nest.

Parus Linnaeus. L. *parus,* "a titmouse." **P. atricapillus** Linnaeus: BLACK-CAPPED CHICKADEE; L. *ater,* "black"; L. *capillus,* "hair of the head." **P. atricristatus** Cassin: BLACK-CRESTED TITMOUSE; L. *ater,* "black"; L. *cristatus,* "crested." Now believed to be conspecific with *P. bicolor.* **P. bicolor** Linnaeus: TUFTED TITMOUSE; L. *bi(s),* "two"; L. *color,* "color"; because the buffy tint on the sides gives at least his underparts two colors. **P. carolinensis** Audubon: CAROLINA CHICKADEE; ML. *carolinensis,* "of Carolina," a more southern bird than the Black-capped. **P. cinctus** Boddaert: SIBERIAN TIT or GRAY-HEADED CHICKADEE; L. *cinctus,* "girdled"; as the bird is not banded in any way, the meaning is not clear. **P. gambeli** Ridgway: MOUNTAIN CHICKADEE; for William Gambel (see Appendix). **P. hudsonicus** Forster: BOREAL CHICKADEE; ML. *hudsonicus*, of Hudson's Bay, alluding to its northern range. **P. inornatus** Gambel: PLAIN TITMOUSE; L. *inornatus*, "unadorned." In contrast to "bicolor" above, "inornatus" is a uniformly gray bird. **P. rufescens** Townsend: CHESTNUT-BACKED CHICKADEE; L. *rufescens*, "reddish" for the color of the back. **P. sclateri** Kleinschmidt: MEXICAN CHICKADEE; for P. L. Sclater (see Appendix). **P. wollweberi** (Bonaparte): BRIDLED TITMOUSE; for Wollweber (see Appendix).

Passer Brisson. L. *passer*, "sparrow." **P. domesticus** (Linnaeus): HOUSE SPARROW; L. *domesticus*, "house." The species that the Romans called *passer*. **P. montanus** (Linnaeus): EURASIAN TREE SPARROW; L. *montanus*, "mountain," although the bird is not partial to mountains.

Passerculus Bonaparte. L. *passerculus*, "little sparrow." **P. sandwichensis** (Gmelin): SAVANNAH SPARROW; ML. *sandwichensis*, "of Sandwich Bay" in the Aleutians whence the first specimen. **P. sandwichensis princeps** Maynard: IPSWICH SPARROW; L. *princeps*, "chief." Originally described as a full species. As it is considerably larger than the Savannah Sparrow, with which it was compared, the designation *princeps* no doubt refers to its size.

Passerella Swainson. L. *passer*, "sparrow"; L. *-ella*, "little"; hence "little sparrow" for the genus which has one of our largest sparrows. **P. iliaca** (Merrem): FOX SPARROW; L. *iliacus*, "relating to colic," from L. *ilia*, "the groin" or "lower intestine," the anatomical seat of the Roman bellyache. It is remotely possible that the taxonomist who named the bird had in mind "flanks," as this portion of the bird's anatomy is conspicuously streaked.

Passerina Vieillot. L. *passerina*, "sparrow-like." **P. amoena** (Say): LAZULI BUNTING; L. *amoena*, "lovely." **P. ciris** (Linnaeus): PAINTED BUNTING; Gr. *ciris*, name of the bird into which Scylla, the daughter of Nisus, king of Megara, was transformed. Minos, the king of Crete, had beseiged Megara for six months to no avail. This was because the city was unconquerable as long as a purple lock of hair remained intact upon the head of Nisus. Scylla, who had plenty of time on her hands, whiled it away by looking over the enemy encampment from one of her father's battlements. Her interest gradually became concentrated on one individual, King Minos, and then quite rapidly evolved into an obsessive fixation. What would please Minos more than conquering the city? And most surely he would be most pleased with anyone who would make this possible. So the lovelorn damsel clipped the purple lock from her father's sleeping head and in the dead of night made her way to Minos' tent and demanded an audience. Was Minos gratified? Enough to conquer the city, yes, but to reward Scylla? No. He was overcome with moral revulsion, spurned the maiden and took off in his fleet in high dudgeon for Crete. Scylla, being a girl of spirit and now having no place to go, followed the fleet into the sea and grabbed hold of a rudder. Her father, who had now been changed into a sea eagle, spied her and beset her with bill and claw. She lost her hold and was just about to disappear beneath the waves when the gods who had all the time been watching the drama got into the act. They changed Scylla into a ciris, a bird which has not been identified, although it is still pursued upon sight by the sea eagle. The reason Linnaeus decided to name the painted bunting after the heroine is no doubt because of its purple head, but, if so, he seems to have been confused about who had the purple lock. As for the gods getting into the act, it shows their understanding of the strength of passionate love. **P. cyanea** (Linnaeus): INDIGO BUNTING; Gr. *cyaneos*, "dark blue," for the male's plumage. **P. versicolor** (Bonaparte): VARIED BUNTING; L. *versus*, "change"; L. *color*, "hue," "tint."

Pedioecetes Baird. Gr. *pedion*, "a plain"; Gr. *oiketes*, "inhabiting." Now merged in *Tympanuchus*.

Pelagodroma Reichenbach. Gr. *pelagos*, "the sea"; Gr. *dromos*, "running." **P. marina** (Latham): WHITE-FACED STORM-PETREL; L. *marinus*, "of the sea."

Pelecanus Linnaeus. L. *pelicanus*, from Gr. *pelekan*, "woodpecker," referring to the bird's pecking habits and also "pelican." The name applied to birds notable for their bills, as W. Turner writing in 1544 used Pelicanus as a synonym for the Shovelard or Spoonbill. **P. erythrorhyncos** Gmelin: AMERICAN WHITE PELICAN; Gr. *erythros*, "red"; Gr. *rhyncos*, "beak." At least it is of an orange color. **P. occidentalis** Linnaeus: BROWN PELICAN; L. *occidentalis*, "western." As it is a New World species.

Perdix Brisson. L. *perdix*, "a partridge," mentioned by Pliny. **P. perdix** (Linnaeus): GRAY PARTRIDGE. Perdix was apprenticed to his uncle, Daedalus, an exceptionally skilled craftsman. After contemplating the spine of a fish, Perdix proved himself to be an apt pupil by inventing the saw. When he followed this by inventing the compass, Daedalus, overcome with envy, seized the opportunity to push his talented nephew from a high tower. Minerva, who was partial to inventiveness, happened to witness this episode. Before Perdix could touch the ground, she changed him into a perdix and now, clothed in feathers but still retaining his name, he flew away unscathed. In spite of the fact that this is recorded in Ovid's *Metamorphoses*, MacLeod suggests that the youth may have been named for the bird rather than vice versa.

Perisoreus Bonaparte. Gr. *perisoreuo*, "to heap up," alluding to the bird's acquisitive habits. **P. canadensis** (Linnaeus): GRAY JAY or CANADA JAY; ML. *canadensis*, "Canadian," for the range.

Petrochelidon Cabanis. Gr. *petra*, "a rock"; Gr. *chelidon*, "a swallow"; nesting sites are often on rocky cliffs. *Petrochelidon* has been combined with *Hirundo*.

Peucedramus Henshaw. Gr. *peuce*, "pine"; Gr. *dram*(ema), "a running"; for the habitat in the pine woods. **P. taeniatus** (DuBus de Gisignies): OLIVE WARBLER; ML. *taeniatus*, "striped," referring to the black eye stripe of the male.

Phaethon Linnaeus. Gr. *Phaeton*, "Phaeton," the son of Phoebus, was allowed by his father, whom he wore down by his whining begging, to drive the chariot of the sun. His incapacity to control the flight of the horses almost resulted in the burning of both heaven and earth. Just why such superb flyers as the tropic birds should have to bear the name of one most noted for ineptness in the air can be explained by giving credit to Linnaeus for a wry sense of humor. **P. aethereus** Linnaeus: RED-BILLED TROPIC BIRD; Gr. *aether*, "the upper air." **P. lepturus** Daudin: WHITE-TAILED TROPIC BIRD or YELLOW-BILLED TROPIC BIRD; Gr. *leptos*, "thin"; Gr. *oura*, "tail."

Phainopepla Baird. Gr. *phainos*, "shining"; Gr. *peplos*, "robe"; for the glitter of the plumage. **P. nitens** (Swainson): PHAINOPEPLA; L. *nitens*, "shining," emphasizing the bright reflecting plumage.

Phalacrocorax Brisson. L. *phalacrorax*, "cormorant." The word was used by Pliny and means "bald crow." Gr. *phalakros*, "bald"; Gr. *korax*, "crow or raven." "Bald" probably refers to the white-headed appearance of the breeding plumage of the common European subspecies, *P. carbo sinensis*, which probably acquired its name in the same way our bald eagle did. To those familiar with land birds, it looked like a balding, white-headed, ocean-going crow. **P. auritus** (Lesson): DOUBLE-CRESTED CORMORANT; L. *auritus*, "eared," for the inconspicuous crest above the eyes. **P. carbo** (Linnaeus): GREAT CORMORANT; L. *carbo*, "charcoal," for the color of the bird. **P. olivaceus** (Humbolt): OLIVACEOUS CORMORANT; L. *oliva*, "an olive," for the color. **P. pelagicus** Pallas: PELAGIC CORMORANT; Gr. *pelagos*, "the sea." **P. penicillatus** (Brandt): BRANDT'S CORMORANT; L. *penicillus*, "a painter's brush" (a pencil of hairs), hence *penicillatus*, "pencil-like," i.e., ending in a tuft for the crest of feathers. **P. urile** (Gmelin): RED-FACED CORMORANT; *urile*, possibly a Russian place name of or in the area of the Kurile Islands.

Phalaenoptilus Ridgway. Gr. *phalaina*, "a moth"; Gr. *ptilon*, "a feather"; for the light texture of the wing feathers. **P. nuttalii** (Audubon): COMMON POORWILL; for Thomas Nuttall (see Appendix).

Phalaropus Brisson. Gr. *phalaris*, "a coot"; Gr. *pous*, "foot"; hence "coot-footed" for the lobes on the toes like those of a coot. **P. fulicaria** (Linnaeus): RED PHALAROPE; L. *fuliga,* "a coot," as the bird's feet are coot-like. **P. lobatus** (Linnaeus); RED-NECKED PHALAROPE or NORTHERN PHALAROPE; L. *lobatus,* "lobed."

Phasianus Linnaeus. Gr. *phasianos,* "a pheasant," for the river Phasis in Colchis, the area where the bird ranged. **P. colchicus** Linnaeus: RING-NECKED PHEASANT; ML. *colchicus;* a double locality name.

Pheucticus Reichenbach. Probably Gr. *phycticos,* "painted with cosmetics," as if the male's breast was rouged. **P. ludovicianus** (Linnaeus): ROSE-BREASTED GROSBEAK; ML. *ludovicianus,* "of Louisiana," the locality of the original specimen. **P. melanocephalus** (Swainson): BLACK-HEADED GROSBEAK; Gr. *melanos,* "black"; Gr. *cephale,* "head"; for the color of the male's head.

Philacte Bannister. Gr. *philos,* "loving"; Gr. *akte,* "sea coast." The genus has been combined with *Chen.*

Philohela Gray. Gr. *philos,* "loving"; Gr. *helos,* "a bog." *Philohela* is no longer kept separate from *Scolopax.*

Philomachus Merrem. Gr. *philos,* "loving"; Gr. *mache,* "combat"; for the aggressive dance of the males in the breeding season. **P. pugnax** (Linnaeus): RUFF; L. *pugnax,* "quarrelsome," from L. *pugnus,* "fist"; repeating the idea that the bird is addicted to violence, although it has sublimated this inclination into a dance.

Phoenicopterus Linnaeus. Gr. *phoinix,* "crimson"; Gr. *pteron,* "wing." **P. ruber** (Linnaeus): GREATER FLAMINGO or AMERICAN FLAMINGO; L. *ruber,* "red," for its reddish plumage.

Phylloscopus Boie. Gr. *phyllon,* "leaf"; Gr. *scopos,* "one that looks about, a watchman." **P. borealis** (Blasius): ARCTIC WARBLER; L. *borealis,* "northern," for the breeding range.

Pica Brisson. L. *pica,* "magpie." **P. nuttallii** (Audubon): YELLOW-BILLED MAGPIE; ML. *nuttalli* for Thomas Nuttall (see Appendix). **P. pica** (Linnaeus): BLACK-BILLED MAGPIE L. *pica,* "magpie."

Picoides Lacépède. L. *picus,* "a woodpecker"; Gr. *oides,* a contraction of *o,* "the," and *eidos,* "like," to mean "resembling." **P. albolarvatus** (Cassin): WHITE-HEADED

WOODPECKER; L. *albus*, "white"; L. *larvatus*, "masked."
P. arcticus (Swainson): BLACK-BACKED THREE-TOED WOOD-
PECKER; L. *arcticus*, "northern" (see *Gavia, arctica*). **P.
arizonae** (Hargitt): ARIZONA WOODPECKER; ML. *arizonae*,
"of Arizona," its residence. Now merged in *P. stricklandi*.
P. borealis (Vieillot): RED-COCKADED WOODPECKER; L. *borealis*, "northern," Gr. *boreas*, "the north wind." Boreas,
the North Wind, fell in love with Orithyea but her father,
Erechtheus, and the people of Athens wanted nothing to do
with another northerner after Tereus' villainry became
known. Orithyea, herself, was not entranced but rather repelled by the rough ways of her suitor. Not to be thwarted
by the proprieties of permission of relatives or reluctance on
the part of the object of his devotion, Boreas, in a great gust
of wind, swooped down and carried her off. No subsequent
accounts suggest it was an unhappy marriage. Vieillot evidently fumbled the naming of this bird, which has its range
in the southeastern United States. The A.O.U. *Check-list*,
in citing his description, has noted (*dans le nord des Etats-
Unis* = southern States). The A.O.U. suggests that Vieillot
was confused. Even if he thought the bird came from the
northern United States, he overdid it a bit. Northern Canada
would be a better justification for the name. **P. nuttallii**
(Gambel): NUTTALL'S WOODPECKER for Thomas Nuttall
(see Appendix). **P. pubescens** (Linnaeus): DOWNY WOOD-
PECKER; L. *pubescena*, "downy," i.e., with the hairs of pu-
berty and not quite so virily unkempt as *villosus*. **P. scalaris**
(Wagler): LADDER-BACKED WOODPECKER; L. *scalaris*, "lad-
der-like"; L. *scals*, "a flight of stairs"; alluding to the plumage of the back. **P. stricklandi** (Malherbe): STRICKLAND'S
WOODPECKER for H. E. Strickland (see Appendix). **P. tri-
dactylus** (Linnaeus): NORTHERN THREE-TOED WOOD-
PECKER; Gr. *trias*, "three"; Gr. *daktylos*, "toe." **B. villosus**
(Linnaeus): HAIRY WOODPECKER; L. *villosus*, "hairy," from
its rather shaggy appearance especially about the head.

Pinguinus Bonnaterre. ML. *pinquinus*. Bonnaterre chose this
name in 1790 when he placed the Great Auk in a genus of
its own. He most likely derived it from F. *pingouin* which

in an earlier form was *penguyn*, which may have come from Breton *pengouin* (white head) or E. *penguin*. The latter is from Welsh *pen* (white), *gwyn* (head), Breton and Welsh being closely related Celtic languages. The name was used by the fishermen of both countries for the Great Auk which had a large white patch in front of its eye. It was also probably used for more than one bird, and sailors are probably responsible for its initial bestowal on the birds of the Southern Hemisphere now commonly known as penguins. Skeat points out that "Sir F. Drake gave a certain island the name of Penguin Island in 1587 from the penguins he found there." Weekley quotes Richard Hawkins, c. 1600, "Pengwyns, which in Welsh, as I have been enformed, signifieth white head. From which derivation . . . some doe inferre that America was first peopled with Welshmen." This "inferres" that the Welsh and the Breton fishermen named the bird through their acquaintance with it about the fishing banks of New Foundland and not from the days when it wintered on the coasts of their homeland. If the above stretches into a credibility gap, one may opt for L. *pinguis,* "fat," "stout"; L. *-inus,* "-like," hence; "fat-looking." **P. impennis** (Linnaeus): GREAT AUK; L. *-im,* "without"; L. *penna,* "feather," in the singular, and L. *pennae,* "wing," in the plural. Linnaeus gets no accolade here, as the bird had feathers, although short and tough, and wings, although it did not fly in the air, which reminds us of Coues who lamented "His Grace, THE AUK, or GAREFOWL, who lost the use of his wings, and perished off the face of the earth in consequence."

Pinicola Vieillot. L. *pinus,* "pine"; L. *colere,* "inhabit." **P. enucleator** (Linnaeus): PINE GROSBEAK; L. *enucleator,* "one who 'shells out,'" from the bird's way of husking the pine seeds.

Pipilo Vieillot. ML. *pipilo,* from L. *pipo,* "to chirp or peep." **P. aberti** Baird: ABERT'S TOWHEE for James W. Abert (see Appendix). **P. chlorurus** (Audubon): GREEN-TAILED TOWHEE; Gr. *chloros,* "green"; Gr. *oura,* "tail." **P. erythrophthalmus** (Linnaeus): RUFOUS-SIDED TOWHEE; Gr. *erythros,* "red"; Gr. *opthalmos,* "eye." For the color of the iris of the adult in most of North America, although it is white or orange in the southeastern United States. **P. fuscus** Swainson: BROWN TOWHEE; L. *fuscus,* "dark brown," for the color of the plumage. The Green-tailed T. was formerly put in the genus *Chlorurus.*

Piranga Vieillot. *Piranga,* a native name for some kind of South American bird. **P. flava** (Vieillot): HEPATIC TANAGER; L. *flava,* "yellow," referring to the color of the female, which possibly was found and described before the male. **P. ludoviciana** (Wilson): WESTERN TANAGER; ML. *ludoviciana,* "of Louisiana." Wilson in naming the bird for its locality was not referring to the state but to the Louisiana Territory from which the bird described by him was brought back by Lewis and Clark who collected it in Idaho. **P. olivacea** (Gmelin): SCARLET TANAGER; L. *oliva,* "olive." We again have the color of the female, which seems to have been settled upon due to possible confusion with the Summer Tanager, which already had preempted the term for the color red. **P. rubra** (Linnaeus): SUMMER TANAGER; L. *rubra,* "red," for the entirely red plumage of the male.

Pitangus Swainson. *Pitangus,* a native Brazilian name for the bird. **P. sulphuratus** (Linnaeus): GREAT KISKADEE or KISKADEE FLYCATCHER; L. *sulphur,* "sulphur"; L. *-atus,* "having"; for the bright yellow underparts.

Platypsaris Sclater. Gr. *platys,* "broad"; Gr. *psar,* "a starling." In poor light from the rear without binoculars, at a distance it might look like a fat starling. The genus has been merged with *Pachyramphus.*

Plectrophenax Stejneger. Gr. *plectron,* "something to hit with, a cock's claw"; Gr. *phenax,* "a cheat." According to MacLeod the word was originally *Plectophanes,* the latter stem from Gr. *phaino,* "to display." So the whole word meant "showy claw" for the bird's long hind claw. MacLeod goes on to say that Stejneger changed *Plectrophanes* to *Plectrophenax* for technical reasons. From here it seems that Stejneger for taxonomic "technical reasons" moved the Snow Bunting from the genus *Emberiza,* where Linnaeus had placed it, into a new genus of his own designation, which he misspelled. In its present permanently embalmed state the term may roughly be translated to mean "something to hit a cheat with." **P. hyperboreus** Ridgway: MCKAY'S BUNTING; L. *hyperboreus*, "beyond the north wind," for the bird's far-northern range (see *Larus hyperboreus*). **P. nivalis** (Linnaeus): SNOW BUNTING; L. *nivalis*, "snowy," for its white plumage and its appearance during the season of snow.

Plegadis Kaup. Gr. *plegadis*, "a sickle or scythe." **P. chihi** (Vieillot): WHITE-FACED IBIS. Chihi is possibly a South American native name for the bird. **P. falcinellus** (Linnaeus): GLOSSY IBIS; L. *falx*, "sickle," for the shape of the bill; L. *-ellus*, "little"; this gives us the little sickle sickle.

Pluvialis Brisson. L. *pluvialis*, "rainy" (see Plover). **P. dominica** (Müller): LESSER GOLDEN-PLOVER or AMERICAN GOLDEN-PLOVER; ML. *dominica*, for St. Domingo on Hispaniola where the first specimen was obtained in 1776. **P. squatarola** (Linnaeus): BLACK-BELLIED PLOVER; squatarola is a Venetian name for the bird.

Podiceps Latham. A contraction of the ML. *podicipes* from L. *podex*, *podicis*, "rump"; L. *pes*, "foot." **P. auritus** (Linnaeus): HORNED GREBE; L. *auritus*, "eared," for the tufts on the head. **P. grisegena** (Boddaert): RED-NECKED GREBE or HOLBOELL'S GREBE; L. *griseus*, "gray"; L. *gena*, "cheek"; for the color of the cheek in breeding plumage. **P. nigricollis** Brehm: EARED GREBE or BLACK-NECKED GREBE; L. *niger*, "black"; L. *collis*, "neck," which it has in its breeding plumage.

Podilymbus Lesson. Lesson coined the word by combining the first syllable of ML. *podiceps*, a generic name for grebes; and the last part of *Colymbus*, a generic name for loons and grebes, from Gr. *kolumbos*, "a diving bird," mentioned by Aristotle. *Colymbus* was formerly used as a generic term for some of our grebes and as a generic term for the loons (divers) in Britain. It has been suppressed by the International Commission on Zoological Nomenclature. **P. podiceps** (Linnaeus) PIED-BILLED GREBE.

Polioptila Sclater. Gr. *polios,* "gray"; Gr. *ptilon,* "feather"; as the primaries are edged with gray. **P. caerulea** (Linnaeus): BLUE-GRAY GNATCATCHER; L. *caerulea,* "blue," for the blue back. **P. melanura** (Lawrence): BLACK-TAILED GNAT-CATCHER; Gr. *melas,* "black"; Gr. *oura,* "tail"; as it has more black in the tail than the former.

Polyborus Vieillot. Gr. *poly* "many"; Gr. *borus,* "gluttonous" or "devouring"; hence an unfussy eater. **P. plancus** (Miller); CRESTED CARACARA; Gr. *plancus,* a "kind of eagle."

Polysticta Eyton. Gr. *poly stictos,* "many-spotted," despite the fact that it is not, although the birds are curiously marked. **P. stelleri** (Pallas): STELLER'S EIDER for George W. Steller (see Appendix).

Pooecetes Baird. Gr. *poe,* "grass"; Gr. *oiketes (oecetes),* "dweller." **P. gramineus** (Gmelin): VESPER SPARROW; L. *gramineus,* "of the grasses," for the habitat.

Porphyrula Blyth. Gr. *porphyrion,* "water hen," from Gr. *porphyreos,* "purple"; L. *-ula,* "little." **P. martinica** (Linnaeus): PURPLE GALLINULE; ML. *martinica,* "of Martinique," where the bird was first found.

Porzana Vieillot. I. *porzana,* "the crake." **P. carolina** (Linnaeus): SORA; ML. *carolina,* "of Carolina."

Progne Boie. Gr. *Progne,* who was changed into a swallow (see *Pandion*). **P. subis** (Linnaeus): PURPLE MARTIN; L. *subis,* "name of an unknown bird."

Protonotaria Baird. L. *protonotarius,* "an authorized scribe," from Gr. *protos,* "first"; L. *notarius,* "a note taker." As Coues puts it: "Why?" **P. citrea** (Boddaert): PROTHONO-TARY WARBLER; L. *citrus,* "the citrus tree," hence to the fruit of the tree and its color, which is a roundabout way of getting to yellow, the bird's color.

Psaltriparus Bonaparte. Gr. *psaltria,* "a harpist"; L. *parus,* "a titmouse." **P. minimus** (Townsend): BUSHTIT; L. *minimus,* "least." Coues calls them "dwarfs among pygmies."

Pterodroma Bonaparte. Gr. *pteron,* "wing"; Gr. *dromos,* "running." **P. hasitata** (Kuhl): BLACK-CAPPED PETREL. As there is no such word as *hasitatus* in Latin, MacLeod speculates, "It first appears in Forster's unpublished plates as the name of a species of *Procellaria,* and was adopted by Kuhl in 1820. In 1863, however, Schlegel (in his account of *Procellaria neglecta*) refers to Kuhl's *Procellaria haesitata* which suggests that *hasitata* is a mistake for *haesitata*. If so, *haesitata* appears to be coined from L. *haesito,* hesitate, and having the meaning of 'uncertain,' the idea being that it was uncertain whether the bird belongs to a distinct species." Now it is so classified with the past uncertainty carried in the uncertain spelling. **P. inexpectata** (Forster): MOTTLED PETREL or SCALED PETREL; L. *inexpecta,* "unexpected," evidently to the describer, as it is infrequently close to shore.

Ptychoramphus Brandt. Gr. *ptyk,* "a fold"; Gr. *ramphos,* "beak"; alluding to the ridges across the bill which are evident only when the bird is in the hand. **P. aleuticus** (Pallas): CASSIN'S AUKLET; ML. *aleutica,* "Aleutian Islands," one of the breeding sites.

Puffinus Brisson. ML. *puffinus,* E. *puffin.* The use of the word puffin as the generic term for shearwaters is attributed to Ray, "the father of English natural history," 1628–1705. He should not be criticized for contributing to confusion as in his day "puffin" was used indiscriminately for the puffin, the razorbill and the shearwater. He had no way of knowing which bird would eventually take over the word "puffin" for its exclusive use. Then, too, Linnaeus and his successors generally adapted terms already in use rather than invent new ones for the binomial nomenclature. Once given a binomial name, the law of priority decrees that no change be made despite seeming inappropriateness or original error. The original name is maintained to avoid confusion, at least among taxonomists. **P. assimilis** Gould: LITTLE SHEARWATER; L. *assimilis,* "similar," so called on account of its resemblance to the Madeiran Little Shearwater which at the time was *Puffinus obscurus* (a species) but is now *P. assimilis baroli* (a subspecies) for the Marchese Farloti di Barol of Turin. As the species *P. assimilis* cannot look like a species that does not exist, its name has to mean that it "looks like itself" which is probably less ridiculous than having the bird look like the Marchese. Thus a valid revision of classification makes the original name meaningless. **P. bulleri** Salvin: BULLER'S SHEARWATER or NEW ZEALAND SHEARWATER; for Sir Walter L. Buller (see Appendix). **P. carneipes** Gould: FLESH-FOOTED SHEARWATER or PALE-FOOTED SHEARWATER; L. *carnis,* "flesh"; L. *pes,* "foot"; for the color of the feet. **P. creatopus** Coues: PINK-FOOTED SHEARWATER; Gr. *kreatos,* "flesh"; Gr. *pous,* "foot"; for the color of the feet, a repetition using Greek roots. **P. gravis** (O'Reilly): GREATER SHEARWATER; L. *gravis,* "heavy," for its large size. **P. griseus** (Gmelin): SOOTY SHEARWATER; ML. *griseus,* "gray," which is not as appropriate as the common name for this sooty black bird. **P. lherminieri** Lesson: AUDUBON'S SHEARWATER; for F. J. L'Herminier (see Appendix). **P. puffinus** (Brünnich): MANX SHEARWATER (see *Puffinus*). **P. tenuirostris** (Temminck): SHORT-TAILED SHEARWATER or SLENDER-BILLED SHEARWATER; L. *tennis,* "thin"; L. *rostrum,* "beak."

Pycnonotus Boie. Gr. *pycnos,* "solid, strong"; Gr. *notos,* "back." **P. jocosus** (Linnaeus): RED-WHISKERED BULBUL; L. *jocosus,* "full of fun," possibly for its liveliness. Given authentic status as a North American bird in the *Auk* (vol. 85, no. 1, 1968), it is locally common in South Miami, Florida, where it has been "free" since 1955.

Pyrocephalus Gould. Gr. *pyros,* "fire"; Gr. *cephale,* "head." **P. rubinus** (Boddaert): VERMILION FLYCATCHER; L. *rubinus,* "ruby," for the red plumage of the male.

Pyrrhuloxia Bonaparte. Gr. *pyrrhoulis,* "the bullfinch," of Aristotle, from Gr. *pyrrhos,* "flame-colored"; Gr. *loxias,* "crooked." The genus is not included within *Cardinalis*.

Quiscalus Vieillot. ML. *quiscalis,* "quail." There are several spellings of the ML. term. See Quail, another form of the word, in the list of common names. The use of a word meaning "quail" seems out of place for a genus in the family Icteridae. **Q. major** Vieillot: BOAT-TAILED GRACKLE; L. *major,* "larger." **Q. mexicanus** (Gmelin): GREAT-TAILED GRACKLE; ML. *mexicanus,* "of Mexico," where the bird is common. **Q. quiscula** (Linnaeus): COMMON GRACKLE; ML. *quiscula,* another spelling for the generic term adding to the variety by changing the gender. We have been unable to determine why *quisquilla, quaquila, quaquara,* and *quaquadra* were passed by as they are all equally inappropriate.

Rallus Linnaeus. ML. *rallus,* "a rail"; F. *rale,* "a rail"; OF. *raale,* "to make a scraping noise"; L. *raelare,* "to scrape." **R. elegans** Audubon: KING RAIL; L. *elegans,* "elegant." **R. limicola** Vieillot: VIRGINIA RAIL; L. *limus,* "mud"; L. *colo,* "to inhabit." **R. longirostris** Boddaert: CLAPPER RAIL; L. *longus,* "long"; L. *rostrum,* "bill."

Recurvirostra Linnaeus. L. *recurvo,* "to bend backward"; L. *rostrum,* "bill." **R. americana** Gmelin: AMERICAN AVOCET; ML. *americana,* "American," to distinguish it from the European.

Regulus Cuvier. L. *regulus,* "little king." **R. calendula** (Linnaeus): RUBY-CROWNED KINGLET; ML. *calendula* from L. *calendus,* "glowing," for the ruby crown. **R. satrapa** Lichtenstein: GOLDEN-CROWNED KINGLET; Gr. *satrapes,* "a ruler" who wears a golden crown.

Rhodostethia MacGillivray. Gr. *rhodon,* "rose"; Gr. *stethos,* "breast." **R. rosea** (MacGillivray): ROSS' GULL; L. *roseus,* "rosy," hence the rosy rosebreasted.

Rhynchopsitta Bonaparte. Gr. *rhynchos,* "beak"; Gr. *psittake,* "parrot." **R. pachyrhyncha** (Swainson): THICK-BILLED PARROT; Gr. *pachys,* "thick," and *rhyncha* repeated for good measure. Here we find the scientific term means the same as the common name.

Riparia Forster. L. *riparia,* "bank of a stream," for the nesting site. **R. riparia** (Linnaeus): BANK SWALLOW; L. *riparia,* see above.

Rissa Stephens. Ic. *rissa,* "kittiwake." **R. brevirostris** (Bruch): RED-LEGGED KITTIWAKE; L. *brevis,* "short"; L. *rostrum,* "bill," for its small bill. **R. tridactyla** (Linnaeus): BLACK-LEGGED KITTIWAKE; Gr. *treis,* L. *tris,* "three"; Gr. *daktylos,* "finger or toe." Not so named for the three front toes which are like those in other gulls, but because the rear toe is abnormally small, making the three normal ones stand out in contrast.

Rostrhamus Lesson. L. *rostrum,* "beak"; L. *hamus,* "a hook."

R. sociabilis (Vieillot): SNAIL KITE or EVERGLADE KITE; L. *sociabilis,* "gregarious," for its nesting in loose colonies.

Rynchops Linnaeus. Gr. *rhynchos,* "a beak"; Gr. *ops,* "face." **R. niger** Linnaeus: BLACK SKIMMER; L. *niger,* "black," for the color of the upper parts.

Salpinctes Cabanis. Gr. *salpinctes,* "a trumpeter." **S. obsoletus** (Say): ROCK WREN; L. *obsoletus,* "indistinct," for the dull coloration.

Sayornis Bonaparte. Gr. *ornis,* "bird"; for Thomas Say (see Appendix). Gr. **S. nigricans** (Swainson): BLACK PHOEBE; L. *nigricans,* "blackening." **S. phoebe** (Latham): EASTERN PHOEBE; Gr. *Phoebe,* "one of the twelve Titans"; imitative of the bird's call. **S. saya** (Bonaparte): SAY'S PHOEBE; doubly honoring Thomas Say.

Scardafella Bonaparte. I. *scardafella,* "scaley appearance." The genus is included in *Columbina* now.

Scolopax Linnaeus. Gr. *scolopax,* "the woodcock." **S. minor** Gmelin: AMERICAN WOODCOCK; L. *minor,* "smaller," in comparison with the Eurasian Woodcock. **S. rusticola** Linnaeus: EURASIAN WOODCOCK; ML. *rusticola,* "a country dweller."

Seiurus Swainson. Gr. *seio,* "to wave"; Gr. *oura,* "tail." **S. aurocapillus** (Linnaeus): OVENBIRD; L. *aurum,* "gold"; L. *capillus,* "hair"; for the gold crown. **S. motacilla** (Vieillot): LOUISIANA WATERTHRUSH; L. *motacilla,* "wagtail" (see *Bombycilla*). **S. novaboracensis** (Gmelin): NORTHERN WATERTHRUSH; ML. *Novaboracensis,* "of New York," where the bird was first found.

Selasphorus Swainson. Gr. *selas,* "light"; Gr. *phoros,* "carrying." **S. platycercus** (Swainson): BROAD-TAILED HUMMINGBIRD; Gr. *platys,* "broad"; Gr. *kerkos,* "tail." **S. rufus** (Gmelin): RUFOUS HUMMINGBIRD; L. *rufus,* "reddish." **S. sasin** (Lesson): ALLEN'S HUMMINGBIRD; of *sasin,* Alexander Wetmore says: "Lesson in his original description of Allen's hummingbird called it the Sasin, from 'Sasime' or 'Sasin,' from a French edition of Cook's third voyage. I do not know what the word means."

Setophaga Swainson. Gr. *setos,* "a moth"; Gr. *phago,* "to eat."

S. ruticilla (Linnaeus): AMERICAN REDSTART; L. *ruticilla,* "red tail."

Sialia Swainson. Gr. *sialis,* "a kind of bird." **S. currucoides** (Bechstein): MOUNTAIN BLUEBIRD; Sp. *curruca,* "the linnet"; Gr. *oides,* "like." **S. mexicana** Swainson: WESTERN BLUEBIRD; ML. *mexicana,* "Mexican," as the first specimen came from Mexico. **S. sialis** (Linnaeus): EASTERN BLUEBIRD; Gr. *sialis,* see above.

Sitta Linnaeus. Gr. *sitte,* "nuthatch." **S. canadensis** Linnaeus: RED-BREASTED NUTHATCH; ML. *canadensis,* "Canadian," for its breeding range although this is only partially in Canada. **S. carolinensis** Latham: WHITE-BREASTED NUTHATCH; ML. *carolinensis,* "of Carolina," although it breeds wherever there are deciduous trees in the United States. **S. pusilla** Latham: BROWN-HEADED NUTHATCH; L. *pusilla,* "very small." **S. pygmaea** Vigors: PYGMY NUTHATCH; L. *pygmaeus,* "a pigmy," "dwarfish," from Gr. *pygme,* "the fist," which was a measure of length from the elbow to the closed fist. It refers to the bird's small size.

Somateria Leach. Gr. *soma,* "body"; Gr. *erion,* "wool"; for the thick down on the body. **S. fischeri** (Brandt): SPECTACLED EIDER; for Gotthelf Fischer (see Appendix). **S. mollissima** (Linnaeus): COMMON EIDER; L. *mollissima,* "softest," for the down. **S. spectabilis** (Linnaeus): KING EIDER; L. *spectabilis,* "showy," referring to the conspicuous orange knob on the front of the head of the male bird in the breeding season which makes it a "spect"acular bird.

Speotyto Gloger. Gr. *speos,* "a cave"; Gr. *tyto,* "a night owl." Former genus for the Burrowing Owl, which is now placed in *Athene.*

Sphyrapicus Baird. Gr. *sphyra,* "a hammer"; L. *picus,* "a woodpecker." Picus loved Pomona and spurned the importunities of Circe. Lacking the guile of Ulysses and possibly ignorant of the proclivity of the one he disdained for turning those she found indifferent into some specimen of the animal kingdom, Picus ended up as a woodpecker. MacLeod disagrees with Ovid, stating that it is his belief that the woodpecker had a name before the youth's transformation.

S. ruber (Gmelin): RED-BREASTED SAPSUCKER; L. *ruber*, "red". **S. thyroideus** (Cassin): WILLIAMSON'S SAPSUCKER; Gr. *thyreos*, "a shield"; Gr. *oidos*, "like"; as the black breast of the male resembles a breastplate. **S. varius** (Linnaeus): YELLOW-BELLIED SAPSUCKER; L. *varius*, "variegated," for the mixed plumage.

Spinus Koch. Gr. *spinos*, "a linnet" or a similar bird. The genus has been merged with *Carduelis* in the sixth edition of the A.O.U. *Check-list* (1983).

Spiza Bonaparte. Gr. *spiza*, "a finch." **S. americana** (Gmelin): DICKCISSEL; ML. *americana*, "American," to distinguish it from others in the genus *Emberiza*, where it was originally placed, as they were European.

Spizella Bonaparte. I. *spizella*, "a finch," diminutive from L. *spiza*, "a finch," from the same in Greek. **S. arborea** (Wilson): AMERICAN TREE SPARROW; L. *arbor*, "a tree." **S. atrogularis** (Cabanis): BLACK-CHINNED SPARROW; L. *atrogularis*, "black-throated." **S. breweri** Cassin: BREWER'S SPARROW; for Thomas M. Brewer (see Appendix). **S. pallida** (Swainson): CLAY-COLORED SPARROW; L. *pallida*, "pale." **S. passerina** (Bechstein): CHIPPING SPARROW; L. *passer*, "sparrow"; L. *-ina*, "like." **S. pusilla** (Wilson): FIELD SPARROW; L. *pusillus*, "smallest," although three spizellas are smaller.

Sporophila Cabanis. Gr. *sporos*, "seed"; Gr. *philos*, "loving." **S. torqueola** (Bonaparte): WHITE-COLLARED SEEDEATER; L. *torquis*, "a twisted neck chain," for the white neck band.

Steganopus Vieillot. Gr. *steganos*, "closed or water-tight"; Gr. *pous*, "foot"; for the partially webbed feet. The genus now has been merged with *Phalaropus*.

Stelgidopteryx Baird. Gr. *stelgis*, "a scraper"; Gr. *pteryx*, "wing"; for the stiff recurved hooks on the first primary. **S. serripennis** (Audubon): NORTHERN ROUGH-WINGED SWALLOW; L. *serra*, "a saw"; L. *pennis*, "wings"; a reference to the roughened edges on the primaries. Formerly the species was treated as conspecific with **S. ruficollis** (Vieillot): SOUTHERN ROUGH-WINGED SWALLOW; L. *rufus*, "reddish"; L. *collum*, "neck." Although lacking in North American birds, some races in South America have a rufous throat. A South America bird was first given the name.

Stellula Gould. L. *stellula*, "little star." **S. calliope** (Gould): CALLIOPE HUMMINGBIRD; Gr. *Calliope*, "the muse responsible for epic poetry." So one of the smallest birds is named for the sponsor of the greatest form of poem.

Stercorarius Brisson. L. *stercorarius*, "having to do with dung," alluding to the scavenging habits of the bird which at times feeds on offal. **S. longicaudus** Vieillot: LONG-TAILED JAEGER; L. *longus*, "long"; L. *caudas*, "tail"; for the lengthened central tail feathers. **S. parasiticus** (Linnaeus): PARASITIC JAEGER; for its pursuit of other sea birds till they disgorge. **S. pomarinus** (Temminck): POMARINE JAEGER; Gr. *poma*, "a lid"; Gr. *rhynchos*, "beak"; for the rim at the base of the bill. Erratic spelling.

Sterna Linnaeus. ML. *sterna*, latinized by Turner in 1544 from OE. *stern*, *starn*, or *tern* from AS. *stearn*, "a tern." **S. albifrons** Pallas: LEAST TERN; L. *albus*, "white"; L. *frons*, "forehead"; for the white feathering above the bill. The species is now considered to be conspecific with *S. antillarum* and bears the latter's name. **S. aleutica** Baird: ALEUTIAN TERN; ML. *aleutica*, "Aleutian Islands," where it breeds. **S. anaethetus** Scopoldi: BRIDLED TERN; a mistake for Gr. *anaisthetos*, "stupid," "without sense," as the bird was supposed to let itself be approached without taking alarm. **S. antillarum** (Lesson): LEAST TERN; ML. *antillarum*, "of the Antilles"; for the region from which the species was first described. **S. caspia** Pallas: CASPIAN TERN; ML. *caspia*, "Caspian Sea," site of the first specimen. **S. dougallii** Montagu: ROSEATE TERN; for Dr. MacDougall of Scotland who provided the first specimen in 1812 (see Appendix). It seems rather singular to leave out the first syllable of the name of the man who is supposed to be honored in perpetuity. **S. elegans** Gambel: ELEGANT TERN; L. *elegans*, "elegant." **S. forsteri** Nuttall: FORSTER'S TERN; for John R. Forster (see Appendix). **S. fuscata** Linnaeus: SOOTY TERN; L. *fuscus*, "dark," for the color of the plumage. **S. hirundo** Linnaeus: COMMON TERM; L. *hirundo*, "a swallow," for its resemblance in shape and flight to a swallow. **S. maxima** Boddaert: ROYAL TERN; L. *maximus*, "largest." If Boddaert, who described this tern in 1783, had looked up the measurements of the Caspian Tern described in 1770, he would probably not have used the term *maximus*. **S. nilotica** Gmelin: GULL-BILLED TERN; L. *nilotica*, "of the Nile," whence came the type specimen. **S. paradisaea** Pontoppidan: ARCTIC TERN; LL. *paradisus* from Zend (old Persian), *pairidaeza*, "an enclosure, a park," from Zend, *pairi*, "around"; Zend, *diz*, "to mold"; hence "form a wall of mud around," which was the way the old Persians made a park. The word was first used in Greek in the Septuagint for the 'Garden of Eden' which translated the Old Testament from Hebrew into Greek. Tradition says the Septuagint is so called because it was translated by seventy-two Jews in seventy-two days for Ptolemy II of Egypt in the third century B.C. It is the biblical version used in the Greek Church. Erik Pontoppidan (1698–1764) attained eminence as a theologian, bishop of Bergen, and as a scientist, author of *A Natural History of Norway*. Possibly his dual career influenced his naming of the bird in the hope that he could convey the idea that so beautiful a creature belonged in that perfect home beyond the sky. **S. sandvicensis** Latham: SANDWICH TERN or CABOT'S TERN; ML. *sandvicensis*, "of Sandwich," Kent, England, whence came the first specimen. **S. trudeaui** Audubon: TRUDEAU'S TERN; for J. Trudeau (see Appendix).

Streptopelia Bonaparte. Gr. *streptos*, "twisted"; Gr. *pel(e)ia*, "a kind of dove"; in reference to the black and white patch on the side of the neck in the European species. **S. chinensis** (Scopoli): SPOTTED DOVE; ML. *chinensis*, "of China," where it is native, having been introduced into the United States. **S. risoria** (Linnaeus): RINGED TURTLE-DOVE; L. *risor*, "a laugher," for the bird's call.

Strix Linnaeus. L. *strix*, Gr. *strigx*, "a screech owl," which members of this genus are not. **S. nebulosa** Forster: GREAT GRAY OWL; L. *nebulosa*, "clouded," as it has the color of a dark cloud. **S. occidentalis** (Xántus de Vesey): SPOTTED OWL; L. *occidentalis*, "western," for its range in western

United States. **S. varia** Barton: BARRED OWL; L. *varia*, "variegated," for the plumage.

Sturnella Vieillot. L. *sturnus*, "a starling"; L. *-ella*, "little"; hence "little starling," although both members of this genus are about two inches larger than the starling proper, *Sturnus*, in the following genus. **S. magna** (Linnaeus): EASTERN MEADOWLARK; L. *magna*, "large," so we end up with "large little starling," which is about as confusing as a scientific term can be. **S. neglecta** Audubon: WESTERN MEADOWLARK; L. *neglecta*, "neglected." So named by Audubon in 1844 as a word of censure for the ornithologists who had named *magna* in 1758 and whom he felt were guilty of inordinate procrastination in identifying this bird.

Sturnus Linnaeus. L. *sturnus*, "a starling." **S. vulgaris** Linnaeus: STARLING; L. *vulgaris*, "common," for its ubiquity.

Sula Brisson. Ic. *sulan*, "gannet." Originally the term meant "an awkward fellow" and possibly was applied to the bird because of its awkward gait. Cf. Nor. *sula*, "gannet." **S. bassanas** (Linnaeus): NORTHERN GANNET; ML. *bassanas* for Bass Rocks, a breeding place of the species in the Firth of Forth. **S. dactylatra** Lesson: MASKED BOOBY or BLUE-FACED BOOBY; Gr. *dactyl*, "finger or toe"; L. *atra*, "black." This looks like an error as the webbed feet are yellow. **S. leucogaster** Boddaert: BROWN BOOBY or WHITE-BELLIED BOOBY; Gr. *leukos*, "white"; Gr. *gaster*, "the belly." **S. nebouxii** Milne-Edwards: BLUE-FOOTED BOOBY; for Adolphe S. Neboux (see Appendix). **S. sula** Linnaeus: RED-FOOTED BOOBY; for *sula* (see above).

Surnia Dumeril. May be an arbitrary word invented by Dumeril in 1806. Coues suggests it is modern Greek for "owl." **S. ulula** (Linnaeus): NORTHERN HAWK-OWL; L. *ulula*, "screech owl," imitative of the bird's cry. Cf. L. *ululare*, "to cry or howl"; Gr. *alala*, "an outcry."

Synthliboramphus Brandt. Gr. *synthlibo*, "compress, small"; Gr. *ramphos*, "beak." **S. antiquus** (Gmelin): ANCIENT MURRELET; L. *antiquus*, "old," hence gray-headed for the hoary appearance of the head. **S. craveri** (Salvadori): CRAVERI'S MURRELET for Frederico Craveri (see Appendix). **S. hypo-**

leucus (Xántus de Vesey): XANTUS' MURRELET; Gr. *hypo-*, "below;" Gr. *leukon*, "white;" for the white underparts.

Tachybaptus Reichenbach. Gr. *tachys*, "quick" or "swift"; Gr. *baptus*, "dipped"; for its habit of suddenly ducking beneath the water. **T. dominicus** (Linnaeus): LEAST GREBE; ML. *dominicus*, "of St. Domingo," on Hispaniola, the site of the first specimen.

Tachycineta Cabanis. Gr. *tachys*, "swift"; Gr. *kineo*, "to move"; hence swift mover. **T. bicolor** (Vieillot): TREE SWALLOW; L. *bicolor*, "two colored." **T. thalassina** (Swainson): VIOLET-GREEN SWALLOW; Gr. *thalassina*, "like the sea," for the sea-green color of the plumage.

Tangavius Lesson. ML. *tangavius*, probably a combination of a Tuni South American native word, *tanger*, and L. *avis*, "bird." Recently merged with *Molothrus*.

Telmatodytes Cabanis. Gr. *telma*, "a swamp"; Gr. *dytes*, "an inhabitant." The former genus of the Marsh Wren, now put into *Cistothorus*.

Thalasseus Boie. Gr. *thalassa*, "the sea." The species previously placed in this genus have been transferred to *Sterna*.

Thryomanes Sclater. Gr. *thryon*, "a reed"; Gr. *manes*, "a cup," for the nest. **T. bewickii** (Audubon): BEWICK'S WREN; for Thomas Bewick (see Appendix).

Thryothorus Vieillot. Gr. *thryon*, "a reed"; Gr. *thouros*, "rushing." **T. ludovicianus** (Latham): CAROLINA WREN; ML. *ludovicianus*, "of Louisiana," the site of the original specimen.

Toxostoma Wagler. Gr. *toxon*, "a bow"; Gr. *stoma*, "a mouth"; literally "bow mouth" for the curved beak. **T. bendirei** (Coues): BENDIRE'S THRASHER; for Charles E. Bendire (see Appendix). **T. curvirostre** (Swainson): CURVE-BILLED THRASHER; L. *curvus*, "curved"; L. *rostrum*, "beak." **T. dorsale** Henry: CRISSAL THRASHER; ML. *dorsalis*, "of the back," which is not distinctive. The correct name for this bird has been debated. There is clear evidence that Henry intended the name to be *crissale* (ML. *crissale*, "of the crissum," referring to the distinctive rufous undertail coverts), but that through a printer's error "*dorsale*" was applied to this thrasher as well as to a junco, both in the same publication. Henry reissued the page, substituting *crissale* for *dorsale*. But, under the rules of the International Code for Zoological Nomenclature, the original name, even if clearly an error, must stand. A lengthy petition procedure may be used to seek changes, and this is now underway for this name. Perhaps 125 years after Henry tried to rectify the error the matter will be settled. **T. lecontei** Lawrence: LE-CONTE'S THRASHER; for John L. LeConte (see Appendix). **T. longirostre** (Lefresnaye): LONG-BILLED THRASHER; L. *longus*, "long"; L. *rostrum*, "bill." **T. redivivum** (Gambel): CALIFORNIA THRASHER; L. *redivivus*, "revived," as the bird was rediscovered after a lapse of time. **T. rufum** (Linnaeus): BROWN THRASHER; L. *rufum*, "reddish."

Tringa Linnaeus. Gr. *tryngas*, "a sandpiper." **T. flavipes** (Gmelin): LESSER YELLOWLEGS; L. *flavus*, "yellow"; L. *pes*, "foot," for the color of the feet and legs. **T. melanoleuca** (Gmelin): GREATER YELLOWLEGS; Gr. *melanos*, "black"; Gr. *leucos*, "white"; as black and white approximate the contrasting color of the upper parts. **T. solitaria** Wilson: SOLITARY SANDPIPER; L. *solitarius*, "solitary."

Troglodytes Vieillot. Gr. *troglodytes*, "cave dweller," from Gr. *trogle*, "hole"; Gr. *dytes*, "a diver"; for the bird's diving into cover. **T. aedon** Vieillot: HOUSE WREN; Gr. *aedon*, "a songstress" from Aedon, the daughter of Pandereus, who was changed into a nightingale by the gods but into a wren by Vieillot. **T. brunneicollis** Sclater: BROWN-THROATED WREN; ML. *brunneus*, "dark brown"; L. *collum*, "neck," for the light brown on the front of the neck. Now considered to be part of the large complex of *T. aedon*. **T. troglodytes** Linnaeus: WINTER WREN or simply WREN, as it is known in the Old World, where there are no other species.

Trogon Brisson. Gr. *trogon*, "a gnawer," for the toothlike edge of the bill. **T. elegans** Gould: ELEGANT TROGON or COPPERY-TAILED TROGON; L. *elegans*, "elegant."

Tryngites Cabanis. Gr. *tryngas*, "a sandpiper"; Gr. *-tes*, "having to do with." **T. subruficollis** (Vieillot): BUFF-BREASTED SANDPIPER; ML. *subruficollis*, "reddish below the neck." As all the underparts are the same buff color, it is difficult to see the need for the word "neck."

Turdus Linnaeus. L. *turdus,* "a thrush." **T. migratorius** Linnaeus: ROBIN; LL. *migrator,* "wanderer."

Tympanuchus Gloger. Gr. *tympanon,* "a drum"; ML. *nucha,* "neck"; for the exposed skin on the bird's neck. **T. cupido** (Linnaeus): GREATER PRAIRIE-CHICKEN; so named for the tufts of feathers on the neck which are supposed to resemble the wings of Cupid; not for the bare skin of the air sacs, as the nakedness of Cupid was not so circumscribed. **T. pallidicinctus** (Ridgway): LESSER PRAIRIE-CHICKEN; L. *pallidus,* "pale"; L. *cinctus,* "banded"; as it is more lightly barred than *T. cupido.* **T. phasianellus** (Linnaeus): SHARP-TAILED GROUSE; Gr. *phasianos,* "a pheasant," from the river Phasis in Colchis, which flows into the Black Sea. Thus we see that naming a bird for its range was done by the ancient Greeks, L. *-ellus,* "little"; the grouse was somewhat like a small pheasant.

Tyrannus Lacépède. L. *tyrannus,* "a tyrant." **T. couchii** Baird: COUCH'S KINGBIRD, for General D. N. Couch (see Appendix). **T. crassirostris** Swainson: THICK-BILLED KINGBIRD; L. *crassi,* "thick" or "heavy"; L. *rostris,* "beak." **T. dominicensis** (Gmelin): GRAY KINGBIRD; ML. *dominicensis,* "of Hispaniola," site of original specimen. **T. forficatus** (Gmelin): SCISSOR-TAILED FLYCATCHER; ML. *forficata,* "forked" from L. *forfic,* "scissors." **T. melancholicus** Vieillot: TROPICAL KINGBIRD; L. *melancholicus,* "melancholy"; from Gr. *melangkolia,* from Gr. *melan,* "black"; *khole,* "bile." When there was too much of this in a body, the one afflicted with ML. *melancholia,* showed symptoms of ill temper, sadness and depression. As the bird is lively and has a rather loud two-syllable call, we can only infer that *melancholicus* indicates Vieillot's disposition rather than the bird's. **T. savana** Vieillot: FORK-TAILED FLYCATCHER; Sp. *sabana,* "a plain"; reference to its habitat. **T. tyrannus** (Linnaeus): EASTERN KINGBIRD; see above for *tyrannus,* **T. verticalis** Say: WESTERN KINGBIRD formerly ARKANSAS KINGBIRD; L. *verticalis,* relating to the L. *vertex,* "the top of the head,"

which has a bright red patch. **T. vociferans** Swainson: CAS-
SIN'S KINGBIRD; L. *vociferans*, "voice carrying," for its loud
call.

Tyto Billberg. Gr. *tyto*, "a night owl." **T. alba** (Scopoli): COM-
MON BARN-OWL; L. *alba*, "white."

Uria Brisson. Gr. *ouria*, one of the most overworked words in
the Greek language, which in various contexts might mean
"a fair wind," "a guardian," "a boundary," "a trench for
hauling up ships," "a buffalo," or (as we take it to mean
here) "a dark water bird with a long and narrow bill." **U.
aalge** (Pontoppidan): COMMON MURRE; D. *aalge*, "the
murre." **U. lomvia** (Linnaeus): THICK-BILLED MURRE or
BRÜNNICHS MURRE; Faroese, *lomvia*, "some kind of small
diving bird."

Vanellus Brisson. ML. *vanellus*, "a little fan," for the way the
broad wings beat the air, from L. *vannus*, "a fan" (note
misspelling). **V. vanellus** (Linnaeus): NORTHERN LAPWING;
a repetition.

Vermivora Swainson. L. *vermis*, "worm"; L. *voro*, "to eat."
V. bachmanii (Audubon): BACHMAN'S WARBLER for John
Bachman, its discoverer (see Appendix). **V. celata** (Say):
ORANGE-CROWNED WARBLER; L. *celata*, "concealed," for
the orange crown which is not easy to see. **V. chrysoptera**
(Linnaeus): GOLDEN-WINGED WARBLER; Gr. *chrysos*,
"gold"; Gr. *pteron*, "wing." **V. crissalis** (Salvin and God-
man): COLIMA WARBLER; ML. *crissalis*, "pertaining to the
crissum, the undertail coverts, which are yellow." **V. luciae**
(Cooper): LUCY'S WARBLER for Lucy Baird, daughter of
Spencer Baird (see Appendix). **V. peregrina** (Wilson): TEN-
NESSEE WARBLER; L. *peregrina*, "wandering," hence migratory. So named by Wilson who, having obtained only two
specimens in his lifetime, considered it a very rare bird. **V.
pinus** (Linnaeus): BLUE-WINGED WARBLER; L. *pinus*, "a
pine tree." Wilson says that William Bartram discovered the
bird and sent it to Edwards who confused it with the Pine
Creeper of Catesby and gave it an inappropriate name. Linnaeus copied the error. **V. ruficapilla** (Wilson): NASHVILLE
WARBLER; L. *rufus*, "reddish"; L. *capillus*, "hair"; for the

dull reddish crown of the male. **V. virginiae** (Baird): VIR-
GINIA'S WARBLER; for Mrs. Virginia Anderson, wife of Dr.
W. W. Anderson, a collector, who first found the bird (see
Appendix).

Vireo Vieillot. L. *vireo,* "a small bird, possibly the greenfinch.
V. altiloquus (Vieillot): BLACK-WHISKERED VIREO; L. *altus,*
"high"; ML. *loquus,* "chatterer," as the bird calls constantly
from the high trees. **V. atricapillus** Woodhouse: BLACK-
CAPPED VIREO; L. *atri,* "black"; L. *capilla,* "hair"; for the
black cap. **V. bellii** Audubon: BELL'S VIREO; for J. G. Bell
(see Appendix). **V. flavifrons** Vieillot: YELLOW-THROATED
VIREO; L. *flavus,* "yellow"; L. *frons,* in this case "front" for
the yellow throat. **V. gilvus** (Vieillot): WARBLING VIREO; L.
gilvus, "yellowish." **V. griseus** (Boddaert): WHITE-EYED VI-
REO; ML. *griseus,* "gray," not too apt. **V. huttoni** Cassin:
HUTTON'S VIREO; for William Hutton (see Appendix). **V.
olivaceus** (Linnaeus): RED-EYED VIREO; L. *olivaceus,* "olive-colored." **V. philadelphicus** (Cassin): PHILADELPHIA
VIREO; ML. *philadelphicus,* for the city within whose
boundaries the first specimen was found. **V. solitarius** (Wilson): SOLITARY VIREO; L. *solitarius,* "solitary." Wilson, who
first described the bird from one collected in Bartram's
Woods in Philadelphia, was familiar with the bird as a migrant under which circumstances it is generally seen alone.
Noting this fact most likely suggested the name to him. **V.
vicinior** Coues: GRAY VIREO; L. *vicinior,* "more neigh-
borly." Coues who named the bird said, "It is unnecessary
to compare *vicinior* with any other species, it is so very
dissimilar from them all." This rules out the supposition that
it was named for its close similarity to other vireos. So it is
possible that the name was suggested by the bird's constant,
pleasant and far-reaching song making it an easily recognized neighbor.

Wilsonia Bonaparte. For Alexander Wilson (see Appendix).
W. canadensis (Linnaeus): CANADA WARBLER; ML. *canadensis,* "Canadian," for most of the breeding range. **W.
citrina** (Boddaert): HOODED WARBLER; LL. *citrina,* "lemon-
colored." **W. pusilla** (Wilson): WILSON'S WARBLER; L. *pus-*

illa, "very small," though it is not noticeably so. There are twenty-four warblers that are larger, most of them by one quarter of an inch; seventeen the same size and four smaller.

Xanthocephalus Bonaparte. Gr. *xanthos,* "yellow"; Gr. *cephalos,* "head." **X. xanthocephalus** (Bonaparte): YELLOW-HEADED BLACKBIRD; a repetition.

Xema Leach. ML. *xema,* "name of an unknown bird." **X. sabini** (Sabine): SABINE'S GULL for Edward Sabine, named by his brother, Joseph (see Appendix).

Zenaida Bonaparte. For his wife, Zenaida (see Appendix under Zenaide). **Z. asiatica** (Linnaeus): WHITE-WINGED DOVE; L. *asiatica,* "Asian." Linnaeus based this bird on "the Brown Indian Dove" of Edwards whose specimen came, according to him, from "Indiis," though he should have indicated it was Jamaica in the West Indies. This unclear identification of the place possibly confused Linnaeus. **Z. aurita** (Temminck): ZENAIDA DOVE; L. *auritus,* "eared," for the dark line of feathers above and below the ear coverts which suggests an ear's outline. **Z. macroura** (Linnaeus): MOURNING DOVE; Gr. *macros,* "long"; Gr. *oura,* "tail." We suggest that the literal meaning "Zenaida's long tail" be taken to refer to the rear end of the bird, as this is its outstanding characteristic.

Zonotrichia Swainson. Gr. *zone,* "a band"; Gr. *trichias,* "a thrush." **Z. albicollis** (Gmelin): WHITE-THROATED SPARROW; L. *albus,* "white"; L. *collum,* "neck." Close but missed again as the bird has a white throat and not a white neck. Possibly Gmelin should not be blamed as he had to depend on the sometimes erratic Edwards who recorded that the specimen came from "Pensilvania." **Z. atricapilla** (Gmelin): GOLDEN-CROWNED SPARROW; L. *atrus,* "black"; L. *capilla,* "hair"; for the black band around the golden crown. **Z. leucophrys** (Forster): WHITE-CROWNED SPARROW; Gr. *leucos,* "white"; Gr. *ophrys,* "eyebrow"; for the white line that goes back over the eye. **Z. querula** (Nuttall): HARRIS' SPARROW; L. *querula,* "plaintive," for the whistle-like song.

Biographical Appendix

Abert, James William (1820–1897). Served in the United States Army as an officer, rising from lieutenant to major. While on duty in the southwestern part of the United States he collected birds, among which was the towhee named in his honor by Baird.

Adams, Edward (1824–1856). G. R. Gray in 1859 named the Yellow-billed Loon for "the late Mr. Adams, Surgeon of H.M.S. Enterprise, commanded by Capt. Collinson, in the voyage made by him through the Behring Straits." "Dr. Adams is reported to have died on the coast of Africa," says a note from Alexander Wetmore.

Aiken, Charles E. H. (1850–1936). A taxidermist who lived in Colorado Springs. He made contributions to ornithological publications.

Alexandre, Dr. We know only that he discovered the Black-chinned Hummingbird in the Sierra Madre of Mexico. Boucier and Mulsant named the species in his honor in 1846.

Allen, Charles Andrew (1841–1930). A collector in California who secured several new species. Henshaw described what he thought was a new species collected by Allen in 1877 and named it for him. When it was found that the hummingbird had been described in 1830, Allen's name was dropped from the scientific term but retained in the common one.

Anderson, Virginia. Mrs. William W. Anderson, nee Mary Virginia Childs. Her husband, Dr. William Wallace Anderson (1824–1911), a native of South Carolina, served as a surgeon in the United States Army from 1849 until his resignation in 1861, and in the Confederate Army until 1865 when the whole army resigned. While stationed in New Mexico in 1860, he discovered a new warbler named by Baird for Mrs. Anderson, which seems a roundabout way of honoring the bird's discoverer, although it was most likely done at her husband's request.

Anna, Duchess of Rivoli (1806–1896). Wife of Prince Victor Massena, son of Marshal André Massena, Duc de Rivoli and Prince d'Essling, a marshal of France under Napoleon. The type specimen of Anna's Hummingbird was in Prince Victor's collection. It was acquired by the Academy of Natural Sciences of Philadelphia in 1846. Lesson named the bird in her honor in 1829. Audubon, who met her in Paris in 1828, was impressed by her beauty and charm.

Audubon, John James (1785–1851). Audubon was born in Haiti, brought to France where he was legally adopted by his father, John Audubon, and educated. He came to America when eighteen years of age to manage his father's estate at Mill Grove on the outskirts of Philadelphia. Although remaining here only about a year, the two most important events in his life took place; he met his future wife, Lucy Bakewell, and developed his lifelong preoccupation with American birds. For forty years he roamed the country east of the Rocky Mountains making notes and drawing the birds. He visited England to raise funds and get help for publishing *Birds of America* (1827–1838). The illustrations and descriptions of birds were a monumental achievement and inspiration of lasting influence. His *Ornithological Biography* (1839) and *Synopsis of the Birds of North America* (1839) with MacGillivray established his reputation. In order to include in his work the birds west of the Rockies, he worked out an amicable arrangement with John Townsend to use his collection of western birds. During his career Audubon named dozens of birds, frequently honoring his friends and associates. Nuttall was so honored twice with a magpie and a poorwill, as was Bachman with a warbler and an oyster-catcher. Townsend was commemorated three times with a solitaire, a bunting and a fox sparrow. All were named for men who had befriended him or whom he admired. No bird bears the name of the one who did the most for him, his wife, Lucy. Northwood suggests that she may have been honored indirectly, as Baird's daughter was named for Lucy Audubon, and a warbler was named for Lucy Baird by J. G. Cooper in 1861.

Bachman, Dr. John (1790–1874). Dr. Bachman was a minister of Charleston, South Carolina, and a close friend of Audubon whose two sons married Bachman's daughters. Audubon named the warbler which Bachman discovered after him as well as the Black Oystercatcher and a sparrow. Audubon says, "My friend Bachman has the merit of having discovered this pretty little species of warbler, and to him I have the pleasure of acknowledging my obligations for the pair which you will find presented in the plate,—I myself have never had the good fortune to meet with any individuals of this interesting Sylvia."

Baird, Lucy Hunter (1848–1913). Daughter of Spencer F. Baird, q.v. When she was thirteen years old, Dr. J. G. Cooper named a warbler for her. She collected bibliographical material for her father which formed the basis for the book authored by Dr. W. H. Dall.

Baird, Spencer Fullerton (1823–1887). Baird was secretary of the Smithsonian Institution, first United States Fish Commissioner, and organizer of the zoological work of the Pacific Railroad Surveys. Author of *Catalogue of North American Mammals, Catalogue of North American Birds;* co-author with Brewer and Ridgway of *Land Birds* and *Water Birds.* He described and named several genera and many species of birds. This was done in the ninth volume of the *Pacific Railroad Reports.* Coues says, "This . . . volume, published in 1858, represents the most important and decided single step ever taken in North American ornithology in all that related to the technicalities of the science. It effected a revolution in classification and nomenclature, nearly all the names of our birds being changed in accordance with more modern usages in generic and specific determinations." Northwood relates, "As a boy of seventeen Baird wrote to Audubon about a new bird he had discovered, the Yellow-bellied Flycatcher. Audubon answered, offering to name it and asking for help in collecting species of small mammals for the 'Quadrupeds.' So started a friendship that lasted for the rest of Audubon's career. Baird visited Audubon in New York two years later and became a great friend of the family. Audubon wanted Baird to come with him on the Missouri expedition, but the boy could not get permission from his family." Concerning Baird's Sparrow, Aubudon says, "I have named this species after my young friend, Spencer F. Baird, of Carlisle, Pennsylvania." Coues also named a sandpiper for him.

Barrow, Sir John (1764–1848). A native of England, Secretary of the Admiralty, founder of the Royal Geographical Society and a promoter of Arctic exploration. He was the author of "Historic Arctic Voyages" (1818) and other works. We find his name in Point Barrow and Barrow's Straits. Swainson named Barrow's Goldeneye for him, but the scientific name was preempted although the popular name has been retained. His name is still valid in the scientific name of a subspecies of the Glaucous Gull.

Bartram, William (1739–1823). Called the "Grandfather of American Ornithology" mainly because of his influence on Alexander Wilson. His book of travels as a naturalist was his chief work. His father, John, was world famous as a botanist.

Bell, John Graham (1812–1889). A famous taxidermist of New York who accompanied Aubudon on his Missouri River trip in 1843. Later in California he collected several new species of birds described by Cassin. Bell's Vireo and the Sage Sparrow were named for him.

Bendire, Charles Emil (1836–1897). While an officer in the United States Army, he collected in the west. He was Curator of Oology in the United States National Museum. He was the author of *Life Histories of North American Birds*. Coues named a thrasher in his honor.

Bewick, Thomas (1754–1828). English author and wood engraver, wrote and illustrated *A History of British Birds*. Audubon says, "I honored this species (Bewick's Wren) with the name of Bewick, a person too well known for his admirable talents as an engraver on wood, and for his beautiful work on the *Birds of Great Britain*, to need any eulogy of mine. I have enjoyed the pleasure of a personal acquaintance with him, and found him at all times a most agreeable, kind and benevolent friend."

Blackburn, Anna (1740–1793). "Mrs." according to both Coues and Bent, which raises a question as her brother was Ashton Blackburn. Possibly she married a cousin or retained her maiden name for business purposes. She was a patron of ornithology and had a museum in Fairfield, Lancashire, England. Her brother Ashton collected in the United States before his death in 1780. Possibly he sent the specimen to England which for some time bore her name. She did, nevertheless, achieve scientific ornithological immortality by having her name attached to a type of rail in 1789, which so far the law of priority has not displaced.

Bonaparte, Charles Lucien Jules Laurent, Prince of Canino and Musignano (1803–1857). Naturalist. He was one of eleven children of Lucien, a younger brother to Napoleon. His wife Zenaide q.v., was the daughter of Joseph, Napoleon's older brother, and therefore Charles' cousin. With the decline in the family fortunes after Waterloo, Charles, Zenaide, and uncle/father-in-law, Joseph, came to America where they lived in Bordentown, New Jersey and Philadelphia, Pennsylvania. Here the first of the couple's eight children were born. While residing in the United States from 1822 until 1828, he re-edited a volume with the longest title in American ornithology even without appending the full names of the author, *American Ornithology, or History of*

Birds Inhabiting the United States not given by Wilson. He is considered to be the father of systematic ornithology in America. His name is commemorated in Bonaparte's Gull.

Botteri, Matteo (1808–1877). Born in Yugoslavia, he lived in Mexico from 1854 until his death. The sparrow named for him by Sclater was presumably collected by him near Orizaba in southern Mexico.

Brandt, Johaan Friedrich (1802–1879). An eminent German zoologist who became head of the Zoological Museum at St. Petersburg. He described several birds and mammals from western United States and mammals from western United States and the Pacific coast. The common name of a west coast cormorant commemorates him.

Brewer, Thomas Mayo (1814–1880). Boston publisher and editor. He was well known for his work on *North American Oology* (1857) and was a champion of the House Sparrow upon its introduction in the United States.

Buller, Sir Walter Lawry (1838–1906). A native of New Zealand and a lawyer by profession who became one of the leading authorities on New Zealand birds. He spent the latter part of his life in England. Although Buller never visited America, the New Zealand Shearwater, named for him, appears on the west coast of the United States.

Bullock, William (1775–1840). English traveler and mine owner, proprietor of Bullock's Museum in London. While visiting a mine near Mexico City, he collected a number of birds new to science. Swainson described these and named in his honor Bullock's Oriole, *Icterus galbula bullockii,* now a subspecies.

Cabot, Dr. Samuel (1815–1885). A physician, he was also Curator of the Department of Ornithology at the Boston Society of Natural History. On expedition to Yucatán in the 1840s, he made important ornithological collections and discovered several new species. He described Cabot's Tern as a new species, but it has since been relegated to subspecific status. Most of his work was published in the "Proceedings" and "Journal" of the Boston Society of Natural

History. His ornithological collection is now in the Harvard Museum of Comparative Zoology.

Cassin, John (1813–1869). Curator of Ornithology at the Academy of Natural Sciences of Philadelphia, the institution with which he was connected for twenty-six years. He was one of the leading systematists of his time, possessing what was then rather unusual in this country, a broad knowledge of foreign birds. In all he described 193 species of birds. Many of these were done in connection with the ornithological reports of government expeditions including the Wilkes Exploring Expedition Around the World, the Gillis Astronomical Expedition to Peru and the Perry Expedition to Japan which he accompanied. Several birds have been named in his honor. *Cassinia,* the journal of the Delaware Valley Ornithological Club, also commemorates him.

Clark, Captain William (1770–1838). With his fellow captain in the United States Army, he led the famous expedition which crossed the country in 1804–1806. Shortly after the return of the expedition, he resigned from the army and became the governor of the Missouri Territory. He was a brother of George Rogers Clark, the famous Indian fighter. The diary of Lewis and Clark, *History of the Expedition under the Command of Captains Lewis and Clark,* was published in 1814. Clark's Nutcracker was named for him.

Cooper, William C. (1798–1864). One of the founders of the New York Lyceum of Natural History. He described the Evening Grosbeak. Cooper's Hawk was named in his honor. He was the father of Dr. James C. Cooper, a noted California ornithologist.

Cory, Charles Barney (1857–1921). American ornithologist who was with the Field Museum in Chicago after 1906. He described the shearwater whose common name commemorates him.

Costa, Louis Marie Pantaleon, Marquis de Beau-Regard (1806–1864). This French nobleman began to collect birds and minerals in his boyhood. He later specialized in hummingbirds gathering together an imposing collection. In recognition of this interest, Bourcier in 1839 named a species *Calypte costae* in his honor.

Couch, General Darius Nash (1822–1897). A graduate of the U.S. Military Academy, who participated in the Mexican War and later took a leave of absence in order to lead a zoological expedition to northern Mexico. He is better known as a general in the Civil War.

Coues, Dr. Elliot (1842–1899). Served as a surgeon in the United States Army (1864–1881). He was the author of *Birds of the Colorado Valley, Birds of the Northwest, Key to North American Birds* and many papers. He served on the committee that prepared the first and second editions of the A.O.U. *Check-list of North American Birds.* Coues' Flycatcher bears his name.

Coues, Grace Darlington (1847–1939). Dr. Elliott Coues, while stationed at Fort Whipple near Prescott, Arizona, in 1865 collected a new warbler. He requested his friend Spencer Baird to name it in honor of his sister and this was done. Miss Coues married Charles Albert Page, one time United States Minister to Switzerland, and after his death, Dana Estes, a publisher.

Craveri, Frederico (1815–1890). An Italian scientist of wide interests (chemistry, meterology, mineralogy, zoology). In 1840 he went to Mexico where he assisted in the school of chemistry in the University in Mexico City. During his twenty years in the country he traveled widely, collecting minerals and animals. While on a trip with his brother to examine the guano deposits on islands off the west coast of Baja California, he collected a murrelet which twenty years later Sclater named in his honor. His last thirty years were spent teaching in Turin, Italy.

Degland, Dr. Come Damien (1787–1856). Director of the Museum d'Histoire Naturelle in Lille, France. He was the author of several publications on European birds. Bonaparte in 1850 named the White-winged Scoter in his honor.

Díaz Agustín (1829–1893). Director of the Geographical and Exploring Commission of Mexico which made extensive natural history collections in that country. Ridgway, who described the birds collected in 1886, named the Mexican Duck *Anas diazi* in his honor.

Fischer, Gotthelf (1771–1853). German naturalist and chemist who was professor of Natural History in Moscow about 1804. He was the author of works on natural history and anatomy. The Spectacled Eider bears his name.

Forster, Johann Reinhold (1729–1798). Accompanied Captain Cook on his voyage around the world in 1772. He wrote *Observations made during a Voyage around the World* in 1778. His ornithological fame rests on a treatise on the birds of Hudson Bay for which Nuttall commemorated him by naming a tern in his honor. His son, Johann Georg Adam Forster, was on the voyage with Captain Cook and also published a book, *A Voyage Around the World*.

Franklin, Sir John (1786–1847). British navigator and explorer who perished on his fourth Arctic expedition. He served at Trafalgar and New Orleans. His wife fitted out several ships to search for him. It was finally determined his ship was abandoned and his whole party lost. Franklin's Gull bears his name.

Gambel, William (1819–1849). A protégé of Nuttall who crossed the continent first in 1841. He was the first ornithologist to spend several years in California collecting and describing birds. The Mountain Chickadee and a quail bear his name. He died of typhoid fever while attempting to cross the Sierra in mid-winter.

Hammond, William Alexander (1828–1900). He was Surgeon-General of the United States Army from 1862 until 1864, when he was court-martialed and dismissed, but reinstated in 1878. Through him John Xantus met Spencer Baird and was given an opportunity to do zoological field work in the West. He repaid Hammond by naming a flycatcher for him that was collected at Fort Tejon in California.

Harcourt, Edwin Vernon (1825–1891). An English naturalist who discovered and described in his book, *Sketch of Madeira,* the petrel *Thalassidroma castro* in 1851. "In recognition of his work, the bird was given its common name," according to Alexander Wetmore.

Harlan, Dr. Richard (1796–1843). A prominent physician and naturalist. He was the author of *Fauna Americana,* published in 1825. Audubon says, "Long before I discovered this fine hawk, I was anxious to have an opportunity of honoring some new species of the feathered tribe with the name of my excellent friend Dr. Richard Harlan of Philadelphia. This I might have done sooner, had I not waited until a species should occur, which in size and importance should bear some proportion to my gratitude toward that learned and accomplished friend." And so we have Harlan's Hawk.

Harris, Edward (1799–1863). A companion of Audubon on his Missouri trip in 1843, whom Audubon called "one of the best friends I have in the world." Audubon named a sparrow, a woodpecker and a hawk for him. Although the birds are now classified as subspecies, Harris' name is used for the common name of Harris' Hawk. The woodpecker is a subspecies of the Hairy Woodpecker. In naming this bird Audubon says, "Having been left at liberty to give names to whatever species might occur among the birds transmitted to me by that zealous naturalist (John Townsend), I have honored the present woodpecker with the name of my friend Edward Harris, Esq., a gentleman to whom I am most deeply indebted for many acts of kindness and generosity, and in particular for his efficient aid at a time when, like my predecessor Wilson, I was reduced to the lowest degree of indigence and removed from any individuals to whom I could make known my wants. But, independently of his claim to scientific recognition as the friend and supporter of one who has devoted his life to the study of birds, he merits this tribute as an ardent and successful cultivator of ornithology. . . ."

Heermann, Dr. Adolphus L. (1818–1865). He was an active collector in the western part of the United States and a surgeon naturalist on one of the Pacific Railroad surveys in 1853–1854. Interested particularly in bird eggs, he is credited with introducing the term, "oology." A gull and a song sparrow commemorate him.

Henslow, John Stevens (1796–1861). English botanist, compiler of *Catalogue of British Plants* and *Dictionary of Botanical Terms*. Audubon, in naming the sparrow, says, "In naming it after the Rev. Professor Henslow of Cambridge, a gentleman so well-known in the scientific world, and who has permitted me so to designate it, my object has been to manifest my gratitude for the many kind attentions which he has shown towards me." Henslow was Professor of Botany at the University of Cambridge and helped Audubon obtain the subscription of the University to the "Birds." He recommended Charles Darwin as a naturalist and introduced him to Captain Fitz Roy of the Beagle.

Holboell, Carl Peter (1795–1856). An officer in the Danish Royal Navy, he served as Royal Inspector of Colonies and Whaling and Governor of South Greenland. While in this post he became interested in natural history. He described the Hoary Redpoll, which he named for Hornemann. At one time the Gyrfalcon and the Red-necked Grebe bore his name. Reclassification necessitated changes in nomenclature, causing Holboell's name to be pushed aside as a species name. His name continued to be used as the common name for the grebe until Red-necked, approved by the A.O.U. *Check-list* Committee, gradually took over.

Hornemann, Jens Wilken (1770–1841). Danish scientist and professor at the University of Copenhagen.

Hutton, William. A little known field collector who obtained birds about Washington, D.C. in 1844, 1845 and 1857. He collected in California in 1847 and 1848, where he obtained the vireo that John Cassin named for him.

Kennicott, Mjr. Robert (1835–1866). A founder of the Chicago Academy of Science who collected and explored in northwestern North America. He died on the banks of the Yukon at Fort Nulato, Alaska.

Kirtland, Dr. Jared Potter (1793–1877). A prominent physician and naturalist of Cleveland, Ohio, who founded the Cleveland Medical College. Spencer Baird named the warbler first found near Cleveland in his honor.

Kittlitz, Friedrich Heinrich (1779–1874). A German Naval Officer and explorer whose account of his work in Kamchatka and Alaska was published in 1858. The last twenty-five years of his life were spent at Mainz, where he was probably connected with the university there. Kittlitz Murrelet was first collected by him.

Lawrence, George Newbold (1806–1895). Lawrence worked with Baird and Cassin describing the birds collected on the Pacific Railroad Surveys, mainly the water birds. Cassin named in his honor the goldfinch which bears his name.

Leach, William Elford (1790–1836). An English naturalist who developed a system of arrangement in conchology and entomology. He acquired the specimen of petrel, which was named for him, in a sale of a collection of Bullock's specimens.

LeConte, Dr. John (1818–1891). A native of Georgia, he turned from the practice of medicine to teaching physics and chemistry, mainly in southern colleges from which he took a respite to operate a gunpowder factory in South Carolina during the Civil War. He resumed his academic career teaching physics at the University of California at Berkeley of which he was president from 1875 till 1881. Coues refers to him as Major LeConte, a rank he probably held while supervising the production of anti-Yankee detonation chemicals. The common name of a sparrow commemorates him. He and John L. LeConte were first cousins.

LeConte, Dr. John Lawrence (1825–1883). A leading entomologist in the United States, who specialized in Coleoptera. He was also interested in birds and had a thrasher named for him. Independently wealthy, he never practiced medicine. He was president of the American Association for the Advancement of Science.

Lesson, Clemence, wife of Rene P. Lesson (1794–1849). A French naturalist who originally described the Blue-throated Hummingbird, *Lampornis clemenciae*, and named it for "notre épouse," his wife.

Lewis, Captain Meriwether (1774–1809). One of the leaders of the Lewis and Clark Expedition which crossed the West in 1804–1806 but paused long enough on Saturday, July 20, 1805, near Helena, Montana, to collect a woodpecker. Wilson in describing it named the bird in honor of Lewis. Although the original name has been changed somewhat, the "Lewis" has been maintained. The bird is preserved in Harvard's Museum of Comparative Zoology and may be the only specimen of that famed expedition still extant.

L'Herminier, Dr. Ford J. (1802–1866) and Felix L. (1779–1833). Son and father who lived on Guadeloupe in the West Indies. Audubon's Shearwater was named either for one or both of them.

Lichtenstein, Martin Henrich (1780–1857). German zoologist and traveler, and founder of the Berlin Zoo. An oriole was named for him by Wagler, another German zoologist.

Lincoln, Thomas (1812–1883). When twenty-one years old he accompanied Audubon on his trip to the coast of Labrador. A new sparrow was found and as this was discovered by Lincoln, Audubon named it for him.

MacDougall, Dr. Patrick (1770–1817). Dr. MacDougall of Glasgow, Scotland, obtained the first specimen of the Roseate Tern in the Cumbrey Islands in the Firth of Clyde in 1812. For this he is honored by having the last part of his name, "Dougall," given to the bird.

MacGillivray, William (1796–1852). Author of *A History of British Birds* (five volumes). Of him, Northwood says, "He agreed to revise and correct Audubon's proof for two guineas for each sheet of sixteen pages, about six dollars today. He was well grounded in the anatomy of birds, and Audubon was fortunate to have obtained the services of so able and diligent a worker, who originated modern classification based on anatomy. When the work was well in hand Audubon and his family toured the lowlands of Scotland with MacGillivray as guide."

Mauri, Prof. Ernesto (1791–1836). An Italian naturalist connected with the Botanical Gardens in Rome, Cabanis named the Western Sandpiper in his honor in 1858.

McCown, John P. (1815–1879). The following is from *Life Histories of North American Cardinals, Grosbeaks, Buntings, Towhees, Finches, Sparrows and Their Allies* by Bent, p. 1564: "'I fired at a flock of Shore Larks,' writes

Captain John P. McCown, U.S.A. (1851), 'and found this bird among the killed.' For this, in the first published description of the bird, George N. Lawrence (1851) announced, 'It gives me pleasure to bestow upon this species the name of my friend, Capt. J. P. McCown, U.S.A.'" He served in the U.S. Army, 1840–1869.

McGregor, Richard Crittenden (1871–1936). Came to America from Australia in the eighties, and after collecting birds in California, he was appointed ornithologist in the Bureau of Science at Manila in the Philippines. He published numerous papers on the birds of the Philippines when editor of the *Philippine Journal of Science*. In 1920 he published a condensed *Index to the Genera of Birds of the World*. In 1897 A. W. Anthony named the House Finch, *Carpodacus mcgregori,* in his honor.

McKay, Charles Leslie (?–1883). The following paragraph is from *Birds of Alaska* by Ira N. Gabrielson and Frederick C. Lincoln, p. 12: "Charles Leslie McKay, another Signal Corps man who was stationed at Bristol Bay, also was active in collecting birds. He arrived at Nushagak, then known as Fort Alexander, in the spring of 1881. He continued active until April 19, 1883, when he was drowned in Bristol Bay after a small boat, in which he was traveling, capsized. During this period he collected about 400 specimens which were sent to the National Museum where many are still available. Among others, he secured the first specimens of the bird now known as McKay's Snow Bunting." The common name of this species, but not the scientific one, bears his name.

Neboux, Dr. Adolphe Simon. Little is known about Neboux except that he was Surgeon Major on the French exploring vessel *Venus,* which visited the coast of California in the course of a cruise extending from 1836 to 1839. The Blue-footed Booby named in his honor in 1882 by Milne-Edwards, the eminent French zoologist, was possibly based on a specimen collected on the *Venus* expedition.

Nuttall, Thomas (1786–1859). Born in England, he came to the United States in 1808. He was first interested in botany and was Curator of the Botanical Gardens at Harvard (1822–1832). Later devoting himself to ornithology, he authored *A Manual of the Ornithology of the United States and Canada*, of which Coues says, "Nuttall, like good wine, does not deteriorate with age." On a trip to California by boat he may be identified as the naturalist, Old Curious, in Richard Henry Dana's *Two Years before the Mast*. His name appears in a genus, *Nuttallornis*, and three species; a woodpecker, a poorwill and a magpie as well as a subspecies of sparrow. Audubon, in naming the Yellow-billed Magpie in his honor, says, "I have conferred on this beautiful bird the name of a most zealous, learned and enterprising naturalist, my friend Thomas Nuttall, Esq., to whom the scientific world is deeply indebted for many additions to our zoological and botanical knowledge which have resulted from his labors." Succeeding to an inheritance, he returned to England.

Oberholser, Dr. Harry Church (1870–1963). A leading American systematist who revised some groups and described a very large number of new species and subspecies. His name was commemorated by Phillips when he described the Dusky Flycatcher. After his retirement from the Fish and Wildlife Service, he was Curator of Ornithology at the Cleveland Museum of Natural History.

Paris brothers. They were dealers in natural history specimens in Paris in 1837 when Bonaparte named what is now known as Scott's Oriole for them. They quite likely financed scientific collecting expeditions as part of their business.

Ridgway, Robert (1850–1929). He was on the staff of the Smithsonian Institution in charge of bird collections from 1869 to 1880 and Curator of Birds of the United States National Museum from 1880 to 1929. He served on the committees that published the first, second and third editions of the American Ornithologists' Union *Check-list of North American Birds*. He also served as president of that organization. With Spencer F. Baird and Thomas M. Brewer he wrote *A History of North American Birds* (5 vols., I–III, 1874; IV–V, 1884). He was sole author of *Color Standards and Nomenclature* (1886), *The Birds of North and Middle America* (8 vols., 1901–1919) and many papers. A whip-poor-will bears his name.

Rivoli, Victor Massena, Duc de (1798–1863). Son of one of Napoleon's marshals and owner of an extensive collection of hummingbirds. Lesson named one for him but it was preempted by the name given by Swainson two years earlier, so the scientific name did not stand although the common name has done so. See Anna, Duchess of Rivoli, for another hummingbird, honoring Rivoli's wife.

Ross, Bernard Rogan (1827–1874). Chief factor of the Hudson Bay Company and a correspondent of the Smithsonian Institution. Cassin named the Little Snow Goose for him.

Ross, Sir James Clark (1800–1862). This Scottish polar explorer made several Arctic expeditions and one Antarctic one. With his uncle, Sir John Ross, he determined the position of the North Magnetic Pole. He published *Voyage of Discovery* (1847). Ross' Gull was named in his honor.

Sabine, Sir Edward (1788–1883). An eminent English astronomer and physicist, president of the British Association for the Advancement of Science and of the Royal Society. On a voyage to the Arctic in 1819 with the Ross and Perry expedition as astronomer, a fork-tailed gull was obtained near Melville Bay on the west coast of Greenland. This bird was named in his honor by his brother, Joseph, who in turn is commemorated by having his name attached to one of ten subspecies of the Ruffed Grouse.

Say, Thomas (1787–1843). He accompanied Major Stephen H. Long's expedition to the Rocky Mountains in 1819–1820 as a naturalist and prepared its report on the birds. He was a pioneer in the field of entomology and the author of *American Entomology*, a three-volume work describing the insects of North America, published 1824–1828. The genus *Sayornis* and Say's Phoebe commemorate him.

Sclater, Dr. P. L. (1829–1913). A fellow of the Royal Society, Secretary of the Zoological Society of London (1859–1903). He contributed several volumes to the *Catalogue of*

Birds of the British Museum. The scientific name of the Mexican Chickadee commemorates him.

Scott, Winfield (1786–1866). Commander of the American forces in the Mexican War. In 1854, Couch, one of his lieutenants, thought he found a new bird and described it under the name *Icterus scottii,* but Bonaparte had named it *parisorum* seventeen years previously. The common name, however, has been kept.

Smith, Gideon B. (1793–1867). Audubon, a friend of Smith, gave the common name to Smith's Longspur in honor of his Baltimore friend and editor.

Sprague, Isaac (1811–1895). An artist who accompanied Audubon on his Missouri River trip. Audubon named a pipit for him, saying, "The first specimen of this truly interesting lark was procured by Mr. Isaac Sprague, another of my companions."

Steller, George Wilhelm (1709–1746). A German naturalist who accompanied Vitus Bering, the Danish navigator who was employed by Russia to determine whether or not the coasts of Siberia and Alaska were contiguous. Bering died when the expedition was wintering on Bering Island in 1741–1742. Steller wrote an account of his travels and described birds and mammals, among them Steller's sea cow (extinct) and Steller's sea lion. An eider and jay bear his name. He died in Tiumen, Siberia.

Strickland, Hugh Edwin (1811–1853). An English naturalist, son-in-law of Sir William Jardine. An early taxonomist, it was he who proposed the genus *Cyanocitta* for crested jays. Several birds bear his name.

Swainson, William (1789–1855). Widely traveled and versatile naturalist. Visited the shores of the Mediterranean and South America. He collected, illustrated, and wrote. Among his principal works are *Zoological Illustrations or Original Figures and Descriptions of New, Rare or Interesting Animals* (six volumes); eleven volumes in Lardner's *Cabinet Encyclopedia;* three volumes in Jardine's *Naturalist's Library;* and other works. He wrote on molluscs, fish and animals. Audubon met him in England and was helped by his favorable reviews. They traveled to Paris together and met Cuvier and other French scientists. Audubon failed to obtain Swainson's services as joint author in describing birds. Swainson emigrated to New Zealand in 1841 where he became attorney general. Audubon named a warbler for him and Bonaparte a hawk. We also have his name in the common name for a thrush.

Thayer, John Eliot (1862–1933). An outstanding patron of ornithology who assembled a large collection of birds and a comprehensive ornithological library. His collection is in Harvard University's Museum of Comparative Zoology. The gull named for him has been restored to specific status.

Tolmie, Dr. William Fraser (1818–1886). A physician, educated in Scotland, he was assigned by the Hudson Bay Company to Fort Vancouver in 1833. He was the first to describe a climb on the summit of Mount Ranier. In 1836 he met Townsend, q.v., who discovered a new warbler which he named in Tolmie's honor. Audubon, thinking he was making an initial description, named the bird for MacGillivray. As Townsend's publication preceded Audubon's, the scientific name reverted although the common name has been retained. Tolmie became chief factor in Vancouver for the Hudson Bay Company in 1856 and retired in 1860.

Townsend, John Kirk (1809–1851). Much admired by contemporary ornithologists, he is best known for his *Narrative of a Journey across the Rocky Mountains*. In this he described some of the new birds he found and sent them as specimens, along with some he did not describe, to Audubon, who states he was given "the liberty to name whatever new specimens might occur." This caused confusion in naming MacGillivray's Warbler (see Tolmie, Dr. William Fraser). Audubon wrote of another bird, the Solitaire, "Transmitted to me by my friend, Mr. Townsend, after whom, not finding any description of it, I have named it." This seems to indicate not only that Audubon became a bit more wary in naming birds, but also that the "Tolmie" episode caused no animosity, especially as Audubon also named a bunting for him. It seems that when Townsend was about to publish a description of a new warbler, he found out that Nuttall was about to do the same thing, and had named the warbler for him. Townsend decided that Nuttall's manuscript had priority and that the name should stand. Thus, although he is recorded as its describer, Townsend cannot be charged with naming a bird in his own honor, even if he worked the law of priority a bit overtime.

Traill, Dr. Thomas Stewart (1781–1862). A founder of the Royal Institution of Liverpool, where Audubon visited him and in return for his support said, "I have named this species (Traill's Flycatcher) after my learned friend, Dr. Thomas Stewart Traill, of Edinburgh, in evidence of the gratitude which I cherish toward that gentleman for all his kind attention to me." He became professor of medical jurisprudence at the University of Edinburgh and edited the eighth edition of the *Encyclopedia Britannica*. By exposing the neglect of the Natural History Museum when it was part of the British Museum, he was instrumental in the establishment of the independent Museum of Natural History in South Kensington.

Trudeau, James deBertz (1817–1887). A physician and friend of Audubon, with whom he became acquainted during Audubon's stay in Louisiana. Audubon named the White-winged Dove for him, but his name has been dropped for this bird. It remains, however, in Trudeau's Tern, the type specimen of which he procured for Audubon.

Vallisnieri, Antonio (1661–1730). Italian naturalist, professor of medicine at the University of Padua. Wilson named the Canvasback after one of its main foods, the wild celery *Vallisnieri americana,* which was named in honor of the Italian naturalist.

Vaux, William S. (1811–1882). A member of the Academy of Natural Sciences of Philadelphia and a friend of John K. Townsend, who named a swift he had discovered on the Columbia River in his honor.

Verreaux, J. B. Edouard (1810–1868). A French naturalist

who worked in South Africa (1828–1830) and in China (1832–1837).

Verreaux, Jules P. (1807–1873). Brother of J. B. Edouard. Worked in South Africa (1818–1820), China (1825–1830), the Philippines (1832–1839), and Australia (1842–1847). Bonaparte honored the brothers by naming the White-fronted Dove for them.

Whitney, Josiah Dwight (1819–1896). An eminent American geologist. While he was director of the Geographical Survey of California, a member of his staff, Dr. James G. Cooper, whose father already had a hawk named for him, found a new Elf Owl which he named for the head of the survey, Dr. Whitney.

Wied, Prince Maximilian zu (1782–1867). A German naturalist and traveler who wrote *Journey to Brazil* (1815–1817) and *Journey to Interior of North America* (1832–1834). His name was given to Wied's Crested Flycatcher.

Williamson, Robert Stockton (1824–1882). A lieutenant in the United States Army in charge of the Pacific Railroad Survey in northern California and Oregon. Dr. Newberry, the surgeon on the survey, collected what he thought to be specimens of a new woodpecker, which he named in honor of the leader of the expedition. These specimens, which happened to be all males, were collected in 1857. Six years before this Cassin collected specimens of a new woodpecker which he named *thyroideus*. These specimens happened to be all females, a fact that became evident when *thyroideus* and *williamsonii* were found to be connubially cooperative. So the *williamsonii* was dropped, not in deference to the fair sex, but to the rule of priority. The common name knowing no such restriction has been retained in Williamson's Sapsucker.

Wilson, Alexander (1766–1813). Born in Scotland, the "Father of American Ornithology" came to the United States in 1794. While teaching school in Philadelphia, his interest in birds was encouraged by William Bartram. Traveling throughout the eastern United States collecting birds, he meticulously noted range, habitat and behavior. His observations were published in his nine-volume *American Ornithology* (1808–1814) which was completed by George Ord. Many of the specimens originally described by him in this classic still retain their validity. He was prone to name birds for the places where he found them. A storm-petrel, a plover, a warbler and a genus of warblers bear his name. It has been said that his contemporary, Audubon, was a great artist with a talent for ornithology, but that Wilson was a great ornithologist with artistic talent.

Wollweber. An obscure German naturalist who collected the first specimen of the Bridled Titmouse in Zacatecas, Mexico, which Bonaparte described and named for him.

Wright, Charles (1811–1855). A self-taught botanist who collected plants for Asa Gray of Harvard in Texas, Cuba, Africa, China and Japan. He accompanied the Exploratory Team for the Pacific Railroad as a botanist. When Baird described the new birds found on the railroad survey he named the Gray Flycatcher in Wright's honor. Possibly Wright collected the original specimen.

Xántus de Vesey, Louis Jonas (commonly known as John Xantus) (1825–1894). Born in Hungary, he came to the United States as a young man and enlisted in the army. Stationed as a hospital steward at Fort Tejon, California, he described two new species of birds from his large collection in that area. Later he collected on the Baja California coast and about Colima, Mexico, where he was the United States Consul. He returned to Hungary as custodian of the museum in Budapest, traveled to the East Indies and was active in the International Ornithological Congress in Vienna in 1884. A murrelet and several other birds bear his name.

Zenaide, Princess Zenaide Charlotte Julie Bonaparte (1804–1854). Cousin and wife of Charles Lucien Jules Laurent Bonaparte, Prince of Canino and Musignano, whom she married in 1822 on the eve of their departure for the United States. Here they lived in Bordentown, New Jersey and Philadelphia, Pennsylvania, with her father, Joseph, king of

Spain (1808–1813) till 1828, when they returned to Europe. The close association of mated pairs that gave rise to the old common name of "love bird" for the dove may be the reason Bonaparte wished to link the name of his wife to this ornithological symbol of conjugal bliss. Her name is preserved in the generic name *Zenaida*.

Bibliography

American Ornithologists' Union. *Check-list of North American Birds*. Fifth ed. Baltimore: American Ornithologists' Union, 1957.

American Ornithologists' Union. *Check-list of North American Birds*. Sixth ed. Lawrence, KS: American Ornithologist's Union, 1983.

Audubon, John James. *American Ornithological Biography*. Edinburgh: Adam Black, 1831.

Auk, The. Journal of the American Ornithologists' Union. Washington, D.C. Particularly the Thirty-second Supplement to the *Check-list of North American Birds,* vol. 90, pp. 411–419, 1973.

Bent, Arthur Cleveland. *Life Histories of North American Birds*. 26 vols. New York: Dover Publications, 1961–1968.

British Ornithologists' Union. *Check-list of the Birds of Great Britain and Ireland*. London, 1952.

British Ornithologists' Union. *The Status of Birds in Britain and Ireland*. London: Blackwell, 1971.

Bullfinch, Thomas. *The Age of Fable*. Philadelphia: David McKay, 1898.

Catesby, Mark. *Natural History of Carolina, Florida and the Bahama Islands,* 1731.

Chaucer, Geoffrey. *The Works of Chaucer.* Globe ed. New York: Macmillan, 1919.

Coble, Mary F. *Introduction to Ornithological Nomenclature.* Los Angeles: American Book Institute, 1954.

Coues, Elliott. *Key to North American Birds.* Sixth ed. Boston: The Page Company, 1927.

Darwin, Charles. *The Origin of Species and the Descent of Man,* 1859. New York: Modern Library, new edition.

Driver, Samuel Rolles. *The International Critical Commentary,* section on Deuteronomy. New York: Scribner, 1902.

Eaton, Elon Howard. *Birds of New York.* Albany: New York State Museum, Memoir 12, 1914.

Eisenmann, E., and H. H. Poor. "Suggested Principles of Vernacular Nomenclature." *Wilson Bulletin* 58 (1946): 210–215.

Ellis, Edward S. *Classical Dictionary.* Philadelphia: Penn Publishing Co., 1895.

Evans, A. H. *Turner on Birds.* Cambridge: Cambridge University Press, 1903.

Fisher, James A. *The Shell Bird Book.* London: Ebury Press & Michael Joseph, 1966.

Fisher, James A. "Systematics," in *A History of Birds.* Boston: Houghton Mifflin Co., 1954.

Francis, W. Nelson. "Revolution in Grammar." *Quarterly Journal of Speech,* October 1954.

Greenough, James B., and George L. Kittredge. *Words and Their Ways in English Speech.* New York: Macmillan, 1920.

Grossman, Mary Louise, and John Hamlet. *Birds of Prey of the World.* New York: Clarkson N. Potter, Inc., 1964.

Gruson, Edward S. *Words for Birds. A Lexicon of North American Birds with Biographical Notes.* New York: Quadrangle Books, 1972.

Harting, James Edmund, and Grundy Steiner, ed. *The Birds of Shakespeare.* Chicago: Argonaut, 1965.

Ingersoll, Ernest. "An Adventure in Etymology." *The Scientific*

Monthly, 45, no. 3 (1937): 233–249.

Innes, Mary M. *The Metamorphoses of Ovid.* Baltimore: The Penguin Classics, 1955.

International Ornithological Congress. *XII, Proceedings.* Helsinki (1958): 30–43.

Jaeger, Edmund O. *A Source Book of Biological Names and Terms.* Second edition. Springfield, IL: Charles C. Thomas, 1950.

Jordan, David Starr. *Manual of the Vertebrate Animals of the Northeastern United States.* Thirteenth ed. Yonkers on Hudson, NY: World Book Company, 1929.

MacLeod, R. D. *Key to the Names of British Birds.* London and New York: Sir Isaac Pinman & Sons, 1954.

Mayr, Ernst. *Systematics and the Origin of Species.* New York: Columbia University Press, 1942.

Newton, Alfred, assisted by Hans Gadow. *A Dictionary of Birds.* London: Adam Black, 1896.

Northwood, J. d'Arcy. "Audubon's Firsts." *The Atlantic Naturalist,* 11, no. 5 (1956): 222–229.

Nybakken, Oscar E. *Greek and Latin Scientific Terminology.* Ames, IA: Iowa State College Press, 1959.

Oxford Dictionary of English Etymology. New York: Oxford University Press, 1966.

Oxford English Dictionary. New York: Oxford University Press, 1933.

Palmer, T. S. "Notes on Persons Whose Names Appear in the Nomenclature of California Birds." *The Condor* 30, no. 5 (1928): 261–307.

Peterson, Roger Tory. *A Field Guide to the Birds.* Boston: Houghton Mifflin Co., 1947.

Peterson, Roger Tory. *A Field Guide to Western Birds.* Boston: Houghton Mifflin Co., 1941.

Peterson, Roger Tory. *A Field Guide to Birds of Texas.* Boston: Houghton Mifflin Co., 1960.

Peterson, Roger Tory, Guy Mountfort, and P. A. D. Hollom. *A Field Guide to the Birds of Britain and Europe.* Boston: Houghton Mifflin Co., 1954.

Robbins, Chandler S., Bertel Bruun, and Herbert S. Zim.

Birds of North America. New York: Golden Press, 1966.

Salomonsen, F. *Report of the Standing Committee on Ornithological Nomenclature, 1960.*

Skeat, Walter W. *A Concise Etymological Dictionary of the English Language*. Oxford: Oxford University Press, 1882.

Stout, Gardner D., ed. *The Shorebirds of North America*. New York: The Viking Press, 1967.

Swann, H. Kirke. *A Dictionary of English and Folk Names of British Birds*. London: Witherby & Co., 1913.

Thomson, A. Landsborough. *A New Dictionary of Birds*. London: Thomas Nelson, Ltd., and New York: McGraw-Hill, 1964.

Thomsoń, Helen. *Murder at Harvard*. Boston: Houghton Mifflin Co., 1971.

Wakefield, John. "Birds in Legend." *The Strange World of Birds*. Philadelphia: MacRae Smith Co., 1964.

Wallace, George W. *An Introduction to Ornithology*. New York: Macmillan, 1955.

Weekley, Ernest. *An Etymological Dictionary of Modern English*. Reprint. New York: Dover Publications, 1921.

Wilson, Alexander. *American Ornithology,* vols. 1–9. Philadelphia: 1808–1814.

Woods, Robert S. *An English Classical Dictionary for the Use of Taxonomists*. Pomona, CA: Pomona College, 1966.

Woods, Robert S. *The Naturalist's Lexicon. A List of Classical Greek and Latin Words Used or Suitable for Use in Biological Nomenclature*. Pasadena, CA: Abbey Garden Press, 1944.

Wynne, Owen E. *Biographical Key—Names of the Birds of the World—to Authors and Those Commemorated,* Courtwood, Sandleheath, Fordinbridge, Hants, England: privately printed, 1966.

English/Latin Glossary

Brackets ([ ]) indicate name not used in sixth edition of American Ornithologists' Union *Check-list* (1983).

[Accentor]	*Seiurus aurocapillus*
Albatross	*Diomedia*
Black-browed	*melanophris*
Black-footed	*nigripes*
Laysan	*immutabilis*
Short-tailed	*albatrus*
[Shy]	*cauta*
White-capped	*cauta*
Yellow-nosed	*chlororhynchos*
Anhinga	*Anhinga anhinga*
Ani	*Crotophaga*
Groove-billed	*sulcirostris*
Smooth-billed	*ani*
Auk	
Great	*Pinguinus impennis*
[Little]	*Alle alle*

Auklet
  Cassin's   *Ptychoramphus aleuticus*
  Crested   *Aethia cristatella*
  Least   *pusilla*
  Parakeet   *Cyclorrhynchus psittacula*
  Rhinoceros   *Cerorhinca monocerata*
  Whiskered   *Aethia pygmaea*
Avocet, American   *Recurvirostra americana*
Baldpate   *Anas americana*
Bananaquit   *Coereba flaveola*
[Basketbird]   *Icterus galbula* or *spurius*
Becard, Rose-throated   *Pachyramphus aglaiae*
[Bee-bird]   *Tyrannus tyrannus*
[Bee-martin]   *Tyrannus tyrannus*
[Bellbird]   *Hylocichla mustelina*
[Big Cranky]   *Ardea herodias*
[Bill-willie]   *Catoptrophorus*
                             semipalmatus

Bittern
  American   *Botaurus lentiginosus*
  Least   *Ixobrychus exilis*
Blackbird
  Brewer's   *Euphagus cyanocephalus*
  Red-winged   *Agelaius phoeniceus*
  Rusty   *Euphagus carolinus*
  Tricolored   *Agelaius tricolor*
  Yellow-headed   *Xanthocephalus*
                             xanthocephalus

[Bluebill] for either
  Greater Scaup or   *Aythya marila*
  Lesser Scaup or   *affinis*
  Ring-necked Duck or   *collaris*
  Ruddy Duck   *Oxyura jamaicensis*
Bluebird   *Sialia*
  Eastern   *sialis*
  Mountain   *currucoides*
  Western   *mexicana*
[Blue Crane]   *Ardea herodias*

[Blue Darter] for either
    Cooper's Hawk or
    Sharp-shinned Hawk
[Blue Peter] for either
    American Coot or
    Purple Gallinule
Bobolink
Bobwhite, Northern
[Bogbumper]
[Bonxie]
Booby
    [Blue-faced]
    Blue-footed
    Brown
    Masked
    Red-footed
    [White-bellied]
[Bottle-head]
Brant
    Black
[Bristle Tail]
[Broad-bill] for either
    Greater Scaup or
    Lesser Scaup or
    Northern Shoveler or
    Redhead or
    Ruddy Duck
[Buffalo-bird]
Bufflehead
Bulbul, Red-whiskered
[Bullbat]
Bunting
    Indigo
    Lark
    Lazuli
    McKay's
    Painted
    Snow

Accipiter cooperii
    striatus

Fulica americana
Porphyrula martinica
Dolichonyx oryzivorus
Colinus virginianus
Botaurus lentiginosus
Catharacta skua
Sula
    dactylatra
    nebouxii
    leucogaster
    dactylatra
    sula
    leucogaster
Pluvialis squatarola
Branta bernicla
    bernicla nigricans
Oxyura jamaicensis

Aythya marila
    affinis
Anas clypeata
    americana
Oxyura jamaicensis
Molothrus ater
Bucephala albeola
Pycnonotus jocosus
Chordeiles minor

Passerina cyanea
Calamospiza melanocorys
Passerina amoena
Plectrophenax hyperboreus
Passerina ciris
Plectrophenax nivalis

Varied	*Passerina versicolor*
[Burgomaster]	
Glaucous Gull or	*Larus hyperboreus*
Great Black-backed Gull	*marinus*
Bushtit	*Psaltriparus minimus*
[Butcher-bird] for either	
Loggerhead Shrike or	*Lanius ludovicianus*
Northern Shrike	*excubitor*
[Buzzard]	
Black	*Coragyps atraus*
Mexican	*Polyborus plancus*
Turkey	*Cathartes aura*
[Calico-back]	*Arenaria interpres*
[Camp Robber]	*Perisoreus canadensis*
[Canary]	
[Blue]	*Passerina cyanea*
[Wild] for either	
American Goldfinch or	*Carduelis tristis*
Yellow Warbler	*Dendroica petechia*
Canvasback	*Aythya valisineria*
Caracara, Crested	*Polyborus plancus*
Cardinal, Northern	*Cardinalis cardinalis*
[Catbird]	*Dumetella carolinensis*
Catbird, Gray	*carolinensis*
[Cedar Bird]	*Bombycilla cedrorum*
Chachalaca, Plain	*Ortalus vetula*
[Chaparral Cock]	*Geococcyx californianus*
Chat [Ground]	*Geothlypis poliocephala*
[Long-tailed]	*Icteria virens*
Yellow-breasted	*virens*
[Chebec]	*Empidonax minimus*
[Cherry Bird]	*Bombycilla cedrorum*
[Chewink]	*Pipilo erythrophthalmus*
Chickadee	*Parus*
Black-capped	*atricapillus*
Boreal	*hudsonicus*
Carolina	*carolinensis*

Chestnut-backed	*rufescens*
[Gray-headed]	*cinctus*
Mexican	*sclateri*
Mountain	*gambeli*
Siberian	*cinctus*
Chicken	*Tympanuchus*
Greater Prairie-	*cupido*
Lesser Prairie-	*pallidicinctus*
[Chippy]	*Spizella passerina*
Chuck-will's-widow	*Caprimulgus carolinensis*
Chukar	*Alectoris chukar*
[Clam Bird]	*Haemotopus palliatus*
[Cock of the Woods]	*Dryocopus pileatus*
[Coffin-bearer]	*Larus marinus*
Condor, California	*Gymnogyps californianus*
Coot, American	*Fulica americana*
Cormorant	*Phalacrocorax*
Brandt's	*penicillatus*
Double-crested	*auritus*
Great	*carbo*
Olivaceous	*olivaceus*
Pelagic	*pelagicus*
Red-faced	*urile*
Corn Crake	*Crex crex*
Cowbird	
Bronzed	*Molothrus aeneus*
Brown-headed	*ater*
[Common]	*ater*
[Red-eyed]	*aeneus*
[Cowcow]	*Coccyzus*
Crane	*Grus*
Sandhill	*canadensis*
Whooping	*americana*
Creeper, Brown	*Certhia americana*
[Tree]	*americana*
Crossbill	*Loxia*
Red	*curvirostra*

White-winged	*leucoptera*
Crow	
American	*Corvus brachyrhynchos*
[Carrion]	*Coragyps atratus*
[Common]	*Corvus brachyrhynchos*
Fish	*ossifragus*
Northwestern	*caurinus*
Cuckoo	*Coccyzus*
Black-billed	*erythropthalmus*
[Black-eared]	*minor*
[Ground]	*Geococcyx californianus*
Mangrove	*Coccyzus minor*
Yellow-billed	*americanus*
Curlew	*Numenius*
Bristle-thighed	*tahitiensis*
Eskimo	*borealis*
[Hudsonian]	*phaeopus*
Long-billed	*americanus*
[Spanish]	*Eudocimus albus*
[Cutwater]	*Rynchops niger*
[Dabchick]	*Podilymbus podiceps*
[Daddy-long-legs]	*Himantopus mexicanus*
[Darter	*Accipiter*
Blue	*cooperii*
Little Blue]	*striatus*
[Devil-down-head]	*Sitta*
Dickcissel	*Spiza americana*
Dipper, American	*Cinclus mexicanus*
Dotterel, Eurasian	*Eudromias morinellus*
Dove	
Common Ground-	*Columbina passerina*
Inca	*inca*
Mourning	*Zenaida macroura*
Ringed Turtle-	*Streptopelia risoria*
Rock	*Columba livia*
Spotted	*Streptopelia chinensis*
[White-fronted]	*Leptotila verreauxi*
White-tipped	*verrauxi*

White-winged	*Zenaida asiatica*
Zenaida	*aurita*
Dovekie	*Alle alle*
Dowitcher	*Limnodromus*
Long-billed	*scolopaceus*
Short-billed	*griseus*
Duck	
[Black]	*Anas rubripes*
Black, American	*rubripes*
[Black-bellied Tree-]	*Dendrocygna autumnalis*
Black-bellied Whistling-	*autumnalis*
[Fulvous Tree-]	*bicolor*
Fulvous Whistling-	*bicolor*
[Dusky]	*Anas fulvigula*
[Gray]	*strepera*
Harlequin	*Histrionicus histrionicus*
Labrador	*Camptorhynchus labradorius*
Masked	*Oxyura dominica*
[Mexican]	*Anas platyrhynchos*
Mottled	*fulvigula*
Ring-necked	*Aythya collaris*
Rock	*Histrionicus histrionicus*
Ruddy	*Oxyura jamaicensis*
[Whistling]	*Bucephala clangula*
Wood	*Aix sponsa*
Dunlin	*Calidris alpina*
Eagle	
Bald	*Haliaeetus leucocephalus*
Golden	*Aquila chrysaetos*
Egret	
Cattle	*Bubulcus ibis*
[Common]	*Casmerodius albus*
Great	*albus*
Reddish	*Egretta rufescens*
Snowy	*thula*
Eider	
Common	*Somateria mollissima*
King	*spectabilis*

Spectacled	*fischeri*
Steller's	*Polysticta stelleri*
Falcon	*Falco*
Aplomado	*femoralis*
Peregrine	*peregrinus*
Prairie	*mexicanus*
Finch	
[Black Rosy]	*Leucosticte arctoa atrata*
[Brown-capped Rosy]	*arctoa australis*
Cassin's	*Carpodacus cassinii*
[Gray-crowned Rosy]	*Leucosticte arctoa tephrocotis*
House	*Carpodacus mexicanus*
[McGregor's House]	*mexicanus*
Purple	*purpureus*
Rosy	*Leucosticte arctoa*
[Flamecrest]	*Regulus satrapa*
Flamingo, American	*Phoenicopterus ruber*
Greater	*ruber*
Flicker	
[Common]	*Colaptes auratus*
[Gilded]	*auratus chrysoides*
Northern	*auratus*
[Red-shafted]	*auratus cafer*
[Yellow-shafted]	*auratus auratus*
[Flinthead]	*Mycteria americana*
Flycatcher	
Acadian	*Empidonax virescens*
Alder	*alnorum*
Ash-throated	*Myiarchus cinerascens*
[Beardless]	*Camptostoma imberbe*
Brown-crested	*Myiarchus tyrannulus*
Buff-breasted	*Empidonax fulvifrons*
Coues'	*Contopus pertinax*
Crested, Great	*Myiarchus crinitus*
Dusky	*Empidonax oberholseri*
Dusky-capped	*Myiarchus tuberculifer*

Fork-tailed	*Tyrannus savana*
Gray	*Empidonax wrightii*
Greater	*Contopus pertinax*
Hammond's	*Empidonax hammondii*
Kingbird, Eastern	*Tyrannus tryannus*
[Kiskadee]	*Pitangus sulphuratus*
Least	*Empidonax minimus*
[Olivaceous]	*Myiarchus tuberculifer*
Olive-sided	*Contopus borealis*
Scissor-tailed	*Tyrannus forficata*
Sulphur-bellied	*Myiodynastes luteiventris*
[Traill's]	*Empidonax traillii* plus *alnorum*
Vermillion	*Pyrocephalus rubinus*
Western	*Empidonax difficilis*
[Wied's Crested]	*Myiarchus tyrannulus*
Willow	*Empidonax traillii*
Yellow-bellied	*flaviventris*
[Fly-up-the-creek]	*Butorides striatus*
[Forest Chippy]	*Helmitheros vermivorus*
Frigatebird, Magnificent	*Fregata magnificens*
Fulmar, Northern	*Fulmarus glacialis*
Gadwall	*Anas strepera*
Gallinule	
[Common]	*Gallinula chloropus*
Purple	*Porphyrula martinica*
Gannett, Northern	*Sula bassana*
Gnatcatcher	
Black-tailed	*Polioptila melanura*
Blue-gray	*caerulea*
[Goatsucker]	*Caprimulgus*
[Gobbler]	*Meleagris gallopavo*
Godwit	
Bar-tailed	*Limosa lapponica*
Hudsonian	*haemastica*
Marbled	*fedoa*
[Goldcrest]	*Regulus satrapa*

Goldeneye
    Barrow's   *Bucephala islandica*
    Common   *clangula*
Goldfinch
    American   *Carduelis tristis*
    European   *carduelis*
    Lawrence's   *lawrencei*
    Lesser   *psaltria*
[Goosander]   *Mergus merganser*
Goose
    Barnacle   *Branta leucopsis*
    [Blue]   *Chen caerulescens*
    [Cackling]   *Branta canadensis minima*
    Canada   *canadensis*
    Emperor   *Chen canagica*
    Ross'   *rossii*
    Snow   *caerulescens*
    [Tule]   *Anser albifrons*
    White-fronted, Greater   *albifrons*
Goshawk
    [Mexican]   *Buteo nitidus*
    Northern   *Accipiter gentilis*
Grackle
    Boat-tailed   *Quiscalus major*
    [Bronzed]   *quiscula*
    Common   *quiscula*
    Great-tailed   *mexicanus*
    [Purple]   *quiscula*
Grebe
    [Black-necked]   *Podiceps nigricollis*
    Eared   *nigricollis*
    [Holboell's]   *grisigena*
    Horned   *auritus*
    Least   *Tachybaptus dominicus*
    [Mexican]   *dominicus*
    Pied-billed   *Podilymbus podiceps*
    Red-necked   *Podiceps grisegena*
    Western   *Aechmophorus occidentalis*

Greenlet	*Vireo*
Grosbeak	
Black-headed	*Pheucticus melanocephalus*
Blue	*Guiraca caerulea*
Evening	*Coccothraustes vespertinus*
Pine	*Pinicola enucleator*
Rose-breasted	*Pheucticus ludovicianus*
[Groundchat]	*Geothylpis poliocephala*
Ground-dove, Common	*Columbina passerina*
Grouse	
Blue	*Dendragapus obscurus*
Ruffed	*Bonasa umbellus*
Sage	*Centrocercus urophasianus*
Sharp-tailed	*Tympanuchus phasianellus*
Spruce	*Dendragapus canadensis*
Guillemot	
Black	*Cepphus grylle*
Pigeon	*columba*
Gull	
Black-backed, Great	*Larus marinus*
Black-headed, Common	*ridibundus*
Bonaparte's	*philadelphia*
California	*californicus*
Franklin's	*pipixcan*
Glaucous	*hyperboreus*
Glaucous-winged	*glaucescens*
Heermann's	*heermanni*
Herring	*argentatus*
Iceland	*glaucoides*
Ivory	*Pagophila eburnea*
Laughing	*Larus atricilla*
Little	*minutus*
Mew	*canus*
Ring-billed	*delawarensis*
Ross'	*Rhodostethia rosea*
Sabine's	*Xema sabini*
Thayer's	*Larus thayeri*
Western	*occidentalis*

Gyrfalcon	*Falco rusticolus*
[Hag, Hagdon, Hagdown, Haglet]	*Puffinus gravis*
[Handsaw]	*Ardea*
[Hangnest]	*Icterus*
Harrier, Northern	*Circus cyaneus*
Hawk	
[Black]	*Buteogallus anthracinus*
Black-hawk, Common	*anthracinus*
Broad-winged	*Buteo platypterus*
Cooper's	*Accipiter cooperii*
[Duck]	*Falco peregrinus*
Ferruginous	*Buteo regalis*
[Fish]	*Pandion haliaetus*
Gray	*Buteo nitidus*
[Harlan's]	*jamaicensis harlani*
Harris'	*Parabuteo unicinctus*
[Marsh]	*Circus cyaneus*
[Pigeon]	*Falco columbarius*
Red-shouldered	*Buteo lineatus*
Red-tailed	*jamaicensis*
Rough-legged	*lagopus*
Sharp-shinned	*Accipiter striatus*
Short-tailed	*Buteo brachyurus*
[Sparrow]	*Falco sparverius*
Swainson's	*Buteo swainsoni*
White-tailed	*albicaudatus*
Zone-tailed	*albonotatus*
Hawk-owl, Northern	*Surnia ulula*
Heath Hen	*Tympanuchus cupido*
Hell-diver	*Podiceps*
Heron	
Black-crowned Night-	*Nycticorax nycticorax*
Great Blue	*Ardea herodias*
[Great White]	*herodias*
[Green]	*Butorides striatus*
Green-backed	*striatus*

Little Blue	*Egretta caerulea*
[Louisiana]	*tricolor*
Tricolored	*tricolor*
Yellow-crowned Night-	*Nycticorax violacea*
High-hole	*Colaptes auratus*
[Honeycreeper]	*Coereba flaveola*
Hummingbird	
Allen's	*Selasphorus sasin*
Anna's	*Calypte anna*
Black-chinned	*Archilochus alexandri*
Blue-throated	*Lampornis clemenciae*
Broad-billed	*Cynanthus latirostris*
Broad-tailed	*Selasphorus platycercus*
Buff-bellied	*Amazilia yucatanensis*
Calliope	*Stellula calliope*
Costa's	*Calypte costae*
Lucifer	*Calothorax lucifer*
Magnificent	*Eugenes fulgens*
[Rivoli's]	*fulgens*
Ruby-throated	*Archilochus colubris*
Rufous	*Selasphorus rufus*
Violet-crowned	*Amazilia verticalis*
White-eared	*Hylocharis leucotis*
Ibis	
Glossy	*Plegadis falcinellus*
Scarlet	*Eudocimus ruber*
White	*albus*
White-faced	*Plegadis chihi*
[Wood]	*Mycteria americana*
Jacana, Northern	*Jacana spinosa*
Jaeger	
Long-tailed	*Stercorarius longicaudus*
Parasitic	*parasiticus*
Pomarine	*pomarinus*
Jay	
[Arizona]	*Aphelocoma ultramarina*
Blue	*Cyanocitta cristata*

[California]	*Aphelocoma coerulescens*
[Canada]	*Perisoreus canadensis*
[Florida]	*Aphelocoma coerulescens*
Gray	*Perisoreus canadensis*
Gray-breasted	*Aphelocoma ultramarina*
Green	*Cyanocorax yncas*
[Mexican]	*Aphelocoma ultramarina*
Pinyon	*Gymnorhinus cyanocephalus*
[Santa Cruz]	*Aphelocoma coerulescens*
Scrub	*coerulescens*
Steller's	*Cyanocitta stelleri*
Junco	
Dark-eyed	*Junco hyemalis*
[Gray-headed]	*hyemalis*
[Mexican]	*phaeonotus*
[Oregon]	*hyemalis*
[Pink-sided]	*hyemalis*
[Red-backed]	*hyemalis*
[Slate-colored]	*hyemalis*
[White-winged]	*hyemalis*
Yellow-eyed	*phaeonotus*
Kestrel	
American	*Falco sparverius*
Eurasian	*tinnunculus*
Killdeer	*Charadrius vociferus*
Kingbird	
[Arkansas]	*Tyrannus verticalis*
Cassin's	*vociferans*
Couch's	*couchii*
Eastern	*tyrannus*
Gray	*dominicensis*
Thick-billed	*crassirostris*
Tropical	*melancholicus*
Western	*verticalis*
Kingfisher	
Belted	*Ceryle alcyon*
Green	*Chloroceryle americana*
Ringed	*Ceryle torquata*

[Texas]	*torquata*
Kinglet	
Golden-crowned	*Regulus satrapa*
Ruby-crowned	*calendula*
Kiskadee, Great	*Pitangus sulphuratus*
Kite	
Black-shouldered	*Elanus caeruleus*
[Everglade]	*Rostrhamus sociabilis*
Mississippi	*Ictinia mississippiensis*
Snail	*Rostrhamus sociabilis*
[Swallow-tailed], American	*Elanoides forficatus*
[White-tailed]	*Elanus caeruleus*
Kittiwake	
Black-legged	*Rissa tridactyla*
Red-legged	*brevirostris*
Knot, Red	*Calidris canutus*
[Lanner]	*Falco peregrinus*
Lapwing, Northern	*Vanellus vanellus*
Lark	
Horned	*Eremophila alpestris*
[Shore]	*alpestris*
Limpkin	*Aramus guarauna*
[Log-cock]	*Dryocopus pileatus*
Longspur	
Chestnut-collared	*Calcarius ornatus*
Lapland	*lapponicus*
McCown's	*mccownii*
Smith's	*pictus*
Loon	
Arctic	*Gavia arctica*
Common	*immer*
[Pacific]	*arctica*
Red-throated	*stellata*
Yellow-billed	*adamsii*
Magpie	
Black-billed	*Pica pica*
Yellow-billed	*nuttalli*

Mallard	*Anas platyrhynchos*
Man-o'-war Bird	*Fregata magnificens*
Marsh Hen	*Fulica americana* or *Rallus longirostris*
Martin, Purple	*Progne subis*
Meadowlark	
Eastern	*Sturnella magna*
Western	*neglecta*
Merganser	
Common	*Mergus merganser*
Hooded	*Lophodytes cucullatus*
Red-breasted	*Mergus serrator*
Merlin	*Falco columbarius*
Mockingbird, Northern	*Mimus polyglottos*
Moorhen, Common	*Gallinula chloropus*
[Mother Carey's Chicken]	*Oceanodroma*
[Mud-hen]	*Fulica americana*
Murre	
[Brunnich's]	*Uria lomvia*
Common	*aalge*
Thick-billed	*lomvia*
Murrelet	
Ancient	*Synthliboramphus antiquus*
Craveri's	*craveri*
Kittlitz's	*Brachyramphus brevirostris*
Marbled	*marmoratus*
Xantus'	*Synthliboramphus hypoleuca*
Nighthawk	
Common	*Chordeiles minor*
Lesser	*acutipennis*
Night-heron	
Black-crowned	*Nycticorax nycticorax*
Yellow-crowned	*violacea*
[Nightjar]	*Caprimulgus vociferus*
Buff-collared	*ridgwayi*
Noddy	
Black	*Anous minutus*
Brown	*stolidus*

[Nonpareil]	*Passerina ciris*
Nutcracker, Clark's	*Nucifraga columbiana*
Nuthatch	
Brown-headed	*Sitta pusilla*
Pygmy	*pygmaea*
Red-breasted	*canadensis*
White-breasted	*carolinensis*
Oldsquaw	*Clangula hyemalis*
Oriole	
Altimira	*Icterus gularis*
Audubon's	*graduacauda*
[Baltimore]	*galbula*
[Black-headed]	*graduacauda*
[Bullock's]	*galbula bullockii*
Hooded	*cucullatus*
[Lichtenstein's]	*gularis*
Northern	*galbula*
Orchard	*spurius*
Scott's	*parisorum*
Spot-breasted	*pectoralis*
Osprey	*Pandion haliaetus*
[Ouzel or Ousel]	*Cinclus mexicanus*
Ovenbird	*Seiurus aurocapillus*
Owl	
Barn-, Common	*Tyto alba*
Barred	*Strix varia*
[Bog]	*Asio flammeus*
Boreal	*Aegolius funereus*
Burrowing	*Athene cunicularia*
Elf	*Micrathene whitneyi*
Ferruginous Pygmy-	*Glaucidium brasilianum*
Flammulated	*Otus flammeolus*
Great Gray	*Strix nebulosa*
Great Horned	*Bubo virginianus*
Hawk-, Northern	*Surnia ulula*
[Hoot]	*Bubo virginianus* or *Strix varia*
Long-eared	*Asio otus*

[Monkey] and [Monkey-faced]	*Tyto alba*
Pygmy-, Ferruginous	*Glaucidium brasilianum*
Pygmy-, Northern	*gnoma*
Saw-whet, Northern	*Aegolius acadicus*
Screech-, Eastern	*Otus asio*
Screech-, Western	*kennicotti*
Screech-, Whiskered	*trichopsis*
Short-eared	*Asio flammeus*
Snowy	*Nyctea scandiaca*
Spotted	*Strix occidentalis*
[Whiskered]	*Otus trichopsis*
Oystercatcher	
American	*Haematopus palliatus*
Black	*bachmani*
Parakeet, Paroquet	
Carolina	*Conuropsis carolinensis*
Monk	*Myiopsitta monachus*
Parrot	
[Sea]	*Fratercula arctica*
Thick-billed	*Rhynochopsitta pachyrhynchna*
Partridge, Gray	*Perdix perdix*
Parula	*Parula americana*
Northern	*americana*
Tropical	*pitiayumi*
Pauraque, Common	*Nyctidromus albicollis*
[Peabody Bird]	*Zonotrichia albicollis*
Pelican	
Brown	*Pelecanus occidentalis*
White, American	*erythrorhynchos*
[Peter Bird]	*Parus bicolor*
Petrel (*See also* Storm-petrel)	
Black-capped	*Pterodroma hasitata*
Cape	*Daption capense*
Mottled	*Pterodroma inexpectata*
[Scaled]	*inexpectata*

Pewee
  Eastern Wood-   *Contopus virens*
  Greater   *pertinax*
  Western Wood-   *sordidulus*
Phainopepla   *Phainopepla nitens*
Phalarope
  [Northern]   *Phalaropus lobatus*
  Red   *fulicaria*
  Red-necked   *lobatus*
  Wilson's   *tricolor*
Pheasant, Ring-necked   *Phasianus colchicus*
Phoebe
  Black   *Sayornis nigricans*
  Eastern   *phoebe*
  Say's   *saya*
Pigeon
  Band-tailed   *Columba fasciata*
  Passenger   *Ectopistes migratorius*
  Red-billed   *Columba flavirostris*
  White-crowned   *leucocephala*
Pintail, Northern   *Anas acuta*
Pipit
  [American]   *Anthus spinoletta*
  Sprague's   *spragueii*
  Water   *spinoletta*
Plover
  [American Golden-]   *Pluvialis dominica*
  [Barnyard]   *Tringa solitaria*
  Black-bellied   *Pluvialis squatarola*
  Common Ringed   *Charadrius hiaticula*
  [Gray]   *Pluvialis squatarola*
  Lesser Golden-   *dominica*
  Mountain   *Charadrius montanus*
  Piping   *melodus*
  [Ringed]   *hiaticula*
  Semipalmated   *semipalmatus*
  Snowy   *alexandrinus*

[Thick-billed]	*wilsonia*
[Upland]	*Bartramia longicauda*
Wilson's	*Charadrius wilsonia*
Poor Joe	*Ardea herodias*
Poorwill, Common	*Phalaenoptilus nuttallii*
Prairie-Chicken	
Greater	*Tympanuchus cupido*
Lesser	*pallidicinctus*
Preacher Bird	*Vireo olivaceus*
Ptarmigan	
Rock	*Lagopus mutus*
White-tailed	*leucurus*
Willow	*lagopus*
Puffin	
Atlantic	*Fratercula arctica*
[Common]	*arctica*
Horned	*corniculata*
Tufted	*cirrhata*
Pygmy-owl	
Ferruginous	*Glaucidium brasilianum*
Northern	*gnoma*
Pyrrhuloxia	*Cardinalis sinuata*
Quail	
California	*Callipepla californica*
Gambel's	*gambelii*
[Harlequin]	*Cyrtonyx montezumae*
Montezuma	*montezumae*
Mountain	*Oreortyx pictus*
Scaled	*Callipepla squamata*
Rail	
Black	*Laterallus jamaicensis*
Clapper	*Rallus longirostris*
King	*elegans*
Virginia	*limicola*
Yellow	*Coturnicops noveboracensis*
[Rain Bird]	*Coccyzus*
Raven	
Chihuahuan	*Corvus cryptoleucus*

Common	*corax*
[White-necked]	*cryptoleucus*
Razorbill	*Alca torda*
Redbird	*Cardinalis cardinalis*
[Redbreast]	*Turdus migratorius*
Redhammer	*Colaptes auratus cafer*
Redhead	*Aythya americana*
Redpoll	
[Arctic]	*Carduelis hornemanni*
Common	*flammea*
Hoary	*hornemanni*
[Hornemann's]	*hornemanni*
Redstart	
American	*Setophaga ruticilla*
Painted	*Myioborus picta*
[Reed-bird]	*Dolichonyx oryzivorus*
[Rice-bird]	*Dolichonyx oryzivorus*
[Roadrunner]	*Geococcyx californianus*
Greater	*californianus*
[Robert o' Lincoln]	*Dolichonyx oryzivorus*
Robin, American	*Turdus migratorius*
[Rubythroat]	*Archilochus colubris*
Ruff, Reeve	*Philomachus pugnax*
Sanderling	*Calidris alba*
Sandpiper	
Baird's	*Calidris bairdii*
[Bartramian]	*Bartramia longicauda*
[Bartram's]	*longicauda*
Buff-breasted	*Tryngites subruficollis*
Curlew	*Calidris ferruginea*
Least	*minutilla*
Pectoral	*melanotos*
Purple	*maritima*
[Red-backed]	*alpina*
Rock	*ptilocnemis*
Semipalmated	*pusillus*
Sharp-tailed	*acuminata*
Solitary	*Tringa solitaria*

Spoonbill	*Eurynorhynchus pygmeus*
Spotted	*Actitis macularia*
Stilt	*Calidris himantopus*
Upland	*Bartramia longicauda*
Western	*Calidris mauri*
White-rumped	*fuscicollis*
Sapsucker	
Red-breasted	*Sphyrapicus ruber*
Williamson's	*thyroideus*
Yellow-bellied	*varius*
Sawbill	*Mergus*
Saw-filer	*Aegolius acadicus*
Scaup	
Greater	*Aythya marila*
Lesser	*affinis*
Scoter	
Black	*Melanitta nigra*
[Common]	*nigra*
Surf	*perspicillata*
[Velvet]	*fusca*
White-winged	*fusca*
[Sea Pigeon]	*Cepphus grylle*
Seedeater, White-collared	*Sporophila torqueola*
[Sewick]	*Empidonax minimus*
[Shag]	*Phalacrocorax auritus*
Shearwater	
Audubon's	*Puffinus lherminieri*
Buller's	*bulleri*
Cory's	*Calonectris diomedea*
Flesh-footed	*Puffinus carneipes*
Greater	*gravis*
Little	*assimilis*
Manx	*puffinus*
[New Zealand]	*bulleri*
[Pale-footed]	*carneipes*
Pink-footed	*creatopus*
Short-tailed	*tenuirostris*
[Slender-billed]	*tenuirostris*

Sooty	*griseus*
[Sheldrake, Sheld Duck]	*Mergus*
[Shite Pote or Poke]	*Botaurus lentiginosus* or
	Nycticorax nycticorax
	or *N. violacea* or
	Butorides virescens
[Shore Lark]	*Eremophila alpestris*
Shoveler, Northern	*Anas clypeata*
Shrike	
[Great Gray]	*Lanius excubitor*
Loggerhead	*ludovicianus*
Northern	*excubitor*
[Sickle Bill]	*Numenius americanus*
Siskin, Pine	*Carduelis pinus*
Skimmer, Black	*Rynchops niger*
Skua-	
[Brown]	*Catharacta skua*
Great	*skua*
Skylark, Eurasian	*Alauda arvensis*
Snake Bird, Snake Killer	*Anhinga anhinga* or
	Geococcyx californicus
Snipe	
Common	*Gallinago gallinago*
[Grass]	*Calidris melanotos*
[Robin]	*canutus*
[Rock]	*maritima*
[Sea]	*Phalaropus*
[Telltale]	*Tringa flavipes* or
	melanoleucus
[Wilson's]	*Capella gallinago*
Snow Bird	*Junco hyemalis*
Snowflake	*Plectrophenax nivalis*
Solitaire, Townsend's	*Myadestes townsendi*
Sora	*Porzana carolina*
Sparrow	
Bachman's	*Aimophila aestivalis*
Baird's	*Ammodramus bairdii*
Black-chinned	*Spizella atrogularis*

Black-throated	*Amphispiza bilineata*
Botteri's	*Aimophila botterii*
Brewer's	*Spizella breweri*
[Cape Sable]	*Ammodramus maritimus mirabilis*
Cassin's	*Aimophila cassinii*
Chipping	*Spizella passerina*
Clay-colored	*pallida*
Dusky Seaside-	*Ammodramus maritima nigrescens*
[English]	*Passer domesticus*
Field	*Spizella pusilla*
Fox	*Passerella iliaca*
Golden-crowned	*Zonotrichia atricapilla*
Grasshopper	*Ammodramus savannarum*
Harris'	*Zonotrichia querula*
Henslow's	*Ammodramus henslowii*
House	*Passer domesticus*
[Ipswich]	*Passerculus sandwichensis princeps*
Lark	*Chondestes grammacus*
LeConte's	*Ammodramus leconteii*
Lincoln's	*Melospiza lincolnii*
Olive	*Arremonops rufivirgatus*
[Pine-woods]	*Aimophila aestivalis*
Rufous-crowned	*ruficeps*
Rufous-winged	*carpalis*
Sage	*Amphispiza belli*
Savannah	*Passerculus sandwichensis*
Seaside-	*Ammodramus maritimus*
Sharp-tailed	*caudacutus*
Song	*Melospiza melodia*
Swamp	*georgiana*
Tree, American	*Spizella arborea*
Tree, Eurasian	*Passer montanus*
Vesper	*Pooecetes gramineus*
White-crowned	*Zonotrichia leucophrys*
White-throated	*albicollis*

Spoonbill, Roseate	*Ajaia ajaja*
[Sprig]	*Anas acuta*
[Stake Driver]	*Botaurus lentiginosus*
Starling, European	*Sturnus vulgaris*
Stilt, Black-necked	*Himantopus mexicanus*
Stork, Wood	*Mycteria americana*
Storm-petrel	
Ashy	*Oceanodroma homochroa*
Band-rumped	*castro*
Black	*melania*
Fork-tailed	*furcata*
[Galapagos]	*tethys*
[Harcourt's]	*castro*
Leach's	*leucorhoa*
Least	*microsoma*
[Madeíra]	*castro*
Wedge-rumped	*tethys*
White-faced	*Pelagodroma marina*
Wilson's	*Oceanites oceanicus*
[Sugarbird]	*Coereba flaveola*
[Summer Redbird]	*Piranga rubra*
Surfbird	*Aphriza virgata*
Swallow	
Bank	*Riparia riparia*
Barn	*Hirundo rustica*
Cave	*fulva*
Cliff	*pyrrhonota*
Rough-winged, Northern	*Stelgidopteryx serripennis*
Tree	*Tachycineta bicolor*
Violet-green	*thalassina*
Swan	
Mute	*Cygnus olor*
Trumpeter	*buccinator*
Tundra	*columbianus*
[Whistling]	*columbianus*
Whooper	*cygnus*
Swift	
Black	*Cypseloides niger*

Chimney	*Chaetura pelagica*
Vaux's	*vauxi*
White-throated	*Aeronautes saxatalis*
Tanager	
Hepatic	*Piranga flava*
Scarlet	*olivacea*
Summer	*rubra*
Western	*ludoviciana*
Tattler, Wandering	*Heteroscelus incanus*
[Teacher Bird]	*Seiurus aurocapillus*
Teal	
Baikal	*Anas formosa*
Blue-winged	*discors*
Cinnamon	*cyanoptera*
[Common]	*crecca*
Green-winged	*crecca*
[Green-winged, American]	*crecca*
[Green-winged, Eurasian]	*crecca*
[Green-winged, European]	*crecca*
[Teeter Bird]	*Actitis macularia* or *Tringa solitaria*
Tern	
Aleutian	*Sterna aleutica*
Arctic	*paradisaea*
Black	*Chlidonias niger*
[Black Noddy]	*Anous minutus*
Bridled	*Sterna anaethetus*
[Brown Noddy]	*Anous stolidus*
[Cabot's]	*Sterna sandvicensis*
Caspian	*caspia*
Common	*hirundo*
Elegant	*elegans*
Forster's	*forsteri*
Gull-billed	*nilotica*
Least	*antillarum*

[Noddy]	*Anous stolidus*
Roseate	*Sterna dougallii*
Royal	*maxima*
Sandwich	*sandvicensis*
Sooty	*fuscata*
Trudeau's	*trudeaui*
[Wilson's]	*hirundo*

Thrasher
Bendire's	*Toxostoma bendirei*
Brown	*rufum*
California	*redivivum*
Crissal	*crissale*
Curve-billed	*curvirostre*
LeConte's	*lecontei*
Long-billed	*longirostre*
Sage	*Oreoscoptes montanus*

Thrush
Gray-cheeked	*Catharus minimus*
Hermit	*guttatus*
[Olive-backed]	*ustulatus*
Swainson's	*ustulatus*
Varied	*Ixoreus naevius*
[Wilson's]	*Catharus fuscescens*
Wood	*Hylocichla mustelina*
[Thunder Pumper]	*Botaurus lentiginosus*
[Tiercel]	*Accipiter gentilis* or *Falco peregrinus*
[Timber Doodle]	*Scolopax minor*
[Tip-up]	*Actitis macularia* or *Tringa solitaria*
Tit, Siberian	*Parus cinctus*
[Titlark]	*Anthus spinoletta*

Titmouse
[Black-crested]	*Parus bicolor*
Bridled	*wollweberi*
Plain	*inornatus*
Tufted	*bicolor*

[Tomtit]	*Parus bicolor*
Towhee	
Abert's	*Pipilo aberti*
Brown	*fuscus*
Green-tailed	*chlorurus*
Rufous-sided	*erythrophthalmus*
[Tree-duck	
Black-bellied	*Dendrocygna autumnalis*
Fulvus]	*bicolor*
Trogon	
[Coppery-tailed]	*Trogon elegans*
Elegant	*elegans*
Tropicbird	
Red-billed	*Phaethon aethereus*
White-tailed	*lepturus*
[Yellow-billed]	*lepturus*
Turkey	*Meleagris gallopavo*
Turnstone	
Black	*Arenaria melanocephala*
Ruddy	*interpres*
Tyrannulet, Northern	
Beardless-	*Camptostoma imberbe*
Veery	*Catharus fuscescens*
Verdin	*Auriparus flaviceps*
Vireo	
Bell's	*Vireo bellii*
Black-capped	*atricapillus*
Black-whiskered	*altiloquus*
Gray	*vicinior*
Hutton's	*huttoni*
Philadelphia	*philadelphicus*
Red-eyed	*olivaceus*
Solitary	*solitarius*
Warbling	*gilvus*
White-eyed	*griseus*
Yellow-throated	*flavifrons*
Vulture	
Black	*Coragyps atratus*

Turkey	*Cathartes aura*
Wagtail	
Yellow	*Motacilla flava*
White	*alba*
[Wake Up]	*Colaptes auratus*
Warbler	
Arctic	*Phylloscopus borealis*
[Audubon's]	*Dendroica coronata*
Bachman's	*Vermivora bachmanii*
Bay-breasted	*Dendroica castanea*
Black-and-white	*Mniotilta varia*
Blackburnian	*Dendroica fusca*
Blackpoll	*striata*
Blue, Black-throated	*caerulescens*
Blue-winged	*Vermivora pinus*
Canada	*Wilsonia canadensis*
Cape May	*Dendroica tigrina*
Cerulean	*cerulea*
Chestnut-sided	*pensylvanica*
Colima	*Vermivora crissalis*
Connecticut	*Oporornis agilis*
Golden-cheeked	*Dendroica chrysoparia*
Golden-winged	*Vermivora chrysoptera*
Grace's	*Dendroica graciae*
Gray, Black-throated	*nigrescens*
Green, Black-throated	*virens*
Hermit	*occidentalis*
Hooded	*Wilsonia citrina*
Kentucky	*Oporornis formosus*
Kirtland's	*Dendroica kirtlandii*
Lucy's	*Vermivora luciae*
MacGillivray's	*Oporornis tolmiei*
Magnolia	*Dendroica magnolia*
Mourning	*Oporornis philadelphia*
[Myrtle]	*Dendroica coronata*
Nashville	*Vermivora ruficapilla*
[Necklace]	*Wilsonia canadensis*
Olive	*Peucedramus taeniatus*

[Olive-backed]	*Parula pitiayumi*
Orange-crowned	*Vermivora celata*
Palm	*Dendroica palmarum*
[Parula]	*Parula americana*
[Parula, Northern]	*americana*
[Parula, Tropical]	*pitiayumi*
Pine	*Dendroica pinus*
Prairie	*discolor*
Prothonotary	*Protonotaria citrea*
Red-faced	*Cardellina rubrifrons*
Swainson's	*Limnothlypis swainsonii*
Tennessee	*Vermivora peregrina*
Townsend's	*Dendroica townsendi*
Virginia	*Vermivora virginiae*
Wilson's	*Wilsonia pusilla*
Worm-eating	*Helmitheros vermivorus*
Yellow	*Dendroica petechia*
Yellow-rumped	*coronata*
Yellow-throated	*dominica*
[Water Belcher]	*Botaurus lentiginosus*
[Water Ouzel]	*Cinclus mexicanus*
Waterthrush	
Louisiana	*Seiurus motacilla*
Northern	*noveboracensis*
[Waterturkey]	*Anhinga anhinga*
[Wavy]	*Chen caerulescens*
	hyperborea
Waxwing	
Bohemian	*Bombycilla garrulus*
Cedar	*cedrorum*
Wheatear, Northern	*Oenanthe oenanthe*
Whimbrel	*Numenius phaeopus*
Whip-poor-will	*Caprimulgus vociferus*
[Ridgway's]	*ridgwayi*
[Whiskey Jack, Whiskey Jay]	*Perisoreus canadensis*
Whistling-duck	
Black-bellied	*Dendrocygna autumnalis*

Fulvus	*bicolor*
Wigeon	
American	*Anas americana*
Eurasian	*penelope*
[European]	*penelope*
Willet	*Catoptrophorus semipalmatus*
Woodcock	
American	*Scolopax minor*
Eurasian	*rusticola*
Woodpecker	
Acorn	*Melanerpes formicivorus*
[Ant]	*Colaptes auratus*
[Arizona]	*Picoides stricklandi*
Black-backed	*arcticus*
Downy	*pubescens*
Gila	*Melanerpes uropygialis*
Golden-fronted	*aurifrons*
[Golden-winged]	*Colaptes auratus*
Hairy	*Picoides villosus*
Ivory-billed	*Campephilus principalis*
Ladder-backed	*Picoides scalaris*
Lewis'	*Melanerpes lewis*
Nuttall's	*Picoides nuttallii*
Pileated	*Dryocopus pileatus*
Red-bellied	*Melanerpes carolinus*
Red-cockaded	*Picoides borealis*
Red-headed	*Melanerpes erythrocephalus*
Strickland's	*Picoides stricklandi*
Three-toed	*tridactylus*
[Three-toed, American]	*tridactylus*
[Three-toed, Arctic]	*arcticus*
[Three-toed, Black-headed]	*arcticus*
[Three-toed, Northern]	*tridactylus*
White-headed	*albolarvatus*
Wood-pewee	
Eastern	*Contopus vireus*

Western	*sordidulus*
Wren	
Bewick's	*Thryomanes bewickii*
[Brown-throated]	*Troglodytes aedon*
Cactus	*Campylorhynchus brunneicapillus*
Canyon	*Catherpes mexicanus*
Carolina	*Thryothorus ludovicianus*
House	*Troglodytes aedon*
Marsh-	*Cistothorus palustris*
[Marsh-, Long-billed]	*palustris*
[Marsh-, Short-billed]	*platensis*
Rock	*Salpinctes obsoletus*
Sedge	*Cistothorus platensis*
Winter	*Troglodytes troglodytes*
Wrentit	*Chamaea fasciata*
[Yellowhammer]	*Colaptes auratus*
Yellowlegs	
Greater	*Tringa melanoleuca*
Lesser	*flavipes*
Yellowthroat	
Common	*Geothlypis trichas*
Gray-crowned	*poliocephala*